Three Years Hard Labour

Three Years Hard Labour

The Road to Devaluation

William Davis

ANDRE DEUTSCH

FIRST PUBLISHED 1968 BY
ANDRE DEUTSCH LIMITED
105 GREAT RUSSELL STREET
LONDON WC1

PRINTED IN GREAT BRITAIN BY
EBENEZER BAYLIS & SON LTD
THE TRINITY PRESS
WORCESTER AND LONDON
SBN 233 96077 5

Contents

A Diary of Three Crisis Years

1964–65

October 15: Labour wins General Election with an overall majority of 5.

October 26: Government White Paper announces 15% import surcharge and export rebates of £70 millions a year.

November 3: Queen's Speech outlines proposals for nationalizing steel, restoring rent controls, abolishing health service prescription charges, and amending trade union law.

November 11: Autumn Budget: Mr Callaghan announces 6d increase in income tax and petrol duty, and increases in national insurance contributions. Prescription charges are abolished.

November 17: Prime Minister announces ban on sale of arms to South Africa.

November 20: Heavy and sustained pressure on sterling begins.

November 23: Bank Rate raised – on a Monday – to crisis level of 7%.

November 25: Central banks club together to provide massive $3,000 million loan in support of sterling.

December 2: International Monetary Fund lends $1,000 million.

December 8: Bank of England curbs bank advances.

December 22: Bank of England gives further substantial support to sterling in forward market.

February 2, 1965: Prime Minister announces appointment of Royal Commission to inquire into trade unions and employers' associations.

February 8: Government White Paper announces setting up of new National Board for Prices and Incomes.

February 10: Mr Callaghan announces that import surcharge will be cut to 10% from April 27.

April 6: Callaghan's second budget raises £164 million in extra taxation, clamps down on expense accounts, introduces corporation tax, and tightens exchange controls on foreign investment.

April 8: Incomes policy outlined in White Paper.

April 29: Bank of England tightens credit squeeze by requesting special deposits from the banks.

May 7: Further IMF drawing of $1,400 million.

June 3: HP terms stiffened. Bank Rate cut from 7% to 6%.

July 27: Cuts in government spending, and further tightening of exchange controls.

July 28: TUC issues statement expressing apprehension about overall effect of the Government's measures on economic expansion.

August: Sterling remains under heavy pressure.

September 10: Big new central bank credit line announced.

September 15: CBI decides 'with great reluctance' to accept proposal for 'early warning' system of increases in prices and incomes.

September 16: George Brown's five year National Plan aims at 25% increase in gross national product by 1970.

November 11: Prime Minister announces economic sanctions against Rhodesia.

1966

January–March: Balance of payments in deficit again.

January 25: White Paper announces proposed Industrial Reorganization Corporation.

February 1: Clearing bank advances frozen at 105% of March 1965 level.

February 3: Government publishes Companies Bill, providing for disclosure of chairman's salaries and contributions to political funds.

February 7: Douglas Jay announces stiffer HP controls.

March 31: Labour wins General Election with an overall majority of 97.

May 3: Budget, delayed by the election, introduces a Selective Employment Tax. Mr Callaghan also announces a 'voluntary' programme restricting investment in the sterling area.

May 16: First official strike of all British seamen since 1911 begins at midnight.

June 13: Eleven central banks make available big new credit line to check fresh run on the pound.

July 1: Seamen's strike ends.

July 3: Frank Cousins resigns from the Government in protest against the incomes policy, which he says is 'meaningless and wrong'.

July 4: Prices and Incomes Bill providing for 'early warning' system.

July 14: Bank Rate raised from 6% to 7% and banks asked to make further special deposits.

July 20: Prime Minister announces wage freeze and stiff deflationary measures. George Brown resigns, but is persuaded to stay on.

August 10: Cabinet reshuffle; George Brown exchanges jobs with the Foreign Secretary, Michael Stewart.

September 13: New swap credit arranged with the United States.

November 30: Import surcharge ends.

September–December: Balance of payments running at a surplus again.

1967

January 9: Unemployment exceeds 600,000. Wage freeze enters period of 'severe restraint'.

January 23: Finance Ministers meet at Chequers to discuss 'interest rates' disarmament.

January 27: Bank Rate cut to 6½%.

February 10: Prince Philip says he is 'sick and tired of making excuses for Britain'.

February 14: Board of Trade announces record export figures.

April 6: Neutral Budget. 'No news is good news', Chancellor says on television.

May 4: Prime Minister announces formal application to join the Common Market.

June 5: Arab–Israeli war begins, Suez Canal closed. Arab embargo on oil to UK.

June 7: HP restrictions on cars eased.

August 16: Good trade figures for July, and Treasury makes reassuring statement on balance of payments prospects. Pound has best day for months.

August 20: Ray Gunter, Minister of Labour, tells trade unions to 'stop equating profits with incest and lechery'.

August 24: Group of Ten agrees on creation of special drawing rights.

August 28: Douglas Jay sacked in Cabinet reshuffle. Mr Wilson takes over DEA. HP controls on cars and domestic appliances eased.

September 1: Arabs lift oil embargo.

September 18: Dock strikes begin in London and Liverpool.

October 3: Gold reserves fall for fourth consecutive month.

October 19: Bank Rate raised by one-half per cent, but pound remains under pressure.

October 6: Governor of the Bank of England attacked by left-wing MP's over speech on unemployment.

October 30: Liverpool dockers return to work, but 6,000 London dockers remain out.

November 5: Pound drops to lowest level for a decade.

November 11–12: Central bankers meet in Basle, approve small loan. Run on pound continues.

November 14: Big trade deficit announced. Pound has worst day ever.

November 18: Sterling devalued from 2.80 dollars to 2.40 dollars. Bank Rate raised to 8%, HP terms tightened, and other measures foreshadowed.

November 22: Gold rush gets under way.

November 27: General de Gaulle vetoes Britain's application for Common Market membership.

November 27: Jim Callaghan resigns as Chancellor, and is replaced by Roy Jenkins.

Introduction

THIS IS NOT an economic textbook. It is a book about a group of politicians with one ambition: to get their hands on the levers of power in Britain, and to transform the nation's economy. They had waited many years for it, and they thought they knew what had to be done – and how they would do it. Their ideas, and their obvious enthusiasm, persuaded millions of people to vote for them. At the end of 'three years hard Labour', the general verdict on their efforts was that they had landed the country in its worst-ever economic mess. The pound had been devalued, election promises lay in ruins, planning had become discredited, and Britain was heavily in debt. Morale was low, and the Labour party was suffering heavy defeats in bye-elections.

One man was universally blamed for this state of affairs: Harold Wilson. He had promised an economic miracle, and had failed to deliver the goods. His Chancellor, Jim Callaghan, had resigned after the forced devaluation of the pound in November 1967 and George Brown, who had created the Department of Economic Affairs in 1964, had left the Government in a huff. But Mr Wilson had remained at No 10 Downing Street, determined to ignore the numerous calls for his resignation. There was talk of a possible Coalition Government, but this was discounted both by him and the Leader of the Opposition, Mr Edward Heath.

James Harold Wilson (he dropped the James when he was still at Oxford) is an economist. He became a don at 21, and entered the House of Commons in July 1945, winning Ormskirk, Lancashire. Lord Attlee made him a junior minister at 29, and President of the Board of Trade at 31. Wilson persuaded Sir Stafford Cripps to devalue the pound in 1949, and in 1950–51 was generally regarded as a leading light on Labour's left-wing, a disciple of the fiery Aneurin Bevan. He dramatically resigned from the Attlee Government in 1951, over the proposed introduction of a one shilling charge for prescriptions from doctors in the National Health Service, but became leader of the Parliamentary Labour Party in February 1963, following the death of Hugh Gaitskell. Twice – in 1964 and again in 1966 – he led his party to victory at the polls.

Yet in 1968 a bitterly disappointed young Socialist expressed a widely held view when he said that 'Harold Wilson has betrayed the idealism of a generation'. Trying to be all things to all men, he had ended up by pleasing none. He had clung to Britain's world role, sacrificed cherished party principles in the unsuccessful battle to maintain the parity of the pound, and rejected most of the radical solutions urged upon him by his followers. He was a master of the headline – but too many headlines had been followed by too many anti-climaxes.

Harold Wilson himself is still inclined to put the blame chiefly on the massive £800 million balance of payments deficit which he 'inherited' from the Conservatives. He also retains a strong feeling that the City – indeed the whole financial world – was involved in some kind of conspiracy against his Labour Government. Jim Callaghan, who was at the Treasury throughout the period, maintains that the Government was always fighting a losing battle. As he sees it, the need to defend sterling against repeated speculative attacks made his task virtually impossible. George Brown, the man who launched the incomes policy and the first drive to change Britain's industrial structure, also says that, 'we were kept in the old strait-jacket because overseas confidence was always held to be paramount and, it was repeatedly claimed to be achievable only by deflation'.

The Opposition, naturally, takes a very different view. In the heated debate which followed devaluation, Mr Edward Heath put the blame on the Government's 'incompetence'. Mr Wilson and his colleagues, he declared, had 'failed the people'.

An independent voice, *The Economist*, makes a more fundamental point. There is a danger, it says, 'that on the central problem of the economy, as far as Britain can decide for itself, this country could become virtually ungovernable'. The country 'wants the economic ends of increasing prosperity all right, but it is adamantly reluctant to will the means. Successive governments in the 1960's have discovered that the electorate is not prepared to tolerate tough, unpopular economic measures, however necessary, for much longer than six months. The country has sought and still seeks, a painless economic miracle to be performed with biblical speed and precision. Any solution that offers the prospect of being a quick, sure-fire panacea attracts mass support, whether it is for a coalition government, a week's "I'm backing Britain" campaign, or the overthrow of Harold Wilson'. I do not go along with this diagnosis, but it certainly merits consideration. Are we really mesmerized by gimmicks, and unwilling to acknowledge that economic miracles cannot be performed overnight? Or has the traumatic experience of the Government's first three years made us realize that 'building a new Britain' takes time and a lot of effort?

Harold Wilson himself admits that he underestimated the size of the economic problem and the time it would take to overcome it. He misjudged the handicap presented by the huge balance of payments deficit bequeathed to him, and the willingness of people to adjust their ideas and arrangements. With the advantage of hindsight, he feels that his Government tried to do too much, too soon. It tackled its 1964 and 1966 manifesto commitments with almost reckless speed, pushing through Bills at the rate of sixty a year for the first forty-four months. It raised pensions and family allowances, and made sure that unemployment would cause far less hardship than it did in the 'thirties. But Harold Wilson failed to obey his own dictum 'The exercise of priorities – this is what Government is about. This is what politics is about. It involves hard and painful decisions.'

Harold Wilson got his priorities wrong, and frequently evaded 'hard and painful decisions'. He was surprised to discover – eventually – that the rank and file failed to appreciate his Government's determination to improve welfare benefits. Surveys conducted in 1968 showed that many working class people were opposed to the increase in family allowances, and to the generous treatment of men who found themselves out of work. The re-introduction of prescription charges, after devaluation, caused far less fuss among voters than it did among Labour MPs.

Harold Wilson was – and is – a superb parliamentary performer. But he lacks the ruthlessness and detachment of the late Clem

Attlee, and the cool arrogance of Harold Macmillan. He can be vindictive, but he is basically a kind man. He wants to be admired, and he is proud of being a 'seven-day-a-week politician'. (In contrast to Roy Jenkins and Reginald Maudling, who are both fond of leisure.) He spends a lot of time 'counting heads', and listening to conflicting advice. The election victories of 1964 and 1966 greatly boosted his self-confidence, and he dominated the Cabinet for many months. But the July 1966 sterling crisis, and the 1967 devaluation, left their mark. So did what he himself has described as the most devastating form of character assassination any British Prime Minister has ever had to endure. As Opposition leader, he had himself done a pretty effective job on Sir Alec Douglas-Home. But his charge has been one of incompetence, in 1968 the charge made most frequently against Harold Wilson was that he 'told lies'.

In July 1968, he decided that enough was enough, and hit back. He made a speech in Newtown, Montgomeryshire, which was strongly reminiscent of the devastating broadsides which were so effective when he was opposition leader. 'We are,' he said 'a Labour Government and proud of it. And I intend to see, through the years ahead, that we go on being a Labour Government. And it is precisely because we are a Labour Government that we have had to face the bitter hostility of those who resent their own loss of power and our being where we are. No other Government can solve the problems of Britain. Or of Wales. They never have. Being a Labour Government means putting Britain first and doing it regardless of short-term popularity. Being a Labour Government means that you are fighting a hostile and bitter Establishment, a deprived Establishment soured by deprivation of office and power, which they had been brought up to believe was theirs by divine ordinance. They have not scrupled nor will they scruple, to turn to their short-term political advantage all the unpopular measures we have had to take to put the economy right, or to exploit the problems, the hardships, the tensions of an era of change.'

He went on to say, somewhat rashly, that 'keen-eyed observers' believed Britain was, after all, on her way to 'an economic miracle'. In his mind, when he said it, was the recent news that productivity was rising smartly and that industrialists were planning to invest more in new plant and equipment than at any time in the past four years. The 'second industrial revolution' was beginning to pay dividends, and he visualized going before the electorate in 1970 and asking for 'the tools to finish the job'.

His critics, predictably, made fun of the prediction. They said it would be a miracle if, by the next General Election, Labour managed to deliver half of what it promised in 1964 and 1966. Roy Jenkins, questioned on television soon afterwards, took a more cautious line than the Prime Minister. He said a miracle was *possible*, but stressed that the country first faced at least two years of 'hard slogging'. He agreed that there could be 'a very sharp turn-around in political prospects' if people could see the economic problem coming right, but added that 'it would be a very rash man who'd come to any firm conclusions for the future, the next election, or the next Parliament'.

Miracles are, by definition, easier to describe than to explain. Since 1945, two countries are said to have performed *economic* miracles – Japan and Germany. Both were devastated and demoralized by war, and began the post-war period with really terrifying problems. And yet, within a few years, their economic performance became the envy of countries like Britain.

Japan, an over-populated group of islands desperately short of food and raw materials, with tiny gold reserves and a geographical base that remains small compared with ours, managed to reach and sustain a rate of expansion which we still dream about. In the ten years to 1965, its growth rate averaged 9·7% – more than three times that of Britain – and Japan became one of the world's leading industrial nations.

Western Germany, ruined and split up at the end of the war, short of raw materials and food which had to be shared with a seemingly endless stream of refugees from the East, and burdened with a currency which no one trusted, achieved a similar transformation. Its growth rate during the ten years to 1965 averaged 6½%. Today, West Germany has the only paper currency which is generally accepted to be as good as gold.

It would be absurd to pretend that Britain is within sight of this kind of performance. But a lot of useful work has been done, and it is not unreasonable to assume – as Mr Wilson does – that the results will become increasingly apparent.

This book is designed to help the reader make up his own mind about what happened in the three years leading up to devaluation.

I have set down the main events, and have attempted to draw some lessons from them.

It cannot be a complete record, nor would I pretend that I have, somehow, managed to stumble on the magic formula that eluded Messrs Wilson, Callaghan, and Brown. But I hope that *Three Years Hard Labour* will make some contribution to a debate which is likely to continue for a long time to come.

Academic economists will no doubt argue that I have been too concerned with personalities. I make no apologies for that. The last few years have surely shown how much the economic management of a democratic country like Britain depends on the decisions of a handful of human beings, each with his own aspirations, gifts, and foibles. Economics is not an exact science, and it exists to serve people – not the other way round. The academic economist is, rightly, concerned chiefly with working out theoretical models. He can afford the luxury of being remote from reality. The politician tries to use economics to help him fulfil the promises he has made to the electorate. He holds the levers of power – and he can throw them into reverse (and all the splendid economic theories with them) at the drop of a hat. It happened in July 1966, and it will no doubt happen again.

As a financial editor, I have naturally been close to both the people and the events. Like millions of people, I hopefully supported the Labour Party in the last two elections. It gives me no pleasure to record the failures and disappointments; one only hopes that the next three years of 'hard Labour' will produce better results.

LONDON, JULY 1968.

PART 1 THE TASTE OF POWER

1 A Hundred Dynamic Days

LABOUR WON POWER for the third time on October 16, 1964, in the closest fought General Election in modern British history. The party's overall majority in the House of Commons was only five – a margin which many people considered impossibly small. But after nearly thirteen years in opposition even a narrow victory tasted deliciously sweet. A year earlier, a glum Jim Callaghan had told me that 'if we don't get in next time, I shall seriously think about leaving politics'. Now he was travelling to London from his Cardiff constituency, to take over as Chancellor of the Exchequer.

The hero of the hour, of course, was James Harold Wilson – who, at 48, had just become the youngest Prime Minister of the century. The Labour Party had won chiefly because many voters felt the time had come for a change of Government. The Tories had run down their battery of ideas and resolve, and did not look like a party which deserved a fourth term of office. Even so, it was generally agreed that they would have kept power but for the superb skill of the tubby, short, silver-haired Yorkshireman who had been elected to lead the Labour movement after the death of Hugh Gaitskell. Wilson had caught the mood of the nation, as Attlee had done in 1945 with his slogan 'let us face the future'. He promised action, and strong leadership.

Only a few years older than John Kennedy, Wilson deliberately cashed in on the youthful and aggressive image created by the American President. Britain was going to have a hundred days of dynamic activity. Harold Wilson was going to 'release the talents and energies of millions of our people', and to put pep into the ailing economy. His self-confidence was impressive. People were ready to listen to a strong personality, a leader. Sir Alec Douglas-Home, the man who had been picked to succeed Harold

Macmillan, was a nice enough chap – but on television he invariably looked nervous, indecisive, and blissfully ignorant of financial and industrial affairs. Harold Wilson, in contrast, never left any doubt that he, at least, knew exactly what was wrong with Britain and what had to be done to put things right. 'The riddle in October', *The Economist* had declared during the summer, 'is the faith voters feel they can put in Harold Wilson.'

A majority of five could hardly be called an overwhelming vote of confidence, but for the new Prime Minister it was good enough. 'I want to make it quite clear', he said on television a few hours after he had kissed hands on his appointment, 'that this will not affect our ability to govern.' Over the whole field of government there would be many changes 'which we have been given a mandate by you to carry out'. The aim was to have a true partnership between Government and people. 'We are', Mr Wilson concluded, 'facing at this time very great problems, but I feel there is nothing we cannot do together.'

The Labour Party had a lot of commitments round its neck. Some, such as the re-nationalization of the steel industry, had been inherited by Mr Wilson. Others, such as the promise to improve old age pensions and abolish the National Health Service prescription charge had been taken on before the election. But Hugh Gaitskell had succeeded in steering the party away from much of its doctrinaire thinking. It was a legacy for which Mr Wilson was extremely grateful. His own commitment was, above all, to change. He was determined to become a historical figure – the man who would drag Britain into the twenty-first century. He considered himself a Socialist, and was quite prepared to sing 'The Red Flag' when the occasion demanded it. He was anti-class and anti-Tory. But he insisted that 'socialism is essentially a pragmatic conception, related to the needs of the age and the world in which we live'. He believed in planning, shared wealth and equal opportunity, but had no time for the old-fashioned doctrinaire recipes for achieving these objectives. His dislike of nationalization was no secret. This is what appealed to the many people who voted for him even though they did not normally support the Labour Party. They had chosen a national leader, a man who could brush aside partisan considerations if it seemed in the country's best interest to do so.

But industrial change demands a reasonably stable financial

background. If the Government was going to introduce reforms, regardless of the howls of protest from vested interests, it needed to be free from constant worry about sterling. The country had to be able to take labour disputes in its stride, and it had to be able to avoid slamming on the economic brakes at regular intervals. Mr Wilson and his colleagues were well aware that this first requirement – a stable financial background – did not exist. Throughout the election campaign, they had made much of the fact that the Conservatives had run up a disturbingly high balance of payments deficit. Voters had accepted that the country was in a financial mess. So had private bankers and speculators in centres like Zurich, Paris and New York. With Labour in power, it did not matter so much who was to blame, but what the new Government intended to do about it. Mr Wilson realized this, but he was not prepared to let the Tories get off that easily. His tiny majority meant that another general election would become more or less inevitable within a year or two. If unpopular measures had to be taken, he was going to make very sure that everyone knew the reason why.

Reginald Maudling, the last Tory Chancellor, has since claimed that the seriousness of the financial position was grossly exaggerated for political reasons. Half the 1964 deficit, he points out, was due to an over-rapid rise in the net outflow of private long-term capital, which reflected exceptional items like Shell's huge investment in Italy's Montecatini group. The other half arose chiefly because, as Chancellor, he was deliberately trying to break out of the stop-go cycle by faster growth. This experiment had long been recommended by many eminent economists, and international financial co-operation had reached a point where it seemed safe to try it. The scheme, Mr Maudling adds, was nipped in the bud by the general election and never had a proper trial. As an explanation of how the deficit arose, this is perhaps fair enough. But to bankers and currency speculators, a deficit is a deficit. When it gets to worrying proportions, they act accordingly. Mr Maudling knew this full well; he would have preferred to make more room for manœuvre by getting the election out of the way in the spring.

Other Tories, needled by Mr Wilson's bitter attacks, have made the point that the Treasury's presentation methods showed the balance of payments in a needlessly unfavourable light. They concentrated on the 'basic' balance of current and long-term capital transactions, and took no account of private short-term capital movements (or 'hot' money). If these had been included, the overall deficit for 1964 would have been some £100 million smaller. It is an interesting point, and it is quite possible that the national interest would have been better served if there had been less frequent use of phrases like 'financial mess' and 'irresponsible Tory policies'. The plain fact is, nevertheless, that when Jim Callaghan moved into the Chancellor's seat he was handed a brief that would have staggered even the most understanding banker.

It forecast that 1964 would end with an £800 million balance of payments deficit, and urged immediate action. The economic policy-makers were called to No 10 Downing Street on Saturday morning – the day after Labour took office. They knew about the Treasury forecast, and they fully recognized what it meant for sterling. They also knew that the change of Government itself had added to the burden. Socialists are never popular with bankers (Mr Wilson once said that, in terms of confidence with the international banking community, a Labour Government is worth £300 million less than a Tory administration) and in spite of all the valiant effort to show that doctrinaire thinking had been discarded, it was clear that the international financial community would be suspicious of the new regime for quite some time to come.

Several of the new Government's top economic advisers suggested that devaluation was the best answer. They argued that Britain was in a 'state of fundamental disequilibrium' – meaning that British goods were uncompetitive at the existing exchange rate – and pointed out that the rules of the International Monetary Fund permitted devaluation under such circumstances. It was all very well to talk of industrial change, of import substitution and science-based industries, but these things would take time. Devaluation would buy that time. It would boost exports, and before long put the balance of payments into surplus. There would be no need for Ministers to keep looking over their shoulders to see how sterling was getting on.

It was an appealing argument, but it ignored the fact that sterling was a world currency, and that heavy deflation – the stop-go so derided by Mr Wilson during the election campaign – would be needed to make it work. Moreover, as the Bank of England was quick to point out, other countries might well decide to devalue their own currencies, so that much of the benefit would be lost. Britain's sterling area partners would be furious, and would probably start to switch their London-held sterling balances elsewhere. Another devaluation might become unavoidable within a year or two. Both the Treasury and the Bank of England considered that the snags outweighed the advantages. So did Mr Wilson, who later in the day had another meeting with Jim Callaghan and George Brown – the two men who had fought him for the party leadership when Gaitskell died, and who were now in joint charge of economic policy. It was an informal get-together without experts, and it ended in a unanimous decision not to devalue.

As a trained economist, Wilson knew the arguments in favour of devaluation. He had advanced them all himself in 1949, when he had persuaded Stafford Cripps to devalue. And no-one needed to tell him that the need for it could be blamed on the Tories. The country would have accepted his explanation without a murmur. But he genuinely believed that it would produce only a temporary gain, and he didn't want the Labour Party to be saddled with the label of 'devaluation party'. He also knew that the Americans would be embarrassed by devaluation. The subject had been brought up a few times during his frequent trips to Washington as Leader of the Opposition, and although he has always denied that the US administration was involved in the decision taken on October 17, or even consulted, there is no doubt that he was thoroughly familiar with its views. When he got down to his discussion with Callaghan and Brown, his mind was already made up. Callaghan quickly agreed. He took the somewhat odd line that there was no public call for devaluation, and went on to argue – more reasonably – that to devalue at that particular point would be bad timing. If Britain was indeed in a state of fundamental disequilibrium, which he doubted, the Tories should have devalued a year earlier. George Brown, who had been impressed by the arguments of convinced devaluers like Sir Donald MacDougall and Nicholas Kaldor, was a bit more hesitant. As the new Economics Minister, it would be his job to defend the cause of the expansionists. If devaluation would give him more elbow room, it might not be a bad thing. Wilson, however, was in no mood to have a long debate. He had made his ruling, and he intended to stick to it.

The obvious next step was to decide what measures should be taken to tackle the ominous payments deficit, and maintain confidence in the existing parity. As it happened, Jim Callaghan had found that contingency plans to deal with the situation had already been prepared by the Treasury before the election. This is normal procedure, designed to ensure that ministers can take action, if and when necessary, which is based on a carefully prepared study of all the practical alternatives.

Reginald Maudling, greatly nettled by Mr Wilson's constant talk about 'the financial mess' which he had left behind, could not resist claiming some of the credit for Labour's forthcoming measures in advance. A week after the election, he wrote in *The Sunday Times*: 'I have no doubt that future months will show an improvement, but the time may now have come to introduce import quotas, surcharges or export subsidies. It was after all with this possibility in mind that I arranged for all the practical implications of such schemes to be worked out in advance.' This understandable, but politically misguided, boast gave Mr Wilson another opportunity to sneer at the Tories and he did not hesitate to take it.

The actual package, presented in a White Paper (promptly dubbed 'The Brown Paper') on the following day combined a 15% import surcharge with tax incentives to exporters. Bank rate, purchase tax and other traditional weapons were ignored. 'Apart from special problems of individual areas and a limited number of industries', the White Paper declared, 'there is no undue pressure on resources calling for action. Moreover the Government reject any policy based on a return to stop-go economics'. Ministers, the paper added, had taken stock of the international financial situation and had satisfied themselves that, with the facilities available, 'the strength of sterling can and will be maintained.'

To most of us who faced the smiling Brown-Callaghan team across a long Treasury table that morning, this seemed an astonishing anti-climax, especially as the Government had chosen the occasion to make public the Treasury's alarming balance of payments forecast. As City Editor of the London *Evening Standard*, I had to meet an edition deadline and I popped out to the ante-office to dictate my story – plus a 600-word article which the *Standard* billed as 'A personal view' on the Chancellor's telephone. 'After all the advance publicity and Mr Wilson's pre-election shouts of crisis', I wrote, 'today's fire-cracker seems a bit of a damp squib. The White Paper predicts a 1964 payments deficit of £700 million, or even £800 million. If this is so, Mr Wilson and his team may yet be forced to resort to a high bank rate and other measures'. Where, I went on to ask, 'is the tough talking we had been led to expect? Where are the detailed plans? Where is the condemnation of restrictive practices which, as much as any capital gains tax, is essential if Britain is to get moving again? Platitudes may work well when you are attacking Governments, but not when you are trying to bring about a major revolution'. The morning papers took much the same line, and *The Economist* that week said that 'the real question is whether there has been half enough of a bloody revolution'. The Government, it thought, 'has done just sufficiently greatly to annoy foreign countries, but hardly anything to enable Britain to sell more competitively in international markets which are going to be made more difficult for us as the result of that annoyance.'

We were, perhaps, a little less than fair because the White Paper had also pledged Ministers to carry out 'a strict review of all Government expenditure', with the object of 'relieving the strain on the balance of payments, and release resources for more productive purposes by cutting our expenditure on items of low economic priority, such as prestige projects'. There was, further a strong hint that Mr Callaghan would shortly be producing an autumn Budget. Even so, it seemed that Mr Wilson had not taken his own diagnosis of our financial ills anything like as seriously as he should have done.

The Prime Minister went on television, a few hours after the Brown-Callaghan double-act, to explain to his partners, the British people, what it was all about. The first essential, he said, was a strong economy. This alone would enable us to maintain the value of the pound, and improve conditions in Britain. We had been living on borrowed money, but this could not go on for ever. The international financial agencies 'and our friends abroad' had the right to expect that we would urgently take measures to ensure that we could stand on our own feet. This meant taking all the steps that a Government could take, all the steps that a people could take, to bring our exports and imports into a reasonable balance. The 'comprehensive' measures announced that morning were aimed at doing this. 'But you know', Mr Wilson added, 'the real drive for our national economic strength and independence is a tougher and inevitably a longer-term job'. This was why the Government had set up the Department of Economic Affairs, and a Ministry of Technology. He and his colleagues had met the industrial leaders on both sides of industry, and they had been left in no doubt of what was needed. We had to reach agreement on a planned incomes policy – incomes rising with production. We had to work out a system which put first things first. The nation's problems could be mastered, but only if we mobilized the energies of all our people, in the job of modernizing Britain by harnessing to our task the scientific revolution of our time. 'I do not', Mr Wilson concluded, 'underrate what this means for all of us. But don't let us think of it as a burdensome duty – it is an exciting, challenging adventure in partnership, in partnership with the Government and the people of Britain'.

The people could not reply to the man on the box in their living-rooms, but had they been able to do so millions would undoubtedly have approved of the sentiments expressed. They were all for modernizing Britain, and improving conditions. The import surcharge and export incentive seemed OK by them: it would hardly involve any sacrifice.

It quickly emerged, however, that the package was *not* OK by our partners in the European Free Trade Association – a 'club' of seven nations, including Britain, set up after the breakdown of Common Market negotiations in 1962. The surcharge represented a flagrant breach of the club's trading rules, and the British Government had not even had the courtesy to despatch special envoys with advance notice of its proposal. The storm of protest which followed took Mr Wilson and his colleagues by complete surprise – the first of many occasions on which they were to be amazed by the behaviour of foreigners who hadn't been let in on the great partnership. The only country which supported the package, it emerged, was the United States. Washington was ready to welcome any measures which would preserve the existing sterling parity, and President Johnson appreciated Mr Wilson's decision not to raise Britain's bank rate during the American election campaign. But America's goodwill did not make up for the fury of Europe.

On November 7 – just three weeks after the election – the

Government presented its ambitious legislative menu for the coming Parliamentary session in the customary Queen's Speech. It presaged no less than nineteen bills – covering industrial retraining, monopolies and mergers, a major review of the social security schemes, the re-nationalization of steel, company law reform, the re-establishment of rent control, facilities for a free vote on capital punishment, and the establishment of a British Ombudsman. George Brown, determined to add another piece of dynamic activity, announced the following day that a further bill, not included in the Queen's Speech, would be brought in to regulate office building.

But it was Jim Callaghan who, a few days later, grabbed the really big headlines with his first mini-Budget. The speed with which it had been prepared was impressive, but the Budget itself turned out to be a costly blunder. (Mr Wilson himself regards it as the biggest mistake of his Government's first three years). I remember, very clearly, the stunned reaction it produced in the office of *The Evening Standard*, in the City, and in industry. My own comment to my Editor was that 'they have gone mad', and the paper's leader writer and I sat down to compose one of the most biting articles I have ever been associated with in my life.

Callaghan had meant well. He wanted to honour Labour's election pledges to raise pensions and abolish prescription charges, and he thought it would impress the bankers if he paid for it by raising income tax and petrol duty. He also believed it would help George Brown with his incomes policy if he foreshadowed a stiffer capital gains tax and a switch to corporation tax. The Gnomes of Zurich, far from being impressed, were astonished by the decision to put old age pensions and the Health Service first at a time of desperate financial crisis. They brushed aside the fact that, overall, the Budget was mildly deflationary. As far as they were concerned, all their fears about Socialist irresponsibility had been confirmed. At home, City businessmen and industrialists were amazed that the Chancellor had failed to foresee the havoc which would be caused by a vague announcement to switch over to a corporation tax in five months' time. The charge of incompetence was levelled against the Labour Government for the first time. Instead of super-efficiency and consistency, the new team had come up with measures which, it was argued, were both ill-prepared and totally irrelevant to the country's main problems.

Mr Wilson gave no sign that he was aware of this feeling when he went to the City a few days later, to speak at the Lord Mayor's banquet. He talked about Britain's role in the world, and assured 'our friends in EFTA' that the Government considered the import surcharge a step in the wrong direction, and would keep it only as long as it was needed, and not a day longer. He re-affirmed the Government's determination 'to keep sterling strong and see it riding high'. But he also said that the Government rejected 'the defeatist doctrine that the only way to keep the pound strong is to keep the economy weak'. Deflation and contraction, far from making the country more efficient and competitive, had the opposite effect. It pushed up costs, discouraged essential investment, and encouraged restrictive attitudes on both sides of industry. It made an incomes policy infinitely harder to achieve. Nor was the Government prepared to accept the unemployment and loss of production that was entailed. None of us who were at the banquet disagreed with this. But we were still left wondering, at the end of Mr Wilson's speech how he was going to cope with the combined impact of an £800 million balance of payments deficit, and the suspicion created in financial markets by his Chancellor's Budget and the controversial surcharge.

2 The First Crisis

THE POUND DID badly in the days following the November Budget, and money was leaving London at a disturbing rate. Lord Cromer, the Governor of the Bank of England, urged the Chancellor to raise Bank Rate by 1%. This, he pointed out, would make it more worthwhile for foreign depositors to leave their funds where they were. Mr Callaghan promised to take the suggestion up with George Brown and the Prime Minister. When he did so, Mr Brown would have none of it. The Bank Rate weapon, he pointed out, was part of the old Tory armoury, which Labour had discarded. An increase would harm industrial investment, and would also lead to dearer home loans. (George Brown, in a widely publicized pre-election gaffe, had promised 3% mortgages.)

Mr Wilson also opposed a change but for rather different reasons. An increased British Bank Rate would almost certainly have forced the Americans to follow suit, and he was anxious not to embarrass President Johnson during the presidential election campaign. Wilson felt he was on good terms with the White House, and that if necessary the President would come to Britain's aid with a sizeable loan. He wanted to do nothing which might affect the goodwill which he was sure existed in Washington. A lengthy cable was dispatched, informing President Johnson of the somewhat awkward situation which the British Government was finding itself in, and asking for his views. The aristocratic Lord Cromer considered this quite unnecessary; he was in constant touch with the Federal Reserve, which is in charge of interest rates policy in the United States, and he was convinced that a 1% Bank Rate increase would cause no bother to the President. He took a dim view of Mr Wilson's indecision, and took little trouble to hide his feelings.

Mr Wilson's attitude was indeed rather puzzling. London's need was obviously greater than Washington's, and a firm decision would have been applauded in the financial world, and grudgingly accepted by George Brown. If, as the Prime Minister believed, President Johnson was ready to protect the pound because it represented the first line of defence for the dollar, a 1% rise in Bank Rate was hardly likely to produce an about turn at the White House. The only possible explanation is that, at this stage, Mr Wilson and his colleagues still had not experienced the frightening swiftness of a major run on a currency, and therefore underrated the risks they were taking. They were determined not to be pushed around by old Etonians like Lord Cromer, and to sacrifice economic expansion to the whim of speculators.

They were soon to learn. When Thursday – the day on which Bank Rate changes are normally made – came and went without a decision, sterling came under heavy pressure. The Bank of England had to use the gold reserves to prop up the exchange rate, and lost millions in a single day. In Geneva, Douglas Jay, the President of the Board of Trade, was kept up until dawn defending the Government's decision to introduce an import surcharge. And when Washington sent its reply to the Wilson cable, it turned out to be completely non-committal. Mr Wilson was beginning to realize that making forceful speeches from the Opposition front bench was a good deal easier than governing. So were Jim Callaghan and George Brown, though at this stage all three men were still inclined to blame their political enemies in the City for much of what was going on in foreign exchange markets. The Prime Minister quickly made up his mind to raise Bank Rate after all, and Sir Eric Roll, a top DEA man who had been dispatched to Washington earlier in the week to 'liaise' with senior officials there, was instructed by telephone to communicate the decision to the White House.

Having done this, Mr Wilson and his colleagues were impatient to translate words into action. George Brown, always the most volatile of the trio, insisted that they should not wait until the following Thursday, November 26, to announce the change. The way to deal with a crisis was to act at once. He suggested that an announcement should be made on Monday morning, and that the increase should be 2%. This, he felt, would show the 'Gnomes of Zurich' once and for all that the Government meant business. His suggestion was adopted. The reaction, however, was somewhat different from the one he had predicted. Bank Rate had not been changed on a Monday since the depression days of 1931. Far from feeling reassured, many people in the financial world concluded that the Government's unusual step was a sign of panic. The situation, they felt, must be worse than expected if the Government considered it imperative to act at once, and to raise the rate to what was then regarded as a crisis level – 7%.

Speculators, as always, were quick to exploit the general uncertainty. Newspapers, too, contributed to the jitters by headlining the daily fluctuations in the pound, and writing long commentaries on the Government's apparent predicament. And businessmen who had signed contracts with overseas customers began to anticipate their foreign currency needs, in case the pound was suddenly devalued. It was the classical pattern, and it was to be repeated several times until the pound finally succumbed in November 1967. Selling of sterling increased, and the Bank of England was again forced to give considerable support. The monthly gold reserve returns, published on December 2, showed a fall of £39 million, to the lowest level for several years. But this was a phoney figure, fixed in order to keep speculators guessing. The true loss was a great deal more than that. The Treasury's statement admitted that Britain had borrowed money from the European central banks, and announced that she was immediately drawing the full £357 million standby credit arranged with the International Monetary Fund some weeks earlier. The pressure on sterling continued, and more and more people began to talk openly about the possibility of an early devaluation.

The Tories, understandably, were rather pleased by Mr Wilson's discomforture. Mr Maudling, in particular, saw an opportunity to repay some of the pre-election abuse. 'In the last few days', he told the Commons, 'there has been a collapse of confidence in the present Government's ability to handle our economic affairs'. The Prime Minister was determined to refute this. Speaking at the Labour Party Conference on December 14, he repeated that no-one should be in doubt about his Government's willingness to take every measure that was necessary. Having been entrusted by the nation with the duties of Government, he and his colleagues intended to govern. No decision would be burked, no decision would be trimmed because of the possibility – 'however remote in our minds' – of an early election. The spirit of Dunkirk, Mr Wilson added, would 'once again carry us through to success'. This said, however, the Prime Minister emphasized – as he had done previously – that 'this is not a return to Selwyn Lloyd'. Unlike their predecessors, ministers did not believe that the way to deal with a kind of crisis which was endemic in the industrial structure which they had inherited, was to bring the whole economy shuddering to a stop. 'The way to a strong pound', Mr Wilson declared, 'is through a strong economy, not by creating unemployment, holding production down, raising costs, deterring investment and creating the insecurity which breeds restrictive practices on both sides of industry'. The faithful nodded their approval, as the bankers had done at the Guildhall banquet less than a month before. But again, the financial world wondered whether the Labour Government really knew what it was up against.

Behind the scenes, Mr Wilson was conducting an increasingly fierce argument with Lord Cromer, who was attempting to rub in the financial facts of life. The Governor suggested sharp cuts in Government spending, and further deflationary measures. The Prime Minister reminded him that there had just been an election, and that he was now dealing with a Labour Prime Minister. He should not, and could not, resort to exactly the same orthodox measures which he had attacked for so long. It was not what the British people had elected him to do. The answer to Britain's problems lay in industrial change, and not in HP controls and increased taxes. If sterling was in trouble, which he conceded was the case, then the right course was to seek financial assistance abroad – and especially in Washington. The Americans, he was sure, would be quite ready to help prevent devaluation. So would most of Europe's bankers. Why didn't Lord Cromer get on with the job of raising the necessary funds?

Lord Cromer went back to the Bank of England in the City, and set about doing just that. He telephoned Charles Coombs, of the Federal Reserve Bank in New York, with whom he always had very close relations. Coombs had already been made aware that Washington was indeed prepared to mount a rescue operation. But it was not willing to do the job alone; the British had to persuade the European central banks to come in on the deal. Lord Cromer promptly put a call through to each of his fellow members in the 'Basle club', as the Bank for International Settlements had become known. Within 24 hours, the Governor had managed to put together a $3,000 million package – an impressive amount by anybody's standards. It was a remarkable performance, and Mr Wilson expressed both relief and somewhat grudging admiration. The Bank of England public relations man made sure that Fleet Street knew where the credit belonged, and reports from Zurich and other centres suggested that the speculators had conceded defeat – at least for the time being – in the face of such united resolve to defend the pound.

Christmas turned out to be a cheerful occasion for Ministers after all. In February, Mr Wilson decided the time had come for another fireside chat with his partners, the British people. The bankers' support operation, he said in a peak-time television broadcast, had given the country a necessary breathing space – but no more than that. We had to use that breathing space to pull Britain through a position of secure and unchallengable economic strength. We would do it. We had faced much tougher propositions when we had been up against it before, and we had won through. We had won through whenever, at moments of national crisis, our people had been given the facts, told the plain unvarnished truth; and told what the national interest required.

'Time after time in our history', Mr Wilson went on, the world, friends and enemies alike, had been prepared to write us off as finished. But time after time – and this had run like a golden thread through our history – a nation which seemed to slumber had called up 'those inner reserves of effort and of character which have enabled us to shake the world with our response'. From now on our approach had to be: from everyone, whatever his position, on whatever side of industry, a full day's work for a full day's pay. Good money, yes, but it had to be earned. We had to pay for skill and expertise, and we had to use it. In every department of management, production, sales, we had to be a lot more professional. In the modern world the gentlemen could not beat the players. This was getting to be a familiar message – and in his DEA office round the corner from the Treasury, the Prime Minister's First Secretary of State was doing his energetic best to see that the gentlemen of the industrial world were turned into centre-forwards.

2

3 Life with Brother

THE FIRST TIME I saw George Brown in action abroad, four months after the 1964 General Election, was at the Beau Rivage Hotel in Geneva, where he and Douglas Jay were staying for the EFTA conference. Half a dozen of us had asked if we could see him, and he bounced into the room during the afternoon. We found it difficult to get a sensible reply to any of our questions. He kept telling us to be 'good patriots', and one could hardly make out what he was saying. When we asked him about rumours that Britain would be cutting its controversial surcharge (a decision which was officially announced a few hours later) he became very aggressive. Out of the blue, I found myself threatened with being 'drummed out of the country'. The storm, however, subsided as quickly as it had blown up and I found myself warmly embraced by the Deputy Prime Minister and First Secretary of State. Early the next morning I was called down to have breakfast in his suite, and Mr Brown told me with disarming candour: 'Anyone can be a bloody fool; I was a bloody fool yesterday'.

This episode, I soon learned, was fairly typical of George Brown's behaviour. He was enthusiastic, but impetuous. He was more energetic than any other Cabinet Minister, but also more erratic and impatient. He was likeable and persuasive, but often indiscreet and moody. He was self-confident, but curiously touchy. He was quick to spot and condemn bad work in others, but hated criticism of himself. Like most people, he was also partial to a drop of gin or Scotch.

George Brown's drinking habits were, right from the start, a favourite topic in company boardrooms and the lobbies of Westminster. But Fleet Street – which he attacked so often, and so vigorously – protected him to a remarkable degree. It invariably referred to his 'odd social behaviour', or simply explained that he was 'tired'. The public only caught occasional glimpses of what this meant when Mr Brown insisted on going through with a radio or TV broadcast, even though he was advised against doing so.

How did he get away with all this for so long? One answer, of course, is that the British love a 'character'. The public image of Harold Wilson was that of an ambitious career politician, a man whose only interest was gaining power – and keeping it. He was respected, but not really liked. Brother George, for all his moods, was warm-hearted and exuberant. His very unpredictability was regarded as an asset: he was not just another stuffy, self-centred politician. Brother George took his shoes off under a banqueting table if his feet hurt, asked his host's wife for a kiss during the main course, and never missed a chance to talk lovingly about 'the people of Swadlincote' – a village in his constituency. To most people, it did not matter in the least that he shocked the upper crust – the Treasury knights and the Foreign Office mandarins. Brother George was blowing away the cobwebs, and if his manner and methods were often unorthodox it was of no consequence. The Prime Minister and other colleagues were naturally aware of this feeling. George Brown's standing in the Labour Party was such that they could not have pushed him out of the Cabinet, even if they had wanted to. They also recognized his undoubted qualities – his quick grasp of essentials, his restless determination, his sudden flashes of charm. Brother George had to be endured, even if he threw frequent tantrums.

Whether, on balance, George Brown did more harm than good in the long period during which he was officially in charge of economic policy is a debatable point. His vigorous advocacy of expansionist policies – enforced by frequent threats to resign if he didn't get his way – helped to delay or water down action which the Treasury considered essential if the balance of payments deficit was to be eliminated. It therefore played a considerable part in bringing on the repeated sterling crises. His equally vigorous advocacy of an early application to join the Common Market helped to persuade Harold Wilson to enter a venture which proved fruitless, but contributed to the factors which eventually forced him to devalue.

As Deputy Premier and First Secretary of State, Brown stuck his finger into every pie – often with expensive consequences. His main asset was that he proved to be a splendid innovator, a man of action who could make the theorist's dream come true. No one contributed more than he did to the process of industrial change which Mr Wilson had pledged the Government to initiate. Brown would unquestionably have been more successful if it had not been for that gaping balance of payments deficit. But by behaving much of the time as if it did not exist, or did not matter, he helped to discredit many of his favourite policies.

The Department of Economic Affairs, of course, had been specially created for him. Brown himself has said that the idea was born in July 1963, when he and Harold Wilson were travelling back to the House of Commons in a taxi, after a private dinner at a London hotel. But in fact, there was nothing very new in the idea of having two parallel economic ministers. In 1945–47, Herbert Morrison had been placed as Economic Co-Ordinator alongside of Hugh Dalton as Chancellor. The experiment had turned out to be notably unsuccessful, and in the end full responsibility had been handed to Stafford Cripps as Chancellor of the Exchequer and Minister of Economic Affairs. For years afterwards, Labour's intellectuals continued to debate the pros and cons. But it did not really become important until Harold Wilson defeated George Brown for the party leadership. Brown took his defeat badly. What would become of him now? The prospect of becoming Deputy Premier, without any departmental responsibility, did not appeal to him at all. Mr Wilson himself was keenly interested in foreign affairs, and indicated that he did not want a strong and independent personality in the Foreign Office if Labour gained power. The Chancellorship was already promised to Jim Callaghan. Any other job would have been junior, and would have been unacceptable.

Creating a new department, in which George Brown's knowledge of the trade union movement and his tremendous enthusiasm could be fully employed, seemed a very obvious solution. The DEA would look after medium- and long-term economic policy, provide the machinery for re-structuring industry, and launch an effective prices and incomes policy. Wilson, who welcomed the prospect of 'creative tension' between the DEA and the stuffy old Treasury, gave him the green light and he began to work at once. The General Election, which many people had expected to take place in the spring of 1964, did not actually come until October – the last possible date. This gave him time to organize discussions, seminars, and conferences with all kinds of people: academics, trade union leaders, industrialists, and even civil servants. One of his first recruits was Sir Eric Roll, who had been Edward Heath's top aide in the 1962 Common Market negotiations and later became the Treasury's man in Washington. He also tried to get Roy Jenkins as Minister of State, but Jenkins turned his offer down. By the time the Labour Party got its hands on the levers of power, George Brown was all ready to swing into action.

Most of the limelight, inevitably, fell on the productivity, prices and incomes policy. Like the DEA itself, this innovation was not new. It had been tried (without conspicuous success) in countries like Sweden, and the Conservative Government had set up a National Incomes Commission in Britain. But Selwyn Lloyd had failed in 1961, partly because he went about it in a clumsy way, but also because he was an old-style Tory. Reginald Maudling was more skilful, but failed because trade unions wanted to see a Labour Government in power. Both had remained keen supporters of the idea.

Trade union goodwill is supposed to be one of the Labour Party's greatest assets – offsetting its unpopularity with bankers – and there were high hopes that Mr Brown's efforts would be crowned with success. The Government certainly staked a lot on it. Economic policies were, for a long time, based on the assumption that incomes could be held down, and many sacrificial offerings were made on the altar of the incomes policy. The Prices and Incomes Board, which was set up by Mr Brown as a kind of semi-official watchdog, explained the *raison d'être* for the policy's existence in its first annual report. 'We either', it said, 'pitch demand so much below the limits of capacity that the uncertainties attendant on its fine regulation are diminished and the power of management and unions to contribute to inflationary pressure are reduced; or secure appropriate behaviour by managements and unions with regard to prices and incomes so that demand can be pitched nearer the limits of capacity and a higher growth rate achieved.' In plain English, do we have lasting deflation and unemployment, or do we start looking beyond the end of our own noses?

The incomes policy was 'sold' to trade union leaders on the

basis that it was a viable alternative to stop-go, and would therefore benefit the whole country. The traditional system of free collective bargaining, George Brown told them, was out of date. It constantly produced inflationary pressures, which then had to be tackled by tough Government action. It was also socially unjust, because the distribution of incomes was decided by organized strength, and not on ethical grounds. Union leaders still had considerable misgivings, but decided to co-operate in the experiment – providing that the *voluntary* principle was applied. Industrial leaders also agreed to take part on this understanding, and in December 1964 George Brown announced his great triumph: the signing of a 'declaration of intent'.

The piece of paper which he happily waved for the benefit of press photographers pledged the Government, the employers' organizations, and the Trade Union Congress to raise productivity throughout industry and commerce; to keep increases in total money incomes in line with increases in real national output; and to maintain a stable general price level.

The declaration of intent, which really marked the beginning of an 'incomes policy period in Britain', was followed by an agreement on the 'machinery of prices and incomes policy' published in February 1965. The main proposal in this was the setting up of the National Board for Prices and Incomes, to examine particular cases of price and incomes behaviour and advise whether they were in the national interest or not. Then in April a further agreed White Paper was published setting out the criteria to be used in determining prices and incomes, and indicating that the average rate of annual increase in money incomes per head must be kept in line with an underlying productivity rise of 3–3½%.

To head his new board, Mr Brown picked a former Tory Minister, Mr Aubrey Jones. He had left politics to become chairman of an industrial concern, Staveley Industries, at £20,000 a year and he first heard about George Brown's offer from a newspaper reporter who telephoned to check a rumour that Jones was the top runner. When the formal approach was made, his attractive wife was firmly against acceptance. Her view, expressed in characteristically vigorous fashion, was that he was doing well enough in his industrial job and that he ought not to get embroiled in a highly complex and controversial notion dreamed up by a Labour Government. He passed this on to Brother George, who promptly turned his charm on her. The two were wined and dined, and sweet-talked. In the end – as so often happens with the fair sex – she relented. Aubrey Jones has since given three main reasons why he said 'yes'.

'The first – a negative one – was the fact that, unknown to me, my name appeared on a list submitted by the Government both to employers and to trade unions, and mine was the only name accepted by both. This being so, I had no honourable alternative but to say "Yes".

'Secondly, the entire job seemed to me to represent a pioneering effort; pioneering in that it was a means by which Government could influence the evolution of life in the country by looking at concrete instances, instead of indulging in general exhortation. Pioneering, too, in the sense that I felt that in this age of large economic units, large trade unions, large firms, some degree of Government supervision was inevitable.

'Thirdly, over the entire post-war period our economic record was dismal. This indicated that the existing means of regulating the economy – monetary and fiscal weapons – were insufficient. Something else was needed to complement them: a prices and incomes policy. And somebody had to get it off the ground!'

Aubrey Jones kept his formal membership of the Conservative Party, and countered suggestions that he had gone over to the 'other side' with the comment that 'the essence of the job is that it must be exercised independently of the Government of the day'.

He recruited a team of economists, and set to work. George Brown, too, put in long hours at the DEA. He held countless meetings with union officials and employers' representatives – alternately charming and threatening them, according to his mood of the moment. His enthusiasm was infectious, but he frequently undid the good he had done early in the day by a sudden, impulsive display of temper. Like Lord Beaverbrook in the second world war, he was fond of 'phoning people at midnight and giving them a piece of his mind. It did not always produce the results he had intended.

Meantime, of course, the Government had run into its first sterling crisis, and it became clear that bankers at home and abroad had little faith in Labour's new wonder weapon.

During the summer of 1965 Treasury officials pointed out to Mr Callaghan that earnings were continuing to rise quite sharply, and came up with proposals for a compulsory warning system on impending wage claims and intended price increases including statutory powers of enforcement. George Brown did not like this at all, and nor did Harold Wilson. But senior advisers stressed that, if nothing was done, sterling was certain to run into serious trouble. The pound was already looking shaky, and the Governor of the Bank of England was pressing for urgent action. Washington, too, felt strongly that the British Government ought to 'put teeth in its incomes policy'. The Administration was prepared to go on propping up the pound, but only if the British showed some 'sense of responsibility'.

At the end of July, Mr Callaghan announced delays in public spending, new exchange control measures, and new curbs on office building and hire-purchase. George Brown, urged to do his bit, reluctantly agreed to talk to the two sides of industry. The meeting lasted more than six hours, and was anything but friendly. Brown carefully explained that confidence in the pound was low, that negotiations were under way for a new support operation, and that the Americans demanded some assurance that the incomes policy could be made to produce results. He was personally still very much in favour of the voluntary principle, but our friends abroad wanted something more definite. He needed to assure them that both the trade unions and the employers were prepared to co-operate. The two sides then withdrew to discuss the situation among themselves. When they returned, the employers' said they were still fundamentally opposed to statutory measures, but were prepared to go along with Mr Brown's proposal on a strictly short-term basis. The TUC's General Secretary, George Woodcock, explained at some length that he felt unable to agree. 'It is impossible', he said, 'to inject into a voluntary long-run policy a quick-acting drug with temporary effects. In essence the method must be long, slow and painful.'

A few months earlier Mr Brown might have said much the same thing himself, but now he found Woodcock's attitude exasperating. Didn't the unions realize what was at stake? Did they really want Washington to withdraw its offer of support? Woodcock was non-committal: he wanted time to consult a wider circle of TUC members. After a phone call to the Prime Minister, Mr Brown agreed to this. But time was short, and on September 1 the Government decided to go ahead with the introduction of an early warning system. The enforcement was to be left to Mr Brown's discretion. The next day (his fifty-first birthday) he went down to the TUC's General Council meeting in Brighton, and stated his case in a blunt, brilliant speech. He promised that he would not make an order to bring the new provisions into effect unless he was convinced that they were necessary to make the prices and incomes policy effective. Before coming to any decision, he would consult the TUC and the Confederation of British Industry. In these circumstances, the TUC approved a proposal by its General Council: all affiliated unions were required to refer pay claims to the Council before proceeding with them. Unions were expected to refrain from any action until they heard the TUC's view.

A few days later on November 25 the Government announced massive new international support for the pound. The amount was not disclosed, but the statement was enough. Sterling had been badly oversold, and the Bank of England mounted a vigorous 'bear squeeze'. Another crisis had been overcome.

Mr Aubrey Jones's board, meanwhile, had been made into a statutory body and was investigating a number of industries. But it was still essentially an inquiry agency, which could only deal with cases referred to the board by the Department of Economic Affairs, and it had no power to enforce its recommendations. It was a situation which Mr Jones found frustrating, but he made the best of it. So did the TUC's special wage-vetting committee. All seemed to be going reasonably well until ten months later. Then the roof fell in.

As before, it was pressure on the pound which suddenly changed the situation. Early in July 1966 Frank Cousins, who had become increasingly unhappy about the whole incomes policy, resigned from the Cabinet and announced that he would actively oppose it. Three weeks later on July 20, the Government found itself in the middle of another major sterling crisis, and called in both sides of industry to announce its bombshell: there was to be a complete standstill on prices and pay increases.

George Brown had already told the Prime Minister that he was resigning over this decision, and the deflationary package which accompanied it, so Mr Wilson himself had to deal with the trade union leaders and employers' representatives. It was a stormy session. George Woodcock told him bluntly that the TUC would 'not accept the freeze'. Wilson replied: 'You know what that means'. Woodcock knew alright, but the prospect of devaluation did not hold the same terror for him as it apparently did for the Prime Minister. Wilson proceeded to explain that if Britain devalued everyone else would follow, and there would be world-wide chaos. Trade would slump, unemployment would soar. Did Woodcock want to take responsibility for putting one and a half million people out of work?

The freeze which lasted for six months, was followed by another six months period of severe restraint, in which pay increases were allowed only in exceptional conditions. George Brown, who had withdrawn his resignation after a few hours of highly-publicized sulking, was spared the embarrassment of having to preside over it. He went off to the Foreign Office, to deal with global problems, though not before declaring in the heated economic debate which followed the July package that 'in order to get through the economic problems I am prepared with the support of my friends' – he gestured at the ministers on the front bench behind him – 'to say to the price fixers and management and the unions that there will have to be some compulsion. We must have a breathing space.'

The July package, and especially the freeze, made nonsense of the National Plan, and everything else the Government had put its faith in for nearly two years. Policies which, by their very nature, took time to produce had been overtaken by short-term pressures.

The freeze was crude, and it was imposed on an arbitrary date and without warning. Aubrey Jones, like most other people associated with the incomes policy, was shattered. But he soon managed to persuade himself that the psychological impact of the freeze might actually help in the long run. 'It has made people face realities', he told me over lunch. 'We must try', he added 'to establish a platform from which we can advance. The important thing is to make sure that, when we do advance, we don't run into the same situation as before.'

In a heated television debate with Frank Cousins a few days later, he insisted that Britain could never return to a strictly voluntary system. He infuriated Cousins with a crack about 'curbing the new barons', and argued that 'some element of sanctions' would always be inevitable. Senior ministers agreed, but were not prepared to be quite so blunt. They told the unions that, when the period of severe restraint was over, they would restore the same sort of system which prevailed before July 20 – a system based chiefly on the vetting process of the TUC and the Government's power of reference to the Prices and Incomes Board. This, indeed is what happened. But there were two differences. First, the TUC committee had to operate on a 'nil norm', instead of $3\frac{1}{2}\%$. Secondly, the Government could use its power of reference to the board to delay settlements for periods of up to seven months. The reserve powers, it was explained, were needed to prevent 'malicious action'.

Whether or not the freeze 'made people face up to realities', it appeared to have one merit which the earlier incomes policy had lacked. On paper, at least, it worked. The Treasury noted in its 1966 economic report that during the eighteen months before the freeze hourly wage rates were rising at an annual rate of 7% – a 'steep' climb which reflected both cash increases and a widespread reduction in the length of the standard working week. Hourly earnings had been rising faster still – by almost 10% – between April 1965 and April 1966, and wage drift (the excess of the rise in earnings over rates, including the effect on earnings of overtime) was considerable. During the period of standstill hourly rates were virtually constant, while over the six months to October 1966 hourly earnings rose by little more than 1% and wage drift was negligible. Prices were also rising strongly in the eighteen months before the standstill. During the freeze manufacturers' selling prices, influenced additionally by lower import prices, did not rise at all. Retail prices rose by $1\frac{1}{2}\%$, but most of this was attributable to the increase in indirect taxes in the July package, to the Selective Employment Tax introduced in May and to normal seasonal factors. There was, moreover, remarkably little labour trouble. The busmen, the railwaymen, the steel workers, and the dockers all had pay claims in the pipeline when the axe fell. None of them, however, had resorted to direct strike action.

Some economists, faced with these facts, said that Britain had carried through a disguised devaluation. Subsequent events, unfortunately, were to show that the freeze simply postponed wage increases. And, of course, the exchange rate of the pound had to be lowered all the same. The freeze taught everyone a lot of useful lessons, but it also produced very considerable disillusionment with the Government's effort to control incomes.

Taking the first three years as a whole, that effort could clearly not be described as a conspicuous success. Indeed, one is entitled to wonder if George Brown's 'baby' was worth all the strain it involved. The original claim that it was an effective means of maintaining full employment had been demolished by the July package. Sir Leslie O'Brien, the new Governor of the Bank of England, accurately summed up the Treasury's judgment when he said, late in 1967, that Britain would have to keep a 'larger margin of unused manpower and resources' until her ministers had worked out effective new techniques – and proved that they could work. Independent economists like Professor Paish, putting it more bluntly, said that we would have to keep a permanent 'pool' of half a million unemployed if we wanted to avoid running into repeated balance of payments troubles. But, having staked so much on the experiment almost from the day it gained office, the Government did not feel inclined to abandon it. Michael Stewart, who followed George Brown at the DEA, eventually handed over to Peter Shore, and Shore in turn handed over to Mrs Barbara Castle.

Armed with the resounding title of Secretary of State for Employment and Productivity, and a new ministry to go with it, Mrs Castle began a valiant attempt early in 1968 to succeed where the men had failed. Fleet Street was fascinated to note that she had learned about her new appointment while standing in a railway station in a nightie, and had a great time speculating about her chances of eventually becoming Britain's first woman Prime Minister. Industrial correspondents nodded sympathetically when she confessed to them that she was 'terrified' of her new job. 'When I went to the Ministry of Transport', she went on, 'I said to myself, I can't do this. Now I am saying to myself, Barbara, you must be crazy'. Her intention, she explained, was to stress the positive side of the incomes policy and to talk direct to the rank and file. 'I want', she said, 'to sit down over a cup of tea and say: "Alright, how would you do it?" Trade union leaders – more used to George Brown's brand of hospitality – reacted with somewhat ungentlemanly scepticism. 'We have', one of them declared at the Scottish TUC conference, 'had enough'.

Several Ministers privately echoed this blunt comment, but the Cabinet as a whole decided to plough on. So did Mr Aubrey Jones. In his Third General Report, covering the period from August 1967 to July 1968, he proudly noted the impressive growth of his little empire and suggested ways of expanding it still further. 'We have not been satisfied', his report said, 'that the Government have been pursuing a sufficiently purposeful strategy for price references to the Board'. Among the things he felt he should be asked to look at was 'the pricing policies of industries or firms orientated towards exports'. He also thought the Board should be told to examine a wide range of other questions – including the salaries of middle management (top management had already been referred to him) and possible schemes for providing wage and salary earners with 'some longer-term benefits to compensate them for any current foregoing of wage increases'.

Tucked away in the Board's report was an estimate of what the movement in prices and incomes would have been in the absence of a policy. 'The average annual increase in earnings in recent years', Mr Jones noted, 'may have been just under 1% less than otherwise it would have been'. To many people, it seemed a meagre reward for all the fuss.

4 Kicking and Screaming

HAROLD WILSON THINKS, in retrospect, that the Department of Economic Affairs should never have had charge of the incomes policy in the first place. It should have been given to the Treasury, and George Brown should have been left to concentrate on the Department's two other functions: planning for controlled economic expansion, and acting as both innovator and co-ordinator in the key task of producing an industrial revolution.

Brown himself would not have accepted this argument in heady days of 1964 and 1965, but armed with the advantage of hindsight he concedes that the incomes policy could well have been managed by the Ministry of Labour, providing that central responsibility had stayed with the DEA. (Understandably, Brown still has very little time for the Treasury.) Such an arrangement would certainly have prevented a good deal of harmful Whitehall in-fighting. Civil servants do not take kindly to any serious encroachment on their preserve, and there is little doubt that the open hostility between the Ministry of Labour and the new department caused immense jealousies at all levels. It's the sort of thing which new ministers invariably tend to ignore until experience has shown them just how much damage it can cause.

In 1964, George Brown still saw himself as the kingpin of the Government's whole industrial and economic policy. He genuinely believed that, as an ex-trade union official he was the best possible man to tackle this exciting new experiment. There was still plenty of energy left for planning and industrial change, he felt – and he did his best to prove it.

Planning, like the incomes policy, was nothing new. It had been employed in wartime, and a Tory Chancellor – Mr Selwyn Lloyd – had made it quite fashionable in 1961. It was Selwyn

Lloyd who first set up the National Economic Development Council (popularly known as Neddy) and tried to gear his policies to a definite growth target. By the time Labour came to power in 1964 planning had long ceased to be a dirty word. Naturally enough, however, Labour embraced it much more warmly than the Conservatives had ever done.

'The Labour Party', Mr Wilson wrote in 1964, 'has believed in democratic economic planning from the day when more than half a century ago its small parliamentary group, led by Keir Hardie, tabled in the House of Commons the Right to Work Bill, which for the first time sought statutory recognition of the right to a reasonable job for all who were able and willing to work'. As Shadow Chancellor, Mr Wilson added, he had outlined a 'four year plan for Britain' early in 1961 – and a few months later Selwyn Lloyd had announced the Tory Government's death-bed conversion to planning. If and when Labour came to power, it would not be content with setting up paper targets. It's planning would mean 'physical and discriminating as well as financial measures'. There would be the 'fullest use of the instrument of taxation' and of the Government's power as one of the biggest bulk purchasers in Britain. Labour would also extend the public sector – 'to occupy the commanding heights' – by the creation of new industries based on science.

George Brown, of course, needed no conversion to the cause of planning. As far as he was concerned, it was the only realistic way to economic progress – just as structural changes in industry were the only answer to Britain's fundamental problems. And, of course, he was in a hurry. Soon after he took over at the DEA, he declared that Britain had 'to carry through, inside two or three years at the most, an industrial and technological revolution that has been going on in other countries for the past decade'. The machinery he had created – on paper – while still in opposition was swung into action. If No 10 Downing Street was to have a hundred days of dynamic activity, then the new powerhouse round the corner (which had been the old Ministry of Defence) was certainly going to play the key part in them.

Addressing the Economic Club in New York six months after the Labour Party took office, Mr Wilson proudly listed its achievements. His ministers he said, had carried through 'one of the biggest revolutions in the machinery of Government which

Britain has ever seen in peacetime'. Central in this reconstruction had been the creation of the DEA, 'charged with preparing a national plan aimed at maintaining a steady expansion in industrial production year by year and, in particular, of strengthening those sectors of the economy which are essential both for increasing exports and for avoiding internal strain.' Another revolution had been the creation of the Ministry of Technology 'to act as a stimulus and goad throughout British industry to the more purposeful application of science of technology in industrial processes'. Concurrently with these moves the Government had 'called in the strongest terms for changes in industrial attitudes: attitudes to restrictive practices on both sides of industry; attitudes of increased aggressiveness in export sales – getting markets, prices, minimum delivery dates, and delivery dates kept when they had been stated, after sales servicing, and the rest; attitudes to science and technology, attitudes in management.' To secure this, the Government had taken various measures which it regarded as 'crucial and strategic in our attack'. Given the response of which the British people were capable, he told the Americans, 'we shall be ready to knock hell out of you'.

Journalists who were present on that occasion reported that the audience had been impressed with Mr Wilson's clear understanding of Britain's shortcomings, and with his determination to do something about them.

The National Plan emerged in September 1965, shortly after sterling had been rescued for the second time by international bankers, and was hailed by Mr Wilson as 'a break-through in the whole history of economic government by consent and concensus'. The Government had certainly been able to secure a remarkable degree of industrial co-operation, and the plan itself was 'welcomed' in the House of Commons by all parties. The Tory-created NEDC had made a vital contribution, and so had the Confederation of British Industry, which some Labour MP's referred to as the 'bosses union'. Neddy had been 're-activated' by the Labour Government, and was serving as an independent top level forum for discussion. It included representatives of employers and trade unionists as well as cabinet ministers, and met at regular intervals. The Confederation of British Industry was a much more partisan organization, but it had been understandably eager to be in on whatever far-reaching decisions were about to be taken. Introducing his plan in a television broadcast (Mr Wilson had, for once, decided to leave it to George) the First Secretary of State began by claiming that 'the plan is not a party political job'. People of all political views – the trade unions, the employers' organizations, particular firms, and many individuals – had helped to prepare it. It's immediate task was to help Britain dispose of her deficit, and repay her debts. Its longer term aim was to make her a stronger and a more prosperous country. If we succeeded, we should be producing one quarter more by 1970 than we had done in 1964, and that extra 25% would give us £8,000 million more by 1970. 'The plan shows', Mr Brown added confidently, 'that, big as this sounds, we can do it'.

The actual document included a long 'check list for action', and a warning from Mr Brown that 'A lot still has to be done'. There would be cuts in Government spending and overseas aid, a major development of fourteen ports, comprehensive studies of ways to increase exports and save imports, and a determined effort to strengthen the government machine for accelerating technological advance throughout industry. Government training centres would be expanded, and full weight would be given to regional considerations in public investment programmes for roads, housing, etc. Managements and unions would attack obstacles to efficiency, and strive for the adoption of more rigorous standards of performance at all levels. Help would be made available for workers moving to jobs in new areas, and the employment exchange service was being improved. It was an impressive statement of intent, though Mr Iain Macleod, as chief spokesman for the Opposition, predictably criticized the Government's failure to make any mention of the need for incentives. The trade unions hailed the plan as 'a framework within which modern economic and social priorities can be realized', and the CBI said it was 'a worthy and worthwhile contribution to economic thinking'. The US Treasury chipped in with the comment that it was 'a longer-range addition to measures thus far taken which should strengthen the position of the British economy both at home and abroad'.

The one reservation most commentators had was about the target of 4% per annum growth. It seemed too ambitious. Since the growth target was the key figure in the entire exercise, this was an important reservation. The Government, after all, had merely plucked a number out of the air, got 'Neddy' to build a model on the national implications, and set down various ways of making the implications come true. If it was going to gear the level of public expenditure to it, and if the trade unions were going to demand an increase in incomes which roughly corresponded to the 4% target, we would probably end up in an awful mess if it turned out that the original number was wrong.

George Brown probably had some doubts himself, but in public he appeared supremely confident. And he lost no time in working his way through the 'check list'. To help him, he had recruited a team of industrial advisers from private industry – men who had held directorships of large companies. Their job was to advise the Government on industrial policy, and to represent the DEA on the so-called 'Little Neddies'. These were Councils for individual industries, designed to bridge the gap between Whitehall and industry. They were neither executive nor negotiating bodies; their main value lay in the fact that they could do in the small most of the things which the central Government could do in the large. They were (and still are) useful in gathering information about a particular industry's activities, spotlighting individual problems, promoting understanding and use of modern management techniques, and helping to eliminate or at least reduce restrictive practices. Like the 'Big Neddy', they had been created under Tory administration (eight were already in existence when the Labour Party took over) but they had been little more than 'talking shops'. The DEA enhanced their status. It recognized that decisions would continue to be made primarily in the boardrooms of individual companies, but felt that the Councils would be more effective than the trade associations in securing the kind of co-operation which, in due course, could lead to action that would benefit both the industry and the individual company. This was a reasonable judgment – but in 1965 Mr Brown probably expected too much from the new Councils. He looked for quick results. What he got was words, rather than action.

This soon turned out to be true of many of the other cogs in the Government's revolutionized machine. Studies and advice poured out on an extraordinary scale, and Britain's structural problems were diagnosed to a quite unprecedented degree. But assessing problems is not the same as actually tackling them. All the talking in the world could not cure the country's ills.

Besides the DEA, the new Ministry of Technology was working hard to discover what was really wrong with British industry. It had assumed responsibility for development contracts in private industry and for the sponsorship of industry's own research associations. It had also taken over from the Board of Trade and the Ministry of Aviation sponsorship functions for a group of key industries – computers, electronics, telecommunications, and machine tools. This, inevitably, produced some over-lapping with the DEA, and with the other Whitehall departments. The Board of Trade, which had already been dealt a blow by the establishment of the DEA, felt particularly hard done by. Senior officials wistfully recalled their brief days of glory under Edward Heath, and made no secret of their feelings about the 'tomfoolery' indulged in by the newcomers. They were fully shared by the President of the Board of Trade, Mr Douglas Jay, who held strong views of his own about the way an industrial revolution should be conducted, and felt that an old-established department like the Board of Trade should play a much more important role than it had been given. Relations between him and Frank Cousins, the first Minister of Technology, were distinctly cool.

An additional source of irritation – not only for the Board of Trade, but for much of industry – were two other newcomers set up by Mr George Brown's DEA. The first of these was Mr Aubrey Jones's Prices and Incomes Board – which, in the course of its investigations, passed all kinds of controversial judgments on the apparent shortcomings of the industry it had been asked to look at. The second was the Industrial Reorganization Corporation – a Government's sponsored body which Mr Wilson promised would take British industry 'by the scruff of its neck and drag it kicking and screaming into the twentieth century'.

The creation of the Prices and Incomes Board had been generally accepted as a necessary evil, but the birth of the IRC was greeted with open hostility. No one disputed that much of British industry was too fragmented, and that bigger units were not only desirable but necessary to deal with growing international competition. But many people saw no reason why a new organization, armed with £150 million of Government money, should be set up to do the job. The Association of British

Chambers of Commerce, in a typical broadside, said it was unnecessary and irrelevant. 'The Government', it declared, 'ought not to create a machine' to perform a function which was already being adequately performed by private enterprise.

There had been no less than eight hundred mergers in the previous twelve months before the IRC was created, and there was every indication that this trend would continue. Merchant banks were perfectly capable of acting as marriage brokers. Government intervention would achieve nothing, and was bound to cause a good deal of ill-feeling. Tory MP's took up this theme in the Commons, and there were rumblings about 'creeping nationalization' and 'big brother throwing its weight about'. ('This', said the Institute of Directors in a statement, 'is not back-door nationalization: it is trap-door nationalization'.)

Ministers did their best to dispense reassurance. The main purpose of the new body, they stressed, was not to invest long-term and thus tie up its funds, and certainly not to act as a as a nationalizing agency. In many instances, it was hoped, the Corporation would be able to bring about desirable changes without using its own funds at all. It had not been set up as a kind of super merchant bank, but as a catalyst, with the special function of promoting rationalization schemes which could yield substantial benefits to the national economy. A leading industrialist, Sir Frank Kearton, would be chairman and other prominent industrialists would be invited to become part-time directors. Some of the left-wing Labour MP's thought this was taking concessions too far. They would have preferred to see the IRC function as a division of the DEA, with a politician in charge as Minister for Reorganization and tough legislation used to back him up. The set-up actually proposed by Mr Brown, it seemed to them, was too modest and certainly too passive.

A bill giving the IRC official status got the Royal Assent in November 1966. But Sir Frank and his team of half-a-dozen aides got down to business long before that. A 45-year-old merchant banker, Ronald Grierson, had been chosen as chief executive and the telephone was soon ringing with inquiries from the City. Anyone with £150 million to spend does not stay unloved for long. When Rolls-Royce was arranging to buy Bristol Siddeley Engines, Grierson was asked if he could put up £20 million. Instead, he got the DEA to request that the Bank of England put a

Rolls-Royce debenture offer at the top of its new issues queue. The IRC got closely involved in many other deals but always kept a tight grip on its purse. By the end of 1967, it had committed less than £45 million of its £150 million allocation.

Having no legal powers to enforce mergers, the IRC was bound to be frustrated in some of the ambitious projects thought up by the DEA. The wool textile industry was a good example. The planners had decided that it could do with complete reshaping. Grierson called in all the leading wool textile men, and talked to them for hours. He pleaded with some of the more enterprising executives to take the initiative, and offered generous IRC help. They listened carefully – but nothing happened. If there had been someone like Joe Hyman (a self-made tycoon who changed the cotton industry with ICI money) among the wool textile men, Grierson would happily have helped him to make a personal fortune. But men of Hyman's quality are few and far between – a factor which invariably tends to be underrated by Whitehall's theorists. The IRC was luckier when it turned its attention to the electrical industry. It helped to bring about a merger between English Electric and Elliot Automation, and it played an important role in the events which led GEC's Arnold Weinstock – a young industrialist whose talents fully equalled those of Joe Hyman – to make a mammoth take-over bid for Associated Electrical Industries. It was also instrumental in bringing British Motor Corporation and Leyland Motors together early in 1968.

Whether or not these latter two could have merged without the £25 million loan provided by the IRC is an open question, but there is no doubt that the money helped. By the time the motor 'wedding' was arranged, Grierson had resigned as chief executive – a decision greeted with some relief at the DEA. A brilliant and highly sensitive man, he had strong views on the IRC's role and was determined to run his own shop. He resented some of Whitehall's directions, and was easily upset by criticism. His first offer of resignation had been made in the early days of the IRC, after a blazing row with George Brown, and had been repeated on a number of occasions afterwards. Grierson maintained that the IRC should act discreetly in the background, relying mainly on persuasion. He strongly disapproved of Mr Wilson's 'kicking and screaming' slogan. The best results, he argued, could be got by making the IRC a forum where directors of large companies could discuss their ideas for mergers and reorganization without feeling that they were talking to the Government, but knowing that public money could be forthcoming. One of the chief factors which finally made him decide to go back to the City was the publication of a so-called Industrial Expansion Bill.

This bill, first heard of in the summer of 1967, was designed to give the Government power to buy shares in private industry. It was produced chiefly because some members of the Government (notably Harold Lever, the wealthy Socialist MP who had become a Junior Minister at the DEA) had grown impatient with the gradualist approach adopted by the IRC and its preference for working independently. Grierson did not know of its existence until he read about it in the newspapers, and when he questioned Michael Stewart – then head of the DEA – he was curtly told that it was none of his business. Grierson considered the new measure to be 'a form of gimmickry' and attributed it to 'a certain financial showmanship which has recently been manifest in Whitehall'. One of its 'real tragedies', he thought, was that 'it elevates a temporary expedient to a major principle of economic administration'.

Grierson was by no means the only one to take a dim view of the latest brain-child. The employers' organizations were up in arms as soon as they heard the news. The CBI journal, *British Industry*, said that private industry was being picked to pay the price of party unity. 'With the Labour Party conference on the horizon', it declared, 'the Government are no doubt feeling the tug of their Socialist consciences. Increased state control is a tasty tit-bit to offer the left-wing of the party, which has had to swallow what to them has been some pretty unpalatable fare of late'. The left-wing was, indeed, hailing it as a great leap forward into socialism. State share buying was the kind of thing it had been advocating for years – and, of course, the 1964 Election manifesto had been quite specific about the need for State participation in industries where the Government had a financial stake through the money it had spent on research. Mr Wilson, however, was reluctant to encourage left-wing jubilation. He was all too conscious of the damaging effect it might have on business confidence. He therefore took care to play down its significance – as he had done when the Government first set up the IRC. The Confederation of British Industry was unimpressed. Its leaders went to see him at 10 Downing Street and passed on the Council's decision to reject the proposals entirely, and to refuse to discuss amendments or modifications to it. They warned that the Government would be unwise to press ahead, and 'put at risk the confidence and goodwill of British industry'. This view, they told him, was held widely. It was not just the opinion of extremists, but the view of 'moderate, intelligent, thinking businessmen'.

The Government responded by delaying publication of the Bill – and when it finally emerged, in January 1968, it proved to be a mouse instead of the roaring lion which the left-wing had expected. It was presented partly as a tidying up operation, and partly as a means of ensuring that the results of research and development produce commercial benefits more rapidly than in the past. State equity participation, far from being a positive boom, was represented as a method of providing the company concerned with genuine risk capital which it might not otherwise secure. The Government, it was made clear, would be extremely chary before venturing to take an equity stake in any given project.

Predictably, there were angry mutterings about 'not having the courage of your convictions' from the Labour backbenches. But by the time the Bill made its appearance, there were bigger things to worry about. Devaluation and its aftermath were holding the centre of the stage. The whole episode was yet another demonstration of the yawning gap between theory and fact. Ministers had talked as if they had, at last, found the ultimate weapon for drastically changing the whole of British industry. What they finally ended up with, however, was hardly the sort of stuff of which revolutions are made.

The revolutionaries were, meantime, beavering away at other fascinating tasks. Mr Aubrey Jones, for example, used a brief to examine bank charges as an excuse for challenging many of the banking world's long-established traditions. 'Over the whole field of banking', he declared, 'there is a myth that requires to be dissipated'. He suggested that they should compete more vigorously for deposits, move into adventurous new fields, and disclose their true profits. The bankers bristled with indignation. They accused Aubrey Jones of basing his report 'on the slenderest possible evidence', and warned that 'these sort of attacks could do a lot of damage'. The Government said that the recommendations would be 'carefully studied'. A year later, however, it had still not taken any action to implement them. The wheels of Whitehall turn slowly, and the Establishment still knows how to fight. Aubrey Jones, having delivered his strictures, moved on to new fields – and more reports which had a good chance of ending up on some dusty shelf.

Another project which the revolutionaries found hard going involved the 'purposive use' of the Government's role as one of the country's biggest bulk purchasers. Before the 1964 General Election, Mr Wilson had talked about this with great enthusiasm. Nationalization was old hat. One could achieve much the same result by various methods which were likely to arouse far less emotion. What mattered was not ownership, but the power it brought. Public spending came to nearly £6,000 million a year. Why not lay down the law to suppliers? Why not tell them that, unless this or that was done, they might lose an important part of their business? When Labour came to power, Mr Wilson declared, he would comb through the trade and navigation accounts and use the Government's purchasing power in order to save imports and to reward the efficient and export-minded.

George Brown and his Under Secretary, Sir Eric Roll, tried to get something done when the DEA first started. But the Treasury had retained control over public spending (a concession which was to handicap the DEA all along the line) and was reluctant to act. Nothing happened, and when George Brown and Sir Eric Roll left the DEA, the whole idea lost its two most powerful advocates. The Treasury and DEA still went through the motions of producing a White Paper, and it duly appeared in May 1967 – two and a half years after Labour took power.

The White Paper said, in effect, that Whitehall gave attention to the whole business long before MP's did, and already made use of its influence. It made much of the practical problems involved, and insisted that there was no question of wielding the big stick. It was 'entirely a co-operative and consultative effort'. Machinery for co-ordinating the work of the various departments, it was pointed out, already existed. The whole tone of the White Paper made it clear that, as far as senior civil servants were concerned, Mr Wilson's great dream was a non-issue.

The economic committee of the Parliamentary Labour Party, which had been working on the subject for some time, was reluctant to leave it there. Robert Maxwell, the millionaire publisher and MP for Buckinghamshire, brought out a 108-page report – prepared at his own expense – a few months later. Predictably, it took a much bolder line than the White Paper. Maxwell came up with no less than six hundred recommendations, chief of which was that Mr Wilson should set up a new body – a Public Sector Purchasing Board. This would advise and co-ordinate buying by all public organizations, and be answerable to the Prime Minister through the Department of Economic Affairs. A part-time advisory board, representing public and private industry, would help. Experienced businessmen and civil servants would staff the board, which would be organized in three sections – central government, local government, and nationalized industries.

Maxwell also suggested the creation of a City liaison committee, a 'star rating' scheme for direct exporters, to identify them instantly to the Government, a larger profit margin for Government contractors, a consultancy organization in Whitehall to carry out efficiency audits throughout the public sector, and savings of £150 million on local authority and hospital board expenditure through more efficient purchasing methods.

The public sector, his report noted, spends 41% of the gross national product, directly employs over 30% of the nation's manpower, owns about 50% of the nation's capital assets, takes nearly 60% of the construction industry's output, and plays a dominant role in electronics, aircraft, pharmaceuticals, electrical engineering, telecommunications and power supply.

This power and influence, Maxwell suggested, should be systematically used by the board to give priority to technological advance, encourage exports and imports substitution, the prices and incomes policy, structural reorganization, and regional development. 'Pressure from an important buyer', he added, 'makes private enterprise more amenable to mergers, speedy reorganization, and to reducing unit costs through improved efficiency'.

Maxwell claimed that the industrialists he consulted were 'by a large majority in favour of the Government using its resources in support of national economic policies, even in a directly discriminatory way as between firms'. He also said that the Prime Minister liked his ideas. The reason why Mr Wilson hasn't done much up to now, he suggested, is that 'having taken over a Government he is operating a Government machine'.

Mr Maxwell's report disappeared into the jaws of the machine, and six months later nothing had emerged. But he remained hopeful; 'I shall be bitterly disappointed,' he said in May 1968, 'if my recommendations are ignored.'

Other Wilsonian ideas which had sounded so exciting before Labour won power – such as the creation of state-owned companies to compete with private enterprise in all kinds of industries – also failed to live up to their promise. But the revolutionaries did manage to score one major triumph: the steel industry was nationalized.

As with everything else, it took much longer to get this done than the faithful had been led to expect. A White Paper outlining the reasons for wanting to re-nationalize steel, and setting out the proposed compensation terms, was produced as early as April 1965 and legislation was promised in successive speeches from the throne. (At the opening of each parliamentary session the Queen reads out a speech prepared by the Government of the day, which lists its proposals for the forthcoming period.) More than two years were to elapse before the steel industry finally passed into public ownership for the second time – but at least the Labour Party had managed to fulfil one of its major election pledges.

The industry was reorganized into four steel-making groups, and a youthful peer – 42-year-old Lord Melchett of Langford, was chosen to run the new British Steel Corporation. A merchant banker and a part-time farmer, Lord Melchett hardly fitted the Labour Party's old cloth cap image, but he seemed the right man for the job. Steel shareholders were paid off in Government stock, and on July 28, 1967, nine-tenth of the nation's steel-making capacity became the property of the taxpayer. Some of the steel-masters declined to serve under the new ruler, but enough adapted themselves to the new situation – after vigorous protest – to become chairmen of the four new groups. A good deal of reorganization followed, and there is no doubt that it helped to equip the industry to face increasingly tough international competition. Labour had reached another 'commanding height'. The taxpayer, though, could be forgiven for wondering if he had acquired such a good bargain. The first accounts, published in April 1968, showed that the fourteen companies which made up the British Steel Corporation made what was, in effect, a staggering loss of £72.7 million in 1967. The real benefits, a spokesman explained, all lay in the future.

Another election pledge which, after a respectable interval, seemed to be well on the way to fulfilment was a really determined effort to tackle regional problems. George Brown still claims this as one of his biggest achievements – so do Messrs Wilson, Callaghan and Jay.

The starting point here was the undisputable facts that some parts of the country – notably Scotland and Wales – lagged behind the rest of the country in living standards. Jobs were harder to come by than in, say, the South-East, and unemployment was well above the average. Every credit squeeze produced disproportionate hardship. On social grounds alone the need for improvement was imperative, but the waste of human resources also seemed a matter for deep concern. The Rhondda Valley, a Labour stronghold which in its colourful history has seen mass sorrow, industrial unrest and violence, was a good example. The textbook said that areas like these had outlived their usefulness. The age of coal had gone, and the Rhondda pits were no longer economical. To a planner it made good sense to abandon the worn-out valleys – to leave them like Western ghost towns after the gold rush is over – and to redeploy the population in thriving, modern industrial centres.

But the Rhondda wasn't a soulless trading estate, with a populace that could be moved around like cattle. The valleys were (and still are) proud of their immense community spirit, and most people were extremely reluctant to leave. They had deep roots there, and the prospect of moving to cities like Coventry or Birmingham was not alluring. There were practical reasons, too. Many people had bought their houses from the National Coal Board and were paying low rates. They would not have been able to find a buyer if they decided to move, and they knew they wouldn't be able to live as cheaply elsewhere. Then there was the matter of educating children. Miners have an almost fanatical desire to give their sons an education, and they do not want to tear them away from schools where they have settled down. What the Rhondda wanted was new industries – factories that would give the area a new lease of life. The Tories had tried to tackle regional problems during their 'thirteen wasted years', and Labour turned to them immediately it won power. First, it created new planning machinery. Regional Advisory Economic Planning Councils and Regional Economic Planning Boards composed of senior officials under the chairmanship of the DEA provided the necessary organization in England. In Scotland and Wales similar machinery was set up by their respective Secretaries of State, while Northern Ireland had its own machinery with similar purposes. The first task, as the DEA saw it, was to collect and analyse basic information about each region's needs, resources and problems; to launch a programme of research projects; and to improve the coverage of regional statistics.

This done, the DEA and other ministries set out to cure the problem of 'imbalance' where it was most acute – in the development areas. To attract new industries, financial incentives were considerably improved. Investment grants were made 20% higher than in the rest of the country, special loans were made available, the banks were asked to take account of the Government's regional policies, and preferential treatment was given in the award of Government contracts. The Board of Trade also stepped up the building of advance factories – plant which is built in the hope of finding a tenant. A major innovation, in 1967, was a scheme to pump £100 million into the development areas through regional employment premiums – increased refunds of Selective Employment Tax.

The benefits of all this activity did not become immediately apparent (in the winter of 1967, unemployment in the Rhondda was still three times the national average and much the same was true of other depressed areas) and the Government's regional policies continued to be subjected to considerable criticism. But Ministers were able to claim that their efforts were, by early 1968, producing some worthwhile results. Mr Tony Crosland, the President of the Board of Trade, said the projects assisted by his department in development areas provided more than 86,000 new jobs during 1966–1967. A whole new motor manufacturing industry had grown up on Merseyside over the past few years. Scotland was the centre of important computer and electronic industries. And a range of new lighter industries had gone into Wales and the North-East to balance the heavy steel and engineering industries, and to help fill the gap as the coal industry contracted. Mr Peter Shore, who had taken over from Mr Michael Stewart at the DEA, added that the Government's measures were running at a level well in excess of £250 million a year – double the expenditure in the previous year and nearly eight times that of 1964–65.

It would be churlish not to acknowledge these achievements. It would be wrong, too, to ignore the other worthwhile work done under the aegis of the DEA. The Department has done much to make industry aware of its shortcomings, to improve industrial techniques and statistics, and to raise the standard of management. The Ministry of Technology has unquestionably helped to bring about badly needed change. Much of this has been done behind the scenes, during a period when the need to defend sterling had to take priority, and has failed to catch the headlines. The fact that some ideas have fallen by the wayside, and that others took a long time to get to the starting gate, should not blind one to the value of taking the country's industrial machine apart, examining every detail, and either putting it together again or trying to find some way of improving it.

The failure of the National Plan was not the DEA's fault. Nor was it to blame for the disappointingly low level of industrial investment – once described by Mr Wilson as the key to Britain's future as an economic power. The Department had done its best to persuade companies to invest in new plant and equipment, but the return to stop-go in July 1966 had made them understandably cautious. Both planners and industrialists learned useful lessons. Mr Wilson, too, had learned something. He continued to talk about 'a new industrial frontier' for Britain for the next generation, but also admitted that there was 'no easy road to economic success'.

The Government's critics may, however, be at least partly right in claiming that much of the reconstruction we saw between 1964 and early 1968 would have taken place anyway. Difficult trading conditions, such as we had throughout the period, always makes businessmen look more closely at their methods. Back in 1961, when Selwyn Lloyd squeezed profits, a large number of companies ordered economy drives and several big American efficiency firms set up subsidiaries in Britain to exploit the potential. The trend towards mergers was gathering pace long before Labour won power, and management was getting to be more professional before the DEA put its oar in. It can be argued, too, that the Government had no need to create two new ministries to tackle industrial problems. If responsibility for the incomes policy had been given to the Treasury (with the day-to-day running in the hands of the Ministry of Labour) the job of promoting industrial efficiency and tackling the regional problem could have been left to a strengthened Board of Trade. Long-term planning could have been placed in the hands of a high-powered Prime Minister's department, working hand in hand with the Treasury and the National Economic Development Council.

Something along these lines would almost certainly have happened if the Conservatives had retained power in 1964. Mr Heath and his Shadow Chancellor, Mr Iain Macleod, are both pledged to abolish the DEA if they win the next election. It is by no means impossible, however, that the Department will have died a quiet death well before then. The DEA was created by George Brown, for George Brown, and it was fighting a losing battle from the moment when he left. The Department was ostensibly 'strengthened' for a while, but neither Michael Stewart or Peter Shore proved a match for the Treasury. When Roy Jenkins, the man who had turned down George Brown's offer to become the DEA's Minister of State in 1964, took over from Jim Callaghan as Chancellor, he quietly pressed for the abolition of the rival Ministry. Tony Crosland, the new President of the Board of Trade, was only too glad to help. With Mrs Castle installed as Minister for Employment and Productivity, early in 1968, the DEA found itself relegated to a minor Department. Planning retained a high place on the Government's list of priorities, but the National Economic Development Council – chaired by the Prime Minister himself and run by Fred Catherwood, a former top DEA man – left little doubt that it considered itself quite capable of dealing with it. The Ministry thought up in a taxi ride less than five years earlier seemed to have lost the battle against the Whitehall Establishment.

5 Hungarian Goulash

FINANCE BILLS ARE not, at the best of times, light bed-side reading. The mixture of legal and financial jargon employed by the authors tends to leave the layman utterly bewildered. The 1965 Finance Bill, which gave effect to Labour's first major tax reforms, even puzzled the professionals. It was easily the most complicated document to emerge from the Whitehall machine for years. A favourite City joke, which was quickly adopted by after-dinner speakers at functions throughout the country, had one weary accountant complaining bitterly to another about countless tortuous passages. 'That's nothing', replied his companion. 'You should have read it in the original Hungarian'. A variation of this – equally popular – referred to the Finance Bill as 'Hungarian goulash'. It always produced guffaws – or, on the brandy and cigars occasions, wild applause. To an American or French visitor, this would have been as inexplicable as the Bill itself. But to thousands of Britons the meaning was very clear: the Government's mysterious Hungarian reformers had loused up a perfectly reasonable tax system.

As a long-standing haven for Continental expatriates (I am one myself) Britain has always had a large number of foreign-born economists, journalists and politicians among its citizens. Virtually all of them, of course, took on British nationality soon after their arrival and, as a rule, became more patriotic than the 'Little Englanders' they used to condemn. But to the British press, a foreigner is a foreigner, whether or not he takes an oath of allegiance to the Queen and goes around waving the Union Jack. The 'Hungarians' aroused Fleet Street's interest and its animosity, and it succeeded in passing on both.

The interest, at least, was understandable. It was unusual that both the Prime Minister and his Chancellor should find themselves with Hungarian-born top advisers. Harold Wilson had Dr Thomas Balogh. Jim Callaghan relied on Dr Nicholas Kaldor. 'Tommy' Balogh was born in Budapest, and came to Britain in 1930 from Harvard. He was a banker for ten years. In the early fifties' he became a one man economic brains trust for the Bevanites, and won Mr Wilson's respect. A dedicated anti-Establishmentarian, keenly interested in politics and world affairs, Balogh had fascinated several generations of Oxford students with his theories. (One often-quoted example of his attitude to students was the day when he heard a young man's essay, and then took it out of the room, and returned as domestic flushing noises sounded. 'It was the only suitable thing to do with it', he explained.) When Labour won power, Harold Wilson invited him to become his special economic adviser at a salary of £6,300 a year. Balogh accepted, and got leave of absence from his college.

From October 1964 until he returned to full-time university work three years later, Tommy Balogh was the eminence grise of No 10 Downing Street – a close confidante of the Prime Minister, and the source of some of Mr Wilson's most cutting remarks on the amateur civil service and business establishment. A strong anti-devaluation man, and an expert on foreign trade, he also played a considerable part in Mr Wilson's decision to defend the existing parity of the pound and to reject an import quota system. Balogh was unpredictable, and never had much difficulty in making enemies. He also liked to have the last word. 'There are three kinds of conversation', a fellow Oxford don once observed: 'dialogue, monologue, and Balogh'.

As far as the Press was concerned, however, the real villain was a Cambridge don – 'Nicky' Kaldor. It was Kaldor, not Balogh, who had inspired the 'Hungarian goulash'. Like his colleague, Kaldor was born in Budapest and came to Britain at an early age. He failed his first examination at the London School of Economics because of his insufficient command of English, but got a First three years later (having, in the meantime, picked up a law degree in Budapest) and was awarded a research fellowship. He stayed at LSE to lecture, and shared a Bloomsbury flat with Balogh. In 1949, he was elected a fellow of King's College, Cambridge. Small, round, genial and immensely popular, he has always presented a complete contrast to the tall, acid, worldly Balogh. He is happiest with theoretical abstraction; Balogh is weak on theory and statistics, but strong on strategy.

Kaldor's initial ventures into tax policy were conducted on foreign soil. As Edward Heath, the Tory Opposition Leader, was later to point out rather gleefully, they did not always have the outcome which had been expected. 'Dr Kaldor', Heath told the Commons, 'has a remarkable reputation of advice to governments. The net result has been: in two, bitter opposition; in one, the Minister resigned; in one, there was a general strike, in the last there was a revolution'.

Kaldor himself admitted, with engaging candour, that his ventures had a chequered history. 'My own role as a tax specialist', he wrote, 'took me to many faraway lands and exotic places to assist in the universal quest for more public revenue; and, since I invariably urged the adoption of reforms which would put more of the burden of taxation on the privileged minority of the well-to-do, and not only on the broad masses of the population, it earned me (and the governments I advised) a lot of unpopularity without, I fear, always succeeding in making the property-owning classes contribute more to the public purse'.

In India men of wealth successfully truncated his proposals for a five-part tax assessment including one on expenditure, income, realized capital gains, property and gifts. In Ceylon his proposals, though on the Statute Book, were not enforced; in Mexico and Turkey they were blocked long before the legislative stage, and in Ghana and British Guiana presentation of his proposals led 'almost immediately to an ugly political situation with an attempt in each case to overthrow the Government by strike action'.

In Britain, Kaldor's views on tax reform first attracted public attention in 1963, when they appeared in a brilliant minority report of the Royal Commission on Taxation. He advocated a corporation tax and a capital gains tax, and argued in favour of taxing expenditure rather than income.

Long before Labour came to power in 1964, he also indicated his intention of declaring war on expense accounts. In November 1964, a few weeks after the general election, he was installed as special adviser to the Chancellor of the Exchequer, at a salary of £4,000 a year, and got an office at Somerset House – the London headquarters of the Inland Revenue. It was the first appointment of its kind in the entire history of the Inland Revenue, and it was viewed with very mixed feelings. But within a short period of time, Kaldor had managed to put some of his pet ideas into effect.

It fell to Mr Callaghan, of course, to break the news. He did so with alacrity: the switch to corporation tax was foreshadowed a few weeks after Labour took office. The result, again, was not quite what had been expected. Industry complained bitterly that, by predicting a major tax change months in advance, and without giving details, the Chancellor had caused endless confusion. The bitterness lasted right until April 7, 1965 – Budget day – and increased when Dr Kaldor's other theories made their debut in Callaghan's Budget speech.

Jim Callaghan, who liked the role of reformer (dynamic activity was not going to be confined to No 10 Downing Street and Storeys Gate), began his oration with the warning that 'I propose to carry out, year by year, a systematic and comprehensive review of every aspect of our tax system. I can see a programme of reform stretching for years ahead'. He went on to announce, first, a stiffer capital gains tax. 'There is little dispute', he said, 'that capital gains confer much the same kind of benefit on the recipient as earnings more hardly won. Yet earnings pay tax in full, while capital gains go free. This is unfair to wage and salary earners'. Broadly, he explained, the tax would be levied on gains realized on all assets, with limited exceptions. Of these exceptions the most important would be the owner-occupied house, and 'goods and chattels realized for not more than £1,000'. Gains on other assets acquired after Budget day and disposed of within twelve months would be treated as ordinary income and taxed at ordinary income and surtax rates. Long-term gains would be taxed at a flat rate of 30%.

Callaghan next dealt with tax avoidance, and came out with a surprise attack on expense account living. 'Many firms', he said, 'are most scrupulous about business entertainment. But there has been widespread criticism for some years of the habit in some circles of lavish entertainment by businessmen of one another on the pretext that it is necessary to create goodwill to secure a customer.

'Something which originally began as the hospitable offering of a modest meal to a client at small expense has grown to such a pitch that luxury penthouse flats are kept, on business expense accounts, yachts are hired and even Scottish landlords can turn a penny by letting their grouse moors.

'And, provided this is done in the name of business entertainment, the taxpayer pays ten shillings or more in every pound of the cost.

'No doubt because of this fact, expense account living, as it has come to be called, is often on a scale which is a scandal and is felt to be so not only by the non-business world but by many firms in industry which have a different code of conduct.

'In my view the time has come to apply a radical solution to a problem which is not only a fiscal but a social one. I propose that, subject to a limited exception for the entertainment of overseas buyers, expenditure on business entertainment incurred after today should in general be completely disallowed for tax purposes.'

Callaghan then turned to corporation tax – which he described rather extravagantly as 'a new landmark in our fiscal history, such as we have rarely been able to create in this country, save under the stringent needs of war'.

Our present method of taxing corporate bodies, he explained, went back to the days before the joint stock company, as we know it, existed. At that stage, income tax was virtually a flat rate tax: it applied to the income of companies and individuals alike, and when a company distributed its income to its shareholders in the form of a dividend, a second lot of tax was not exacted. Since those days, there had been extensive changes both in the tax system and in the status and position of companies. First, the personal income tax had become a graduated tax, differentiated according to the circumstances of each taxpayer, and made progressive by reduced rate belief at lower end of the scale, and surtax at the other end. Secondly, company taxation had been altered by the introduction of profits tax, which was imposed on the whole profits of a company, whether or not distributed, and which was not chargeable to shareholders. These changes had made obsolete the idea that companies and individuals should be treated for tax in the same way. By separating formally the two taxes – namely, the tax on corporations and the tax on individuals – the Labour Government would be bringing the tax system of the United Kingdom 'into line with reality and adopting what has become the general practice throughout the world'. And it would be free to draw up the new company tax 'on principles most conducive to economic growth and efficiency'.

One of these principles, it emerged as Mr Callaghan continued with his marathon speech, was that companies ought to plough back profits for expansion rather than pay them out in dividends. The new corporation tax, he thought, would have that effect. Another principle was that companies ought to invest money at home, rather than in other countries. To secure this, the Government was limiting the circumstances under which it was giving relief for underlying tax – that is, the tax charged by an overseas Government on the profits of an overseas company out of which the dividend is paid and remitted to the United Kingdom. And to back it up, he was introducing new exchange controls on overseas investment. In future, official exchange would be made available only where two criteria were satisfied. First, the project must bring a substantial continuing return to the UK balance of payments (for example, in additional export earnings). Secondly, there must be good prospects that the overall return to the balance of payments would, within the short-term, equal or exceed the capital outflow.

Predictably, Mr Callaghan's formidable package (it included many other, less important, changes) produced a storm of protests from the City, industry, and the accountancy profession. Companies with huge overseas investments were particularly vigorous in their condemnation of the Chancellor's reforms – and they had the more or less open backing of the Governor of the Bank of England. Petitions were hastily organized, and Tory MP's prepared to fight the Government's 'half-baked ideas' in the various stages of the Finance Bill. There is no doubt that the fierce animosity which developed affected sterling; 'confidence' had been struck a severe blow.

Callaghan, who bore the brunt of the attacks, was very much inclined to dismiss the complaints as the inevitable outcry of vested interests. It was, he told friends, the price one had to pay if one wanted to be a reformer. Dr Kaldor, the real author of the package, said nothing and stayed in the background. The British tradition that Ministers take full responsibility, and that criticism of their advisers is improper, protected him to a very large extent from the wrath of those who had to eat his 'Hungarian goulash'.

Neither the Opposition nor the press, however, intended to let him get off quite so lightly. MP's broke with tradition by attacking him in Parliament, and the gossip columns had a field day with Whitehall 'leaks' about the odd goings on in the corridors of power. For example:

> A fellow civil servant overhears Kaldor and Balogh talking in Hungarian, and asks them why.
> 'Security, old boy', is the reply.
>
> Again: Balogh is discussing incomes, and talks about a man's 'home take pay'. Nicky Kaldor interrupts. 'No, no Tommy. Learn to speak English now. It's take home pay'.

Stories like these were perfectly true, but of course they missed the point. Kaldor's record as an advisory economist, his political opinions, and the merits of his tax proposals was a matter for proper public discussion. His Hungarian birth, and the fact that 'inside his head he counts in Hungarian, but thinks in English' were irrelevant and unneccessarily personal.

The SET had a long history, and it fitted in perfectly with the belief, long-held by many people in the Labour Party, that one has to dirty one's hands to be a worker. It also fitted in with Mr Wilson's own feelings about the 'candy floss economy'. These feelings were based, very simply, on the view that manufacturing industry was 'productive' and therefore good, and that the service industries were unproductive, and therefore bad. Modern economics rejects such a distinction, but Mr Wilson – encouraged by Kaldor and Balogh – did not. Kaldor had been working for some time on a tax which would penalize the service industries, by levying a tax on all employees and then making rebates to manufacturing enterprises. He had not, however, expected to see it introduced when it was. He was on holiday in France (with his long report locked away in his office desk) when an urgent summons came from Jim Callaghan. He returned at once, and found both Callaghan and Wilson enthusiastic about his innovation. They informed him that they proposed to announce it in the Budget speech on May 4. (The Budget had been postponed because of the General Election.) Kaldor was surprised, but agreed to co-operate. And a short while later the Chancellor duly produced his block-buster. Manufacturers – defined as firms in which more than half the employees are engaged in manufacturing – were to get back more than they paid; farming and building would get back as much as they paid; while retailers, wholesalers, hotels and export houses and other service organizations would get no rebate. 'Our aim,' Mr Callaghan declared, 'is to get people out of the offices and into the factories.'

Critics scoffed at the implication that factories provided exports while offices did not. Hoteliers pointed out that tourism was one of Britain's top foreign currency earners, and that 'invisible exports' were just as useful to the balance of payments as sales of cars and refrigerators. Others predicted that the new tax would cause endless trouble and confusion. The general verdict was that the SET was the most absurd, and most harmful piece of fiscal legislation ever introduced by a British Government.

'It is', Mrs Margaret Thatcher declared on behalf of the Opposition, 'sheer lunacy. I only wish that Gilbert and Sullivan were alive today so that we could have an opera about it. Why does the Chancellor have to have a system whereby he takes away 25s to repay 32s 6d six months later? This is absolute nonsense – and I really think that the Chancellor needs a woman at the Treasury. If my chief had come to me and put up a cockeyed scheme like that, I would have asked him if he was feeling alright'.

Dr Kaldor, contemplating the furore with quiet amusement from his desk in Somerset House, was feeling perfectly alright. He still had faith in his baby, and so had his chief – Jim Callaghan.

Callaghan had seized on the Selective Employment Tax for one simple reason. Just before the Election, he had been asked what kind of Budget he was likely to come up with. He had replied: 'I see no reason for severe increases in taxation this year; I use words carefully and I stand by them.' A definition of severe? 'No one can give a precise one, but I would say the word means very drastic, or harsh'. Having thus committed himself, he found it rather awkward when, soon after the election victory, the Treasury urged him to take tough deflationary action. A cynic might have argued that, with a comfortable majority safely tucked under his belt for another five years, there was no need to worry about pre-election pledges.

But Callaghan and Wilson both felt that they could not blatantly resort to orthodox deflationary measures. The Selective Employment Tax, they reasoned, would neatly kill two birds with one stone. It would get people into the factories. And it would satisfy the Treasury's demand for deflation, without making voters feel that they had been cheated. Smart? Wilson and Callaghan thought it was brilliant. Twenty-two months and countless protests later, Roy Jenkins stood up in the Commons and explained why he was not only keeping SET going, but increasing it by a staggering 50%. It boiled down to the simple fact that he needed the money. Iain Macleod, the Tory Shadow Chancellor, promptly announced that if his party got to power he would do away with the whole nonsense. But as Jim Callaghan remarked to me, wrily, a few days later: 'I'd like to see the Chancellor who does away with something which produces £500 million a year'. So would I. Dr Kaldor did not need to count in Hungarian to recognize that in the SET he had found a useful way to 'assist in the universal quest for more public revenue'.

There was, however, one Kaldor theory which never made the grade: a tax on wealth. Jim Callaghan had been sold on it three years before he became Chancellor. He told the House of Commons all about it in 1961, and the general expectation was that a Labour Government would tax 'fortunes' of over £20,000 as soon as it won power. In this case, though, the Treasury establishment succeeded in persuading Callaghan that a wealth tax would be more trouble than it was really worth. He stuck to this, despite continued pressure from trade unions and left-wing Labour MP's. And Roy Jenkins endorsed his line, early in 1968, with the comment that 'it would be quite impracticable at present because of the problems of valuation which would be involved'. Instead, the new Chancellor introduced a special charge aimed at the rich, disguised as a tax on incomes but amounting, in the upper ranges, to a levy on capital. It applied to investment income of £3,000 and above received during 1967–68. The charge varied between two shillings in the pound at the lower end of the scale to a top rate of nine shillings on investment incomes of £9,000 or more. This meant that the extremely rich were being forced to pay income tax, surtax and the special charge at a marginal rate totalling 27s 3d in the pound!

The charge, Mr Jenkins made clear, was to be for one year only. But he could not resist pointing out that, like his predecessor, he intended to be a reforming Chancellor. 'This Government', he declared, 'has made a beginning with the reform of direct taxation and I hope to continue the work, more particularly in the field of personal taxation'.

Dr Kaldor – back in his academic job in Cambridge – no doubt greeted this statement with a broad Hungarian smile. But it was Dr Balogh who, early in 1968, was rewarded for his services with a life peerage. 'On receiving it', noted *The Financial Times*, 'he will sever all connections with the Government'. He did just that, but chose the annual economic debate on the Finance Bill, soon afterwards, to make his maiden speech in the House of Lords. Two things, he said, had bedevilled the British economy since the First World War. One was on the way to being mended, although it was not cured. It was the tendency to generate overseas investment 'far beyond Britain's capacity to maintain', due to 'the historical development of London and Britain as the focal point of the world financial and economic system'. The second was far from a solution. It was the consequence of costs rising faster than those of other competitive economies. The prices and incomes policy, Lord Balogh went on, was 'a crucial piece of social reform of which Britain could only be proud'. We might, he thought, have created 'a new order which other countries might imitate, as in the past they have imitated Britain's social and parliamentary institutions'. Some peers, listening to this, noted the absence of similar claims for his colleague's tax reforms. Was he, they wondered, saving it up for the day when Dr Kaldor would join him on the plush Lords benches?

PART 2 STORMY WEATHER

6 Facing The Enemy

THE LABOUR PARTY grew out of the trade union movement, and bosses have always been treated with a good deal of suspicion. The City of London – that 'citadel of capitalism' – has tended to be looked upon as positively wicked. In a mixed economy, however, a Government has to work together with both industrial tycoons and City financiers. Mr Wilson – a former President of the Board of Trade and, subsequently, economic adviser to a City timber firm – was pragmatic enough to accept this – even though he privately remarked to parliamentary colleagues that he hated having to be nice to pompous old Etonians, and made little secret of his rows with Lord Cromer, who was Governor of the Bank of England when he took over.

Jim Callaghan started in a much more uncompromising mood, but constant contact with bankers and economists changed him so much that, long before he left the Treasury, he talked and looked like a City man himself. George Brown stayed clear of the City, and showed a clear preference for industrial managers like Frank Kearton and Fred Catherwood, who had got to the top through sheer ability. He recruited a few able City men, notably merchant banker Ronald Grierson, but when he visited the London Stock Exchange he was greeted with loud boos from the trading floor – and gave them the Churchillian victory sign in return. Most of the other senior ministers distrusted the City from the start (Frank Cousins, the first Minister of Technology, once told me that it made his blood boil to see a stockbroker eating smoked salmon and drinking brandy) and they found that the feeling was mutual.

And yet, the City was surprisingly well-disposed towards Harold Wilson's special brand of 'Socialism' when his Government first took over. During Mr Macmillan's premiership, the

Square Mile had grown so disillusioned with the Tories that the Chairman of the Stock Exchange was moved to declare that the City was 'very nearly at the end of its tether'. Mr Wilson, while in opposition, had made a point of lunching regularly with various City organizations, and explaining his ideas.

He had made a good impression.

When he came to power, television crews went to Throgmorton Street – in the heart of the City – and got some stockbrokers to make critical remarks about the new masters. It looked and sounded hysterical, and was no doubt representative of quite a large number of people who travel from the suburbs to the Square Mile each day. But the City is much more diverse than is generally realized, and there is less fraternization between the various sections than one might think. The City believes in sound financial principles, and likes to be left free to go about its business, but it does not hold uniform opinions on every possible subject. Far from it. The stockbroker often holds very different views than the commodity dealer or shipping expert, and the conversation one gets in one of the Square Mile's umpteen private dining rooms tends to be much more balanced than the prejudiced outbursts shown on the TV screen or quoted in newspapers. The City prides itself on its ability to make reasoned judgments, and to adapt itself to any given situation. It knows that the man who lets his emotions dominate his actions is likely to go bankrupt.

Bankers and other City people accepted Mr Wilson's victory in good spirit because having daily contact with various parts of industry, they knew how much needed to be done and were highly doubtful about the Tory Party's willingness or ability to do the job required. They realized that the new Prime Minister was not going to rush into socialist schemes, and were pleased that he endorsed the City's order of priorities – putting sterling above all else.

There was shocked surprise at Mr Callaghan's first Budget, but this reflected incredulity at the Government's incompetence rather than any implacable bias against socialists. The stiffer capital gains tax, which was directly aimed at the City speculator, was accepted in good spirits.

Indeed, at the end of the Labour Government's first year. Dr Nicholas Kaldor had become known as 'the investor's friend.'

Dr Kaldor had been the chief architect of the tougher gains tax, and the switch to a corporation tax. Both these measures, stockbrokers quickly recognized, had drastically altered the long-term balance of supply and demand. Corporation tax had almost eliminated new issues of ordinary shares; companies found it better to raise new money through fixed interest stocks instead. And the gains tax made existing shareholders determined not to sell. The outcome, inevitably, was a growing shortage of shares – and a rise in prices which was quite out of proportion to the volume of business done. Another development which no-one would have forecast a year earlier was the stock market's keen disappointment when, in November 1965 in the Queen's Speech, no mention was made of steel nationalization. The White Paper published in April had suggested attractive nationalization prices, and speculators were looking forward eagerly to early action. They felt quite cheated when Mr Wilson showed himself in no hurry to go ahead. Why, they asked, can't he stick to his guns?

There was more predictable annoyance when the Prime Minister did stick to his guns over Rhodesia. The City instinctively dislikes economic sanctions – they interfere with free market forces – and it has a lot of sympathy with Rhodesia's cause. When the Labour Government decided to act against Mr Ian Smith's regime, the City immediately voiced its misgivings. It fretted about the loss of export business, the fate of investments in Rhodesia, the consequences of any move to freeze sterling balances, and the reactions of South Africa – a vastly more important market.

As time went on, and the honeymoon with Mr Wilson's Government began to wear off, City organizations also voiced their irritation with many other Labour measures – notably the curbs on overseas investment – and criticized the Prime Minister's apparent softness with the trade unions. One also heard numerous complaints about the new tax laws. Lord Shawcross – once a Labour Minister, but now a highly paid member of several company boardrooms and chairman of the Wider Shareownership Council, expressed a growing City view when he declared that 'the whole of our tax law has become a scandal.' The attacks increased when Mr Wilson announced early in 1966 that he was holding another general election: the City suddenly started to fret about the possibility that, armed with a bigger majority, the Government would become socialist after all.

Wilson did his best to reassure them, even after he had gained a resounding victory. He had little choice: a parliamentary majority of close on a hundred was no more protection against another sterling crisis than a mere five, and he knew that it still paid to make the City 'part of the show'. He donned white tie and tails to preach the virtues of orthodox finance at City banquets, and he invited bankers to 'working dinners' at No 10 Downing Street. In August 1966, shortly after the traumatic sterling crisis which led to a heavy deflationary package and wage freeze, Wilson asked eighteen bankers round to tell him what they thought had gone wrong. For more than an hour they sat in the cabinet room, at the very same table normally occupied by cabinet ministers, and discussed the nation's ills. Some of Mr Wilson's left-wing critics, if they had known of this, would probably have said that Mr Wilson had got together with his *real* Cabinet at last. But the Prime Minister, who had been deeply shaken by the crisis, simply wanted to pick their brains. They all repaired upstairs to dinner afterwards, and the brandy and cigars were passed round until very late in the evening. The occasion had at least one interesting consequence. One of the bankers present told Mr Wilson, during the 'Cabinet' discussions, that some of the Government's closest economic advisers had been spending a good deal of time at cocktail parties held by various business organizations, and had openly advocated devaluation. This, they said, had got round the City – and from there to Zurich and other financial centres. Inevitably, it had added to the market's jitters, making it more difficult to defend the pound. Mr Wilson promptly told some of his 'socialite' advisers to guard their tongues in future.

Mr Callaghan also tried to maintain close contact with the City. As Chancellor, of course, he had to address functions like the annual bankers' dinner at the Mansion House, and he always took Sir William Armstrong and other Treasury knights along with him. But he never quite rid himself of the impression that, behind his back, the City was doing its best to make life difficult for the Labour Government. He still thinks that City people were 'less than helpful'. This may be partly because he had mistrusted them for so long, and partly because they gave him a rough time over measures like the Selective Employment Tax. He also knew that, after the July 1966 crisis, there was a lot of talk about a possible National Government. (One prominent City man offered me a £10 bet that it would happen before the end of the year, and I accepted with alacrity.)

Despite the bonhomie, there was unquestionably a good deal of bitter animosity in the City and some of the Tory diehards did their best to spread gloom and despondency. But both Callaghan and Wilson were too ready to mistake the professional's natural desire to protect his money, and that of his clients, for a blatant attempt to trip up the Socialists at all cost. Harold Wilson never missed an opportunity to lash out at unnamed people who were 'selling Britain short', and to warn anyone who followed them that they would pay a 'heavy price'. In a speech to the Economic Club of New York in 1965, he said that he was, 'not one who believes that this undercurrent of gossip should go unanswered', and went on to quote Don Basilio in Rossini's *Barber of Seville:*

A well-timed insinuation
A suggested intimation—
Half denying, half implying
O'er the town, 'twill soon be flying
Expectation, fear and wonder
Gathering strength like distant thunder
E'er increasing, never ceasing
Is to new invention spurred.

The 'well-timed insinuations' certainly existed, but it was disingenuous to assume that they were invariably inspired by political malice. Many people in the financial world (as in the academic world) judged that Britain's circumstances would make devaluation inevitable sooner or later and decided to act accordingly. British firms with definite commitments in foreign currencies, for example, bought those currencies at once because they knew that devaluation would make it more expensive to do so later on. Foreign companies took similar protective action. They did not accept that businessmen had a patriotic duty to risk losses. In their view, it was up to the Government of the day to maintain confidence in the pound – and if it failed to do so, it had to face the consequences. More determined efforts to cure

Britain's financial problems, they argued, would have disposed of 'well-timed insinuations'.

Overall the City's relationship with the Labour Government during the three years leading up to devaluation was better than might have been expected. There was always a certain amount of underground warfare, but Mr Wilson also got a good deal of co-operation.

Industrialists, too, adapted themselves more readily to the new regime than many people had predicted. Many of them argued, from the very beginning, that the new Government ought to be fought every inch of the way. They felt that industry should have no truck with an administration which seemed to be strongly opposed to all forms of private enterprise. One of the Government's strongest and most persistent opponents was Sir Paul Chambers, the chairman of ICI, Britain's biggest manufacturing group. When George Brown announced that he intended to set up an Industrial Reorganization Corporation, the whole ICI Board publicly attacked his decision. And Sir Paul himself declared, early in 1966, that 'we are getting nearer and nearer to conditions in a planned economy as you have in a Communist state'. He argued that an incomes policy, plus the National Plan, would lead to 'a steady loss of individual liberty so slow that the erosion is hardly noticed.' He also claimed that 'if you are working from a National Plan, which is inevitably static, your objectives will be the wrong objectives.' Sir Paul's views were shared by many other leading industrialists, but relatively few of them advocated a policy of active resistance, or even of non-co-operation. Mr John Davies, a Welshman with a fine temper who became the Confederation of British Industry's first Director General at the age of fifty, took the line that industry and Government had become 'strongly intermeshed' and needed each other's assistance to progress. He had the backing of the CBI's first President, Sir Maurice Laing. 'Whatever our personal views', Sir Maurice told members, 'we see it as the duty of the CBI to be non-political and to endeavour to assist the Government of the day whatever its colour wherever they take action or consider taking action that we see to be in the interest of industry and the nation'. Both of them approved George Brown's famous 'declaration of intent', which really launched the incomes policy, and continued to co-operate in various ways. They fully accepted that the general level of management in Britain left much to be desired, and that industry had to undergo major changes.

There were, of course, plenty of occasions when the two sides clashed fiercely. The CBI opposed steel nationalization, state share buying, and many other Government attempts to 'interfere'. It also resented some of Mr Wilson's colourful language – such as the repeated boast that he would 'drag industry kicking and screaming into the twentieth century'. Labour MP's in turn bitterly resented the CBI's constant claim that too high a proportion of the nation's resources was going on the welfare state. Immediately after the July 1966 package, which included the highly unpopular wage freeze, it called for cuts in hospital, school, and road building, the introduction of prescription charges for medicines supplied under the National Health Services, and the ending of subsidized rents for council houses. MP's angrily retorted that the CBI should mind its own business. Mr Wilson and other ministers also made disapproving noises – but kept in touch. John Davies had every bit as free access to No 10 Downing Street as the TUC's George Woodcock, and Labour's two new ministries – the Department of Economic Affairs and the Ministry of Technology – developed closer links at all levels of industry than any Tory Government had ever done.

But the slanging matches invariably attracted more publicity. For Sir Paul Chambers and many like-minded industrialists, the Selective Employment Tax and Industrial Expansion Bill were really the last straw. In October, 1967, the inevitable happened: they announced the formation of a splinter group 'dedicated to study the fundamental causes of the malaise in the British economy'. Sir Paul explained that the army of planners at the Department of Economic Affairs, and the umpteen committees formed to make 'in depth' studies, had got it all wrong. They were dealing with the consequences of a wrong financial policy, and not its causes. His new group would 'seek to display a blend of the qualities of academic inquiry with the fruits of the intimate practical knowledge of industry possessed by its members'. He, together with Unilever's Lord Cole, Beecham's Henry Lazell and others had got together and decided that 'certain things were being done which are bad for British Industry'. They did not intend to support one party against another; it wasn't a matter of politics, but of sound finance.

There might well be something in Tory policies which they could not support – though, Sir Paul added, it was at present 'not awfully clear' what Tory policies would be. When I asked him why he had set up a separate organization, he explained that the CBI council was much too big. Too many different views had to be accommodated. Not only that, but the CBI was too often forced to make off-the-cuff statements without going too deeply into subjects, because particular sections said: 'This is a good thing, let's do it.' Sir Stephen Brown, who had succeeded Sir Maurice Laing as CBI president and was present at the launching of the new group, added: 'We shall not be automatically committed to accepting the group's findings'. This, indeed, seemed to be the key to the venture. Committees and councils thrive on compromise, and Sir Paul and his friends had grown tired of the CBI's general line. By starting a new group, they could make a right-wing stand without having to secure the CBI council's endorsement. Council members who were sympathetic to the Labour Government, like Cortaulds' Chairman Sir Frank Kearton, did not have to be associated with the views expressed.

Jim Callaghan, predictably, referred to the new group as a cluster of 'sinister men' and produced an equally predictable storm of protest. The CBI's official leadership, meanwhile, went on trying to steer the Government – and Whitehall – in the direction it believed to be right, and making the best of a bad job if they failed to convince the other side. Early in 1968, however, it decided to issue a lengthy document entitled 'Industrial Management and the Next Two Years', in which pride of place was given to what the CBI itself described as 'a catalogue of criticism'. The catalogue, CBI leaders declared somewhat disingenuously, 'is not intended to revive old hostilities nor to justify an attitude of suspicion and helpfulness.' But to many Labour MP's it seemed a carefully calculated attempt to do just that. It began with an attack on Mr Callaghan's fiscal policies, and went on to deal in scathing terms with seven other fields in which, as far as the CBI was concerned, the Government had been tested and found wanting. Corporate taxation, it began, had been revolutionized in a manner so as:

> To penalize success by increasing the total burden of tax on profits whilst making no distinction between profitability and

non-profitability in the field of investment grants: thereby discouraging risk-taking;

To discriminate without proper forethought between distributed and undistributed profits giving rise to unforeseen distortions in the capital market;

To dampen both the willingness to take risks and the exercise of personal initiative by excessive direct taxation;

To prejudice severely investment abroad not only in respect of new ventures but also in the return of existing investment;

To penalize unjustifiably some forms of investments at home whilst subsidizing others;

To deal harshly with the small company and so to stultify at their origin the beginnings of successful enterprises.

Public spending, the CBI went on, had risen in constant terms between 1964 and 1967 by 15% whilst the gross domestic product had risen by 6%. This growth for mainly non-productive purposes had 'throttled back the private sector and has stifled the productive initiative upon which we rely as a trading nation'. Initiative, it seemed had also been stifled by State intervention in matters which the CBI felt were none of the Government's business. Nationalization, taxation, the extension of the role of nationalized industries, regional subsidies – they all had 'played their part in upsetting the exercise of sound business judgment in the management and development of indsutry'.

Regional policies were criticized on the grounds that they were directed towards getting management to install or develop plants in areas where they would not otherwise have gone. 'Industry believes', the CBI declared, 'that the way to deal with the problem is to clear up the mess, to improve communications and generally to rehabilitate the areas in question – not to bribe people to install plants there against sound business judgment'. Other criticisms were directed at the Government's failure to grapple with the 'intransigent action of irresponsible minorities', its tendency to 'allow dogma dressed up as principles' to prevail in dealings with Britain's trading partners, and its habits of 'maintaining over-optimism to a point when, repeatedly, unforeseen misadventure could and did upset our economic equilibrium'.

All this added up to a formidable list of woes, and understandably gave many people the impression that relations between

Government and Industry were on the point of collapse. There was a good deal of talk about a 'Boardroom rebellion' and considerable publicity was given to the fact that many individual companies were stepping up their contributions to Tory Party funds. A lot of publicity was also given to suggestions by Lord Robens and others that Britain would be better off under a Government composed of businessmen. The CBI stressed, however, that it had simply intended to put its views on record and said that it had no intention of refusing to co-operate with ministers. This was endorsed subsequently, by a number of individual industrialists.

Industrial change always involves argument, and there is bound to be continued friction between private enterprise and a Government committed to planning and direct intervention. No-one could pretend that current relations are ideal. But the two sides have learned to appreciate each other's problems, and one would like to think that – despite the occasional clashes – they will continue to give practical acknowledgement to the foolishness of pulling in opposite directions.

7 Callaghan's July Itch

JULY 20, 1966, saw the abrupt death of a myth. For nearly twenty-one months Harold Wilson had been regarded as a political superman. He was the party leader who could work miracles, the sure-footed Premier respected by factory workers, Oxbridge intellectuals and bankers alike. He could talk the language of economists, and he knew exactly what needed to be done – in stark contrast to his predecessor Sir Alec Douglas-Home, who was never allowed to forget a careless remark about tackling sums with a box of matches. The astonishing events of the ten days which led up to July 20 showed that Mr Wilson was not only human, but far from sure-footed when he was under pressure. They had a profound influence on the financial world's judgment of the Labour Government's competence, and of Mr Wilson's own ability to lead Britain into the promised land. Ministerial expressions of confidence were, from that day on, treated with extreme suspicion and I believe this played a key role in the equally remarkable sequence of events which ended in devaluation sixteen months later.

The Prime Minister gave no public indication that he was aware of this when he addressed the nation on television that night. A time of crisis, he declared 'was a time for greatness'. There must be no more 'scrimshanking', no more 'dodging the column', no more accepting 'second best'. The impression left on the viewer was that, as far as Mr Wilson was concerned, the blame for what had happened lay with the nation and not its Government. To some extent, this was true. Throughout the first half of 1966, as in 1965, people had given very little recognition to the fact that Britain's economic problems called for an all-out effort by the whole country. There were a lot of brave words, and committees were created at a record rate, but life was really going on much as before.

This however, reflected to a considerable degree the lack of that firm leadership which Mr Wilson had promised time and time again. And there simply could be no excuse for the incredibly clumsy handling of the delicate situation which had developed at the beginning of July.

The crisis had been in the making for some months. The starting point was Mr Callaghan's post-election Budget, on May 3, and the key factor was the increasingly apparent failure of the incomes policy to produce the kind of results which the Government had hoped for. The Treasury mandarins, who had always been sceptical about the efficacy of an incomes policy, did their best to persuade the Chancellor that a strong dose of deflation was in order. But Mr Wilson, in high spirits after his resounding victory at the polls, did not want to give Ted Heath the satisfaction of being able to say 'I was right'. George Brown supported him, though for different reasons. Brother George still had great faith in the incomes policy – his 'baby' – and he was a fervent growth-man. Deflation was anathema to him.

Faced with this attitude on the part of the Prime Minister and the First Secretary of State for Economic Affairs, Jim Callaghan found himself in a dilemma. He knew that his Treasury advisers were talking sense, but he also had a good deal of sympathy for the views expressed by Harold Wilson and George Brown. Deflation meant unemployment, and he did not want to be accused at the next annual conference of one of the worst crimes in the Labour Party's book – putting people out of work.

I spent an evening with him at No 11 Downing Street shortly before Budget day. He was deeply troubled about the conflict of opinion among those who were determined to be optimistic, and those who were predicting serious trouble for sterling unless the Chancellor poured out some familiar medicine. I told him that I saw no need for severe deflation, because there were already signs of a down-turn in the economy, and suggested that sterling was in no condition to take another easy-going socialist Budget. I had interviewed a number of bankers in New York and Zurich shortly before, and they had all expressed concern about the possibility that the Chancellor might introduce another 'irresponsible' Budget to make good the Government's latest election promises. Mr Callaghan agreed that sterling remained vulnerable, but indicated that he intended to stand up to the Treasury pessimists. I have no doubt that he sounded out many other people in the days that followed.

In the event, the Budget turned out to be much milder than most people had expected. Higher duty on beer and cigarettes had been widely predicted, and there had been much talk of a post-election increase in income tax. By the time Mr Callaghan sat down, however, the forecasters were feeling rather foolish. He had proved them wrong. There was nothing much for the pundits to discuss except the new fangled innovation called a Selective Employment Tax. Potentially, the SET was £300 million worth of deflation. Though a former Chancellor, Reginald Maudling, writing in *The Director* magazine, actually described Mr Callaghan's efforts as 'about the most deflationary budget ever seen', the Government itself did very little to stress the firing power of its new weapon for the benefit of the anxious gnomes of Zurich. On the contrary, it made much of the fact that Tory predictions of drastic post-election measures had been proved false.

Inevitably, financial markets concluded that the Government was still relying far more on the incomes policy than its record to date justified. A day or two after the Budget, a small team from the International Monetary Fund – Britain's principal creditor – arrived in London to go over the books with Treasury officials. The result was kept secret, but rumours spread that the IMF economists were doubtful about Mr Callaghan's chances of making good his Budget promise that Britain would be running a balance of payments surplus by the end of the year. The Treasury dismissed these rumours as unfounded, but the gnomes remained suspicious.

It was against this background that the seamen's strike began in mid-May. Mr Wilson made much of the fact that he intended to stand up to the seamen, for the sake of the incomes policy. The central bankers nodded approvingly; they had long urged the Government to have a showdown with the unions. A big new international credit line was made available on June 13.

The private bankers, the merchants and everyone else who held sterling, however, were much more concerned with the effect which a crippling strike of this kind was bound to have on the trade figures of an island economy. That balance of payments surplus which Mr Callaghan had set his heart on looked even more remote. The next official trade returns showed an alarming rise in imports, and the Treasury indicated that it was beginning to share the doubts about our short-term balance of payments prospects.

Two other events of considerable psychological importance followed in quick succession. The steel nationalization bill was published on July 1, and Frank Cousins resigned from the Government in protest against the incomes policy a few days later. The steel bill had been foreshadowed for months, but it still had quite an impact. The gnomes took it as evidence that the socialists were determined to press on with doctrinaire anti-capitalist policies, regardless of their consequences. It seemed to them totally irrelevant to our immediate problems. The resignation of Frank Cousins finally convinced them that the incomes policy experiment had failed. How could it possibly succeed now that one of Britain's most powerful trade union leaders – a man who had held Government office – had announced his intention to fight it all along the line?

As they saw it, Mr Wilson's best move was to acknowledge defeat and face the alternative: deflation. But, the gnomes asked, would he dare to do so knowing that it would lead to much higher unemployment in the winter? Did a Government which had just nationalized steel have the courage to put a few thousands more people out of work? Mr Wilson must have been aware that these questions were being actively discussed in the financial markets of the world. He did not, however, give the slightest indication that he was concerned about them. His mind was on Vietnam. He planned to go to Moscow shortly, to try to pull off a spectacular peace coup, and he regarded the gossip about sterling as a minor irritation. Let the gnomes talk, and the press speculate. It would all blow over quickly enough. Next door at No 11 Mr Callaghan took much the same line. He told Cabinet colleagues that sterling was being temporarily weakened by rising interest rates in other centres, notably New York, and by the 'window-dressing' which banks all over the world went in for at the half-year mark. Bankers always tried to make their balance sheets look good at this particular time, and funds had been moved away from London for this purpose. They would all come back within a matter of weeks. By that time, too, the trade figures would improve strongly as exports held up by the seamen's strike left British ports. Not least, the deflationary effects of the Selective Employment Tax would make themselves felt. This, plus the formidable credits available to Britain, would take care of the usual autumn strain on sterling. The present period of speculation was nothing more than 'a July itch'.

Whether Mr Callaghan really believed this is open to doubt. He *wanted* to believe it, and he was still willing to err on the side of optimism. But some of his closest Treasury advisers were certainly giving him a very different assessment. Their scepticism was shared by a large number of economists, both at home and abroad, by the Bank of England, and by one important visitor to London – M Pompidou, the French Prime Minister. M Pompidou, a former banker, took a dim view of the British economic scene. He told George Brown that, if he wanted to get Britain into the Common Market, there was nothing for it but to devalue the pound. He communicated this to his banking friends when he returned to Paris, and the French press immediately got wind of it. Devaluation rumours spread like wildfire – with predictable consequences in foreign exchange markets.

When I saw Mr Callaghan in his room at the Treasury shortly after the day of reckoning, July 20, he told me that he had come round to accepting in the first week of July that further deflationary steps were unavoidable. His Treasury advisers, he said, had given him new balance of payments estimates. They indicated that, if nothing more was done, Britain would not be in surplus in 1966, or in 1967 either. The earliest period was 1968. On the basis of this, he had ordered them to prepare appropriate measures. If this was true, it makes Mr Wilson's subsequent behaviour quite inexplicable.

On July 10, the Sunday newspapers severely criticized the Prime Minister for his inactivity. At the same time, some of them printed news stories which suggested that the Treasury and the Bank of England were pressing for immediate action. Mr Callaghan's later remarks to me certainly supported this. It also emerged, subsequently, that the new Governor of the Bank of England, Mr (now Sir) Leslie O'Brien, had gone to No 10 Downing Street on July 9 to give the Prime Minister details of the alarming drain on Britain's gold reserves. The Governor told him that, if the pound was to be saved, it was essential to restrain domestic demand at once. Meanwhile, he thought that

Bank Rate ought to be raised by 1%, on the following Thursday. Mr Wilson, therefore, was hardly unaware of the feeling among the Government's top financial and economic experts. Yet he went out of his way, during the next few days, to play down the sterling troubles. Financial journalists working on daily papers, who had the job of 'following up' the Sunday news stories for Monday's edition, were told by the Chancellor's office that 'if further measures become necessary, they will be taken'. This is a stock formula, which gives absolutely nothing away. But next door, at No 10, Mr Wilson's Press officer, Trevor Lloyd Hughes, was telling political journalists on the same newspapers that the Government saw no need for additional moves to deflate the economy. Reports that the Chancellor was considering a mini-Budget were nonsense. This was duly reported in the next day's papers, and as soon as the financial markets opened on Monday morning sterling began to be sold on a frightening scale.

The Government, it was decided, had lost touch with reality. Oil companies, tobacco firms and other commercial interests with large forward commitments for foreign currencies rushed to protect themselves against the possibility of devaluation. Speculators in Zurich, Paris and other centres jumped on the bandwagon, eager to exploit the panic. A full-scale run was under way. Throughout the day, however, No 10 stuck to its line. Journalists were urged to 'calm down'. Everything, they were assured, was under control.

Mr Callaghan told friends later that he had not been consulted about Sunday night's 'guidance' from No 10, and that he was furious when he realized what had happened. To check the run, he arranged to have a question raised in the House on Monday about the effects of the Selective Employment Tax. The banks, he announced would not be allowed to help companies who ran into liquidity problems – a move which amounted to an intensification of the credit squeeze. If this had been done earlier, it might have helped. But now it was too late. The gnomes were tasting blood.

Mr Wilson, incensed by Fleet Street's criticism, took another decision. Scheduled to speak at a dinner in honour of the Australian Prime Minister on Tuesday night, July 12, he arrived at the coffee stage with a special addition to his prepared speech. 'You, Mr Prime Minister,' he declared, 'will recognize how remote from the realities of Britain's economic situation are the defeatist cries, the moaning minnies, the wet editorials – yes, the Sundays as well – of those who will seek any opportunity to sell Britain short at home or abroad'. He went on: 'To the defeatist rushing for cover, still more to those who seek a short-term gain by speculating against Britain, I say again the value of sterling will be maintained. They have doubted us before and we have shown our utter determination and resolve to keep Britain strong, and sterling strong'.

The guest of honour (Mr Harold Holt) gave no sign that he disbelieved him. But the 'defeatists' and 'speculators' did. They were running for cover again as soon as foreign exchange markets opened the next morning. Mr Wilson's ringing declaration of faith had merely strengthened their impression that the Government was living in a fool's paradise. The next day we had some bad trade figures. They were distorted by the seamen's strike, but coming at a delicate moment such as this they lent weight to the argument that new measures could not be delayed any longer. At Thursday's Cabinet meeting, Mr Wilson suddenly changed course. He told his colleagues that some pretty drastic deflation was going to be needed to save the pound. George Brown was still objecting to heavy deflation, so the Prime Minister decided that the burden would have to be shared by all the departments. This meant more work than the Treasury had already done, so an immediate public announcement of full details was clearly not possible. But Thursday was the normal Bank Rate day, and it was agreed that the Bank of England should go ahead with the first part. Bank Rate was duly raised, and the banks were called upon to make further special deposits – a device which effectively tightened the credit squeeze.

A lengthy argument arose about whether the occasion should also be used to forecast the *rest* of the package. Mr Callaghan was firmly against this, and so were several other ministers. But having made up his mind to act, Mr Wilson was characteristically anxious to get the whole business over with as quickly as possible. Mr Callaghan suggested that, in the circumstances, the Prime Minister had better make the announcement himself. Mr Wilson did so. He told the Commons that afternoon, July 13, that steps were about to be taken to reduce domestic demand, and to cut back overseas expenditure. The financial world's reaction to this took him completely by surprise. Far from feeling reassured, they concluded that the situation must be much worse than anyone had expected. Mr Wilson's dramatic statement struck them as the snap reaction of a puzzled politician to an unexpected situation, rather than a dynamic piece of leadership. Further heavy selling of sterling developed, and there was widespread talk that Mr Wilson was about to devalue. The Governor of the Bank of England paid another visit to No 10 Downing Street, and told him that Britain's gold reserves were being run down at a terrifying rate. The Prime Minister, genuinely alarmed, consulted Jim Callaghan and together they decided that the measures must be brought forward to July 20. This was communicated to the newspapers (Mr Wilson personally rang the editor of *The Financial Times*) and the story appeared as Mr Wilson flew off to Moscow for his Vietnam talks.

The actual job of putting together a thoroughly convincing package was largely left in the hands of Sir William Armstrong, the top man at the Treasury, and Sir Eric Roll, of the Department of Economic Affairs. Sir Burke Trend, who was to have accompanied the Prime Minister on his Moscow trip, stayed behind to watch developments. Jim Callaghan was still in charge, but he was feeling tired, depressed, and confused. He readily agreed that deflation would have to be a good deal heavier than he had originally envisaged, and he was quite prepared to leave most of the details to the professionals. George Brown, hearing of this, telephoned Jim Callaghan from Durham, where he was attending the Miner's Gala. 'Jim', he bellowed, 'I don't know how you can bear looking at your face in the mirror this morning!' The civil servants, obeying their instructions from the Prime Minister, got to work. They contacted top officials in other departments and told them to come up with proposals for effective cuts. Treasury men were kept in their offices until late at night, working out various permutations. Time was desperately short. On Monday, Sir Burke sent a private secretary to Moscow with an up-to-date report. Meanwhile, sterling remained under heavy pressure. By the time Mr Wilson returned, outwardly calm and confident, he was faced with the most serious crisis since the Government took office in October 1964. He had already made up his mind to endorse whatever the Treasury recommended, and found Jim Callaghan completely on his side. George Brown continued to be much more difficult. He was fighting for his incomes policy, his National Plan, and for the thousands of workers who faced unemployment if the Government went ahead. He insisted that, instead of deflating heavily, the Cabinet ought to give very serious consideration to devaluing the pound.

The Prime Minister rejected this out of hand. At the long Cabinet meetings which followed the arguments were fierce. George Brown pressed the case for devaluation, and threatened to resign if he could not get his way. He was supported by several Ministers, including Roy Jenkins and Tony Crosland. They maintained that, if the pound was devalued without further ado, Britain would have a real chance of breaking out of the stop-go cycle. Some deflation would still be needed, but exports would soon pick up and the economy would gather pace again. George Brown also brought up the point made to him by M Pompidou shortly before – namely that devaluation would improve Britain's chances of getting into the Common Market. The country had been hiding behind America's voluminous skirts for far too long, borrowing and deflating so that the pound could remain the first line of defence for the reserve currencies, and so that Washington would have someone to share the role of world policeman. It was time to break away. Mr Wilson countered that the Anglo-American alliance remained of the utmost importance. Devaluation would lead to trouble for the dollar, and probably the collapse of the entire monetary system. Besides, it would do nothing to solve Britain's structural problems. He would have none of it – and, the Prime Minister added, anyone who felt like resigning on this issue was welcome to do so.

Denis Healey and Michael Stewart strongly supported the Prime Minister's views on Britain's present and future relationship with the United States, and Jim Callaghan endorsed his other objections to devaluation. Most of the other Cabinet Ministers were mainly concerned with saving their own programmes from the axe. As the battle of words raged on, and it appeared that Brown faction was gaining ground, the Chancellor began to waver. For several hours, he actually crossed over to the devaluationists. But Mr Wilson managed to win him back, and on Wednesday morning the Cabinet approved what amounted to the toughest set of financial measures since 1949.

The man who, two years earlier, had poured scorn on Tory stop-go had slammed on the brakes, much more viciously than any Tory Chancellor ever had to do. Election promises had been broken and a thousand illusions had been shattered. The National Plan lay in ruins. Home demand had been cut by £500 million. And the trade unionists – the founders of the Labour Party – found themselves saddled with a statutory wage freeze. It was a bitter pill to swallow, and George Brown was not the only member of the Labour Party who found it sticking in his throat. Michael Foot expressed a widely held view when he said that Mr Wilson had produced 'stupid measures to please stupid people'. He supposed that the central bankers 'wouldn't be satisfied until they see us tearing down our hospitals with our bare hands'.

George Brown sulked, and then did what he had so often threatened to do – he resigned. Bill Rogers, Brown's Parliamentary Secretary, and other friends quickly organized a 'round robin'. Nearly a hundred MP's from all sections of the party attached their names, and within hours of handing in his resignation Mr Brown was reading their plea that he should change his mind. Mr Wilson added his own efforts. He stressed the gravity of the crisis, and appealed to Mr Brown's loyalty. Brother George remained unmoved, but he confided to his friends that he was 'deeply touched' by the 'round robin'. Close to midnight, he announced that he would stay on after all.

It was a farcical situation, but then so much of what had happened had all the ingredients of pure farce. While Brother George was writing out his notice, Fleet Street's city editors were being briefed by a top Treasury official. He read out a list of the new measures. 'And cigarettes', he said, 'will go up by 5d a packet of twenty, and tipped by 4d'. We looked puzzled. 'But', one of my colleagues protested, 'cigarettes were not mentioned in the Prime Minister's statement'. It was the official's turn to look puzzled. 'Oh', he exclaimed, 'I am sorry. I was thinking of yesterday's list'. Tobacco, it appeared, had been automatically included in the first rough outline, and had survived several hasty revisions. But it was crossed off at the last moment because someone pointed out that the law of diminishing returns had started to apply. Duty increases were liable to touch off such a large fall in sales that the Treasury would end up with a lower revenue than before. This, at least, was what the manufacturers claimed. There had not been time enough to check their story, so smokers were spared. One could not help feeling, when one heard this explanation, that whisky drinkers (who were being charged another 3s 5d a bottle so that Mr Wilson could defend sterling) were unfortunate not to have an equally persuasive advocate in the Treasury ranks.

The whole package seemed to have been drawn up on a 'hit and miss' basis, and it was clear that very little thought had been given to the impact which individual measures were likely to have on the economy. Jim Callaghan proudly told me, some months later, how he had personally decided on the £50 travel allowance. 'I sent a secretary to all the London travel agencies with instructions to collect as many brochures as possible. The poor girl must have thought I had gone mad. When she got back, I spread all the brochures out on my desk. After an hour of inspection, I decided that it was perfectly possible to have a holiday abroad on £50'. So much for the science of economics!

The farce would have been highly enjoyable if the price had not been so terrifyingly high. As it was, one was left to ponder on the shortcomings of human beings in general, and of politicians in particular. The superman had blustered, then panicked. Cherished principles had been ditched to preserve a national totem pole. Economists and businessmen had been forced to abandon their precious theories. Faced with a wad of bills, Father had said 'turn' – and we had turned. Britain was launched on a new course, and no-one had a clue where she would end up. It was the biggest disappointment yet for the millions who had voted Labour into office.

It is easy to heap all the blame on the Prime Minister's slender shoulders. He had failed to see what was coming, and he had acted foolishly when it must already have been obvious to him that the situation had become extremely serious. His tactics had been astonishingly amateurish. His blunders had cost the country many millions, and he had publicly acknowledged full responsibility for the end result. But was it all Mr Wilson's fault? Mr Callaghan, certainly, could not be absolved from blame. He had been over-optimistic. Given two sets of forecasts, he had always plumped for the cheerful one. This might have been justified at the beginning of May, when he produced his Budget, but there was little excuse for underrating developments like the seamen's strike, the rise in US interest rates (which was bound to attract money away from London), and the resignation of Frank Cousins.

Earlier action would have reassured the bankers. By waiting

until the crisis was well under way, the Chancellor made it inevitable that the Government would have to resort to really drastic measures. He was honest enough to admit during the heated Commons debate on the package, that his strategy in the months before the crisis had been a 'calculated risk'. And he made it clear to me, in our long interview, that he felt badly about the fact that his calculations had been proved disastrously wrong. He said he was extremely weary, and that he had no real desire to stay at the Treasury. 'When the dust has settled', he said 'I am going to look for a nice, quiet job'. The Foreign Office was mentioned, and he described it as 'very peaceful after this place'. If Mr Wilson had been prepared to move him there and then, Mr Callaghan would have been happy to go. But he was needed as a symbol of the Government's determination to 'see things through', and the Prime Minister disapproved of what seemed to him a blatant attempt to lay claim to the Foreign Office.

And what of Messrs Brown, Cousins and Co? For months they had sneered at the warnings of the Treasury and the Bank of England. They were all for the Maudling theory that Britain could break out of her strait-jacket by deliberate *expansion*. The fact that conditions were unsuitable, largely because the Maudling experiment had been ended in an £800 million balance of payments deficit, seemed to escape them. Day after day, hour after hour, they had lectured the Cabinet on the virtues of growthmanship. Harold Wilson and Jim Callaghan had listened because they desperately wanted to believe that, under a Labour Government, the vilified stop-go measures of the Tory years could be banished for good.

Finally, what of the newspapers – the 'moaning minnies' – and the 'defeatists' – the City bankers – who ran for cover in the hour of the country's greatest need? Were they too ready to 'sell Britain short' on every possible occasion? Mr Wilson was not the first Prime Minister to ask these questions, and he will not be the last. Journalists and businessmen will have to search their own consciences about the events of June and July 1966, if they can possibly remember what part they played in them. They were entirely within their rights; this is a free country. But were some of them, at least, a bit too cynical? Did they bother to consider the national interest, or were they solely concerned with looking clever? Did they realize what impact they were having on opinion abroad? Did any of them ever spare a thought for the man on the factory floor, or the old age pensioner? In our kind of society, Governments have only limited power. They can set the pace, but real success comes only when everyone agrees to co-operate. Harold Wilson and his colleagues failed to provide adequate leadership, but very few people can have felt any satisfaction at the end result.

8 Living on Tick

As on two previous occasions, the pound had been 'saved' by borrowing money. No-one quite knew how much we owed at the end of the July 1966 crisis, but it was certainly no secret that Britain was more heavily in debt than she had ever been before. Harold Wilson, the man who poured scorn on Tory Chancellors when they borrowed their way out of trouble, had gratefully accepted all the help he could get.

Committed to defending the existing parity, the Bank of England had in practice been forced to act whenever selling looked like pushing the rate against the dollar below 2·78. It had to buy all the sterling others did not want, and it did so by digging into the official reserves. They had long been inadequate for a world banker, and could not be expected to protect sterling against a long and determined onslaught. The Bank of England, however, had over the years built up an elaborate system of defences in co-operation with the Federal Reserve Bank of New York and others. Technicians like Roy Bridge, working closely with Charles Coombs in New York, did a splendid job in hiding the real extent of the drain of money from London. They disguised official support by spreading their orders for sterling around a number of centres, and around various banks. No-one was every quite sure (and cannot be sure to this day) just how much a speculative attack was costing the authorities. But technical brilliance could not dispose of the basic fact that our gold reserves were weak. Mr Wilson had, in 1964, found himself in the unenviable position of a businessman taking over an over-extended company which is short of ready cash. This much was public knowledge, and currency speculators were certainly not inclined ever to forget it. Britain had £11,000 million worth of overseas assets, but not nearly enough gold and foreign currency to meet all the demands which could be made on us. One way of rebuilding the kitty was to sell at least some of those assets, and indeed this course was urged upon the Labour Government by many of its supporters.

Six months before the July crisis, the independent and respected National Institute of Economics and Social Research had added its voice to those who felt that the Government should reconsider the whole structure of Britain's foreign asset holdings 'in the light of the long haul ahead for the British balance of payments'. Rather than go on suffering the inconveniences and humiliations of short-term indebtedness, the Institute felt, it might be well worth taking more deliberate steps to liquidate some long-term assets. The Chancellor could draw on a lot of sympathy if he followed this line of thinking. He frequently argued, in Cabinet and outside, that if the choice was between unemployment and dipping into the kitty, the Government ought to dip.

But the Bank of England, and the Treasury establishment, raised powerful objections. The Bank argued that it was foolish to 'eat the seed corn', and stressed the psychological damage which the compulsory acquisition of privately owned assets was bound to do. Treasury officials pointed out that Britain's overseas assets provided a large, and still rising, income, without which we should be in a frightful mess. Most of them, they maintained, could not be sold without difficulty and sacrifice, if at all. A more intelligent course was to cut back current and future investment. It would not give the Chancellor any ready cash, but it would make it easier to get Britain out of the red. The Government largely accepted this orthodox reasoning. It made no attempt to get its hands on the vast shareholdings of insurance companies and others in countries like the United States.

Steps were, however, taken to 'liquefy' the portfolio of dollar stocks held by the Government itself. This portfolio, worth $1,250 million, had been acquired during the Second World War from private investors in Britain who had been offered British Government stock in exchange, and when the war ended ministers had hung on to their nest-egg. It included holdings in many well-known American corporations, and it had grown enormously in value. Mr Callaghan decided to use it soon after he got to the Treasury, but was quickly persuaded that he could not just pick up the telephone and instruct a Wall Street stockbroker to dump millions of pounds worth of stock. It would drive down prices against us, and it would certainly upset President Johnson. The whole operation had to be done step-by-step, over a period of time. The Treasury got its way. The process of turning the nest-egg into short-term bonds, and then into ready cash, took more than two years and was conducted in great secrecy. The secrecy unquestionably helped to secure a better average price, but it also meant that few of the people who fretted about sterling during the whole period realized we possessed a useful second line of reserve.

The only other way of raising enough cash to defend the pound against persistent attacks, and to convince speculators that it was futile to dabble in sterling, was to borrow from other central bankers. Britain, for so long a proud banker to the world, became an expert at living on tick. Nine weeks after the July package Mr Callaghan was in Washington to meet our creditors at the annual meeting of the International Monetary Fund.

He was accompanied by a Treasury team, the Governor of the Bank of England – and, of course, a dozen financial editors. Invited to address a press club lunch, the Chancellor said that, after travelling for ten days in North America (we had all been to Montreal the week before, for the Commonwealth Finance Minister's meeting) he had noted two broad impressions, 'one reassuring and the other perhaps less so'. The first, he said, was that 'there seems to be a very genuine feeling over here that the measures we have taken will be successful in getting our overseas payments into balance – I hope even into surplus – next year. I have found that people understand why we are confident that the medicine will work'. There was also a good understanding, Mr Callaghan went on, of the long-range importance of 'the very tough policies we have launched on the prices and incomes front.' But there was another side on the coin. People were concerned – quite rightly – with the effect of these policies of restraint on Britain's future economic growth. They felt that, while a period of slower growth might be an unavoidable result of policies to take the overheating out of the economy and get back into balance on our overseas payments, our future must lie in expanding productivity. They asked, very naturally, how we would achieve that aim. This question, the Chancellor declared, was justified provided it was based on a correct appreciation of where we already stood as an industrial power. It was being asked in the wrong framework if it was linked to the myth, which he had found active in some places, that Britain had been losing out badly in competitive industrial strength and that the new measures would make things still worse. Mr Callaghan then listed a number of British achievements, and claimed that 'we start from a base of considerable industrial power'. Everyone could see that if we were successful in launching a long-term incomes policy after the current period of restraint, our position would be strengthened further. Industrial investment might level off in the short-term, but this was not to say that the process of modernization would come to a halt. Investment would continue, and be stimulated. So would the drive towards greater efficiency. 'The idea that we are facing a period of total inertia and ossification', the Chancellor declared, 'is absolutely contrary to the facts'.

It was a good platform speech, but it didn't tell the whole story. Apart from doubts about our long-term growth, and about the Government's ability to achieve the structural changes everyone regarded as essential, there was considerable scepticism in Montreal and Washington about the Cabinet's willingness to persist with unpopular measures. Unemployment was bound to rise, and the Government's supporters would protest. Mr Callaghan might be prepared to ride out the storm, but would Mr Wilson, Mr Brown and other senior colleagues go along with him? American bankers and economists were doubtful, and they made little secret of the fact. Callaghan himself had to deal with a lot of anxious questions from Mr Henry Fowler, the US Treasury Secretary, M Pierre Schweitzer, the IMF's Managing Director, and other luminaries with a close interest in the stability of the pound. They were happy enough to let him maintain a bold front in public, but at the private dinner parties which went on throughout the week they did some tough talking. The Chancellor assured them that the Government's resounding victory at the General Election had given it the strength to see things through. The Cabinet had learned its lesson, and it would not take any chances. Trade unions leaders and left-wing MP's could howl as much as they wanted to; the balance of payments would come first.

A few days later, Mr Callaghan returned to Britain – and immediately made for the Labour Party's annual conference in

Brighton. He knew that the howling would start right there and then. It did. And because the Chancellor had just been to Washington, it was inevitable that the charge of 'Bankers' ramp' would be hurled at him. 'What', the faithful angrily demanded to know, 'did you tell the bankers?'

Bankers' ramp is a nasty phrase, reminiscent of the early thirties. It was coined by Ramsay MacDonald, and taken up by Labour Party loyalists who resisted the National Government. The phrase conjures up visions of a group of menacing bankers in league with a corrupt Government to make life miserable for the working classes.

Mr Callaghan, in his reply, emphatically denied that the July measures had been forced on the Government from outside. 'We cut back,' he declared, 'not because of a bankers' ramp, but because of the need to pay our way. Unless that is fully understood and accepted we shall continue looking for scapegoats who are not there.' The charge, however, persisted. And it was to be revived when, a year later, Mr Callaghan sent the International Monetary Fund a 'letter of intent' in return for a new stand-by credit. The general view among Labour MP's was that, whatever Ministers might say in public, they were firmly in the clutches of the bankers and were being pushed around by them. Economic policy was not being made at Westminster, but in M Pierre Paul Schweitzer's elegant office in Washington, and at the secret monthly meeting of the Bank for International Settlements in Basle. Mr Michael Foot was loudly cheered when, in a debate on the 1967 'letter of intent', he declared in ringing tones, that if British Chancellors always agreed with the head of the International Monetary Fund, there would be no point in changing Chancellors or Governments. If they always agreed, it would remove from politics most of the major issues which some members were determined should not be removed. 'Some of us,' Mr Foot thundered, 'are determined that we shall not accept the rulings of these bankers on these matters. What bankers like to regard as correct economic behaviour many of us regard as an outrage against humanity – the maintenance of a level of unemployment. We do not accept the bankers' view of that. We are not prepared to have someone dictating to this country what should be the level of unemployment.'

Mr Foot's fervent declaration of independence was directed

not only at M Schweitzer and the 'Basle' club, but also at the traditional enemy of the left-wing: the Governor of the Bank of England. To people like Mr Foot, the Governor embodies all that is wrong with bankers. They see him as a hard-headed brute, wedded to financial orthodoxy, sitting in a sumptuous City parlour and manipulating the levers of power without a mandate from the electorate. This has been the view ever since Montague Norman persuaded Churchill to put the country back on the gold standard in 1925 – with disastrous results. Norman *was* a hard-headed brute, wedded to financial orthodoxy, who was quite unperturbed by the spectacle of a million or two unemployed. For 25 years he ruled the Bank with an iron hand, often taking major financial decisions without consulting Ministers. But the Bank was nationalized in 1946, and Governors since then have exercised a good deal less power.

Labour MP's, however, have continued to be incensed by the speeches which Governors are expected to make at banquets and business lunches. Lord Cromer, an Old Etonian who owed his appointment to Mr Harold Macmillan, infuriated them in 1965 and 1966 by publicly voicing his objections to high Government spending and restraints on overseas investment. Mr Wilson, too, was involved in frequent rows with him, and everyone was much relieved when Lord Cromer decided to step down at the end of his term of office. His successor, Mr (later Sir) Leslie O'Brien, had been educated at a grammar school, and had come up through the ranks. He was not a die-hard Tory, and Mr Callaghan had no qualms whatever about making him Governor. Even Sir Leslie O'Brien, however, found himself faced with demands for his dismissal in October 1967 – a month before the pound was devalued and the 'letter of intent' was dispatched to Washington.

The storm blew up over a speech he had made in Buenos Aires, shortly after the 1967 'bankers' jamboree' in Rio de Janeiro. Sir Leslie told his audience that we needed 'a rather larger margin of unused manpower and resources than in the past'. Mr Wilson and his Chancellor had been saying much the same thing in earlier months, and the Governor thought he was simply stating official policy. He had made the same point, at much greater length, at a Mansion House banquet in the summer, and no one had raised an eyebrow then. His argument, basically, was that the techniques which had been developed to ensure that full employment did not lead to overheating – notably the incomes policy – had not been very effective. It was wrong, therefore, to place too much reliance on them. If we did, we would run smack into another sterling crisis. There was nothing original about this comment, and events of the past couple of years certainly supported it. But Sir Leslie's speech had been made right in the middle of the emotion-charged Labour Party Conference at Scarborough, and Fleet Street had interpreted it in the most controversial way: the Governor of the Bank of England, screamed the headlines, was advocating the creation of a permanent pool of unemployment. Mr Wilson immediately assured the party that the Government's whole policy was 'to secure full employment and to maintain it on a permanent basis', but he refused to sack Sir Leslie – who was utterly bewildered by all the fuss. Jim Callaghan went further: he gallantly defended his protegée. 'I do resent this suggestion that I am nothing but a cipher in the hands of the Bank of England, the Treasury, or anybody else', he declared. 'The Governor of the Bank of England is carrying out a policy laid down by the Government. This is his job and responsibility and it is also his responsibility to tell me when he disagrees with it.'

The argument over what the Governor should or should not be allowed to say will, no doubt, continue for a long time to come. It is far less important, however, than the more fundamental charge that Britain's economic policies, throughout the three years leading up to devaluation, were dictated by the bankers. Does it stand up to closer examination?

The idea that Sir Leslie, or his predecessor, were the shadowy decision-makers certainly does not. Lord Cromer tried to impose his views on Mr Wilson, but was read some stern lectures about democracy. It might have been better, as things turned out, if the Prime Minister had taken more notice of the Governor's advice – but the plain fact is that his stern warnings were largely ignored. Sir Leslie put his views across with rather more diplomacy, and by the time he moved into the Governor's chair Mr Wilson had become more ready to listen. Sterling's continued troubles, after all, made it virtually impossible to dismiss the fears of the financial world out of hand. The infamous £800 million balance of payments deficit had been run up by politicians, not by bankers. The decision to defend the exchange rate of 2·80 dollars to the pound despite this, had been taken by the Cabinet, not by the Bank of England.

The day-to-day defence of the parity was, however, in the hands of the Bank's officials and the Governor knew better than anyone else how much it cost. He also knew, of course, what holders of sterling were fretting about, and what they regarded as the right solutions. If there *was* a dictator it was the parity of the pound – not the man who had the job of maintaining it. Ministers were free to reject the solutions offered by the anxious international financial community. The community, in turn, was free to withdraw funds from London and switch into other currencies. Private bankers and businessmen are paid to look after the money entrusted to them. If their judgment tells them that a currency is heading for trouble, because of the unwillingness of a Government to face facts, they try to play safe. This is how the international capitalist system works, and it cannot be dealt with by delivering long tirades against the 'sell Britain short brigade' and the 'unscrupulous speculator'.

The overriding need to defend sterling until the balance of payments position had been put right was also directly responsible for bringing the International Monetary Fund and the 'Basle club' into the picture. If the deficit had been tackled earlier, and with more vigour, there would have been no cause to involve them in any way. They certainly had no burning desire to tell Mr Wilson how to run the country's business. They were bound to have some say, however, the moment we asked to borrow large sums of money from them. Like any ordinary bank manager, they had a right to request that we should follow 'sensible' policies.

The International Monetary Fund, which became Britain's biggest and best-known creditor, is an institution set up in 1947 to help promote exchange rate stability. The experience of the thirties had taught the world's managers that slumps are threatened when, because of a temporary shortage of reserves, major countries start to vary their exchange rates, or protect themselves through import controls and foreign exchange restrictions. The basic idea behind the Fund was that anyone in trouble should instead be able to resort to short-term borrowing. The Fund's financial resources are supplied by more than a hundred members. Each has a quota expressed in dollars, and determined by the member's economic power. Together the quotas make up a pool, managed by executive directors and a Board of Governors. Resources have been increased, from time to time, to match the growth in world trade, and there is no doubt that the fund has played an important part in the free world's impressive post-war economic development.

Mr Selwyn Lloyd borrowed heavily from the IMF when we ran into trouble in 1961. He did so by drawing a large sum in other currencies (the largest, in fact, ever drawn up to that point) and depositing sterling to the same value. We were also granted a 'stand-by credit', which guaranteed a further agreed amount if required. We never actually had to use it, and the drawing itself was repaid within a year. Selwyn Lloyd had been lucky. His deflationary package had worked, money had come flooding back to London, and he had been able to relax.

The Labour Government tried to do exactly the same as Selwyn Lloyd, but with a great deal less success. Instead of getting out of debt after a reasonable period of time, it ran more and more deeply into it. When the pound was finally devalued, in November 1967, Britain owed the Fund $1,522 million.

M Pierre Paul Schweitzer, the Fund's Managing Director, has described himself to me as 'a hired hand'. Strictly speaking, this is what he is. As Managing Director, he is paid a salary by the pool to administer its operations in accordance with rules. One of these is that, if a borrower has repaid his loan, he automatically reconstitutes his right to draw another sum. Another is that, while loans are outstanding, the executive directors must keep an eye on the way in which the money is being used. The pool, quite rightly, does not want to see loans frittered away on luxuries.

During the Fund's annual meeting in 1966, I filmed a television interview with M Schweitzer at his office in Washington, and pressed him to say how 'multilateral surveillance' (the bankers' favourite phrase) was exercised. What did he think of the charge that economic policy was dictated by him and his colleagues? The interview was shown by the BBC at about the same time as Mr Callaghan defended himself against the shouts of 'bankers' ramp'. This is what M Schweitzer said:

'We never force a policy on anybody. Your Government

knows as well and probably much better than we what's good for the United Kingdom. When we put all this money at your disposal, we just agreed with your Government on what was our common view of desirable policies in the United Kingdom. What specific steps you take is the problem of your Government.

'One very essential point in it was the understanding by your Government to take any additional steps which would be needed in the judgment of your Government, mainly, to achieve in proper time your balance of payments equilibrium. We didn't force anything on you, we just agreed with you on what you should do.'

The publication, in December 1967 after devaluation of the 'letter of intent' signed by the Chancellor was a highly unusual move, but it brought the IMF's procedure into the open. Once an application for a stand-by credit has been made, IMF economists talk to the Government concerned, and make their own assessment of what is needed to re-establish financial stability. On the basis of this, they frame some recommendations. To spare Ministers political embarrassment, it is left to them to incorporate the agreed targets and broad measures in the letter.

As a rule, however, the IMF works in a safeguard in the form of so-called 'trigger clauses'. These lay down ceilings for, say, the supply of credit or the level of Government spending, and carry the threat that non-compliance will lead to cancellation of the stand-by credit. Periodic checks are made, and any serious deviation from the agreed policies usually produces, in the first place, a strong warning from the IMF directors in Washington.

Clearly, then, the fund *does* have a say in the way a borrower runs his economy – and will continue to do so until the stand-by credit is no longer needed. Some countries, however, tend to get more lenient treatment than others. This seldom becomes public knowledge, because the contents of the 'letter of intent' are not normally revealed.

When I visited Washington in January 1968, shortly after all the Commons furore over Jim Callaghan's letter, the IMF officials told me that the Government's decision to depart from normal practice had caused a bit of a bother. Several other member countries had complained that the fund had been 'too soft' with

Britain. There were no trigger clauses in our letter, partly because the IMF did not want to add to the Government's troubles with Labour MP's and trade unionists, and partly because it was recognized that sterling's world currency role called for special treatment. The piece of paper signed by Jim Callaghan left his successor a good deal more room for manœuvre than would have been given to, say, a South American or African country.

M Schweitzer himself repeated that he had 'at no time attempted to tell your Government what to do.' He had not recommended the re-introduction of prescription charges or any other specific measures. 'The figures mentioned in your letter', he added, 'were worked out by your own people. And we were neither consulted about the latest package of economic measures, nor informed about your proposed spending cuts in advance. I first heard about them when I saw Mr Wilson's speech. We are concerned with your overall performance – but the details are entirely a matter for your ministers.'

Mr Roy Jenkins was, in the circumstances, perfectly entitled to claim, as he did, that we had always been our own masters – and that this remained the position. At the same time there is no doubt that, from the day Labour took office, we never enjoyed quite the same freedom as a surplus country like Germany or France. The IMF was looking over the Chancellor's shoulder – and so, for that matter, was the 'Basle club' and the administration of the United States. The 'Basle club', like the IMF has helped us out in the interest of preserving the international monetary system. The Americans spent their dollars because sterling was, to them the first line of defence, and because they wanted Britain to go on sharing the role of world policeman. Neither was motivated by charitable considerations, but they were understandably reluctant to throw good money after bad. Britain had to promise that she would put her house in order, and our creditors reserved the right to withdraw their assistance if that promise remained unfulfilled.

The Bank for International Settlements – the 'Basle club' – was set up by representatives of the central banks as long ago as 1930. Mutual support operations among central bankers, however, first began in their present form as recently as 1961. They arose directly from the biggest post-war wave of speculation in currencies, sparked off chiefly by the revaluation of the German mark. Sterling was the chief sufferer, and the main recipient of aid. It was made clear, however that credits would be available for periods of only three months, or at the most six, and that they could not be regarded as a substitute for policy action to correct basic imbalances in the payments accounts of the countries concerned. This basic principle has been applied throughout – officially the credits were available only to protect us against the possible withdrawal of sterling balances – but during the last few years the Bank of England has managed to secure frequent extensions of the bankers' 'short-term' credits. The Americans have done their bit through a separate 'swap network'. Like the 'Basle club' arrangement, this was developed in 1962 as a means of buying time for hard-pressed Governments. It is operated by the Federal Reserve Bank of New York, and allows the Bank of England to make automatic drawings for three or six months. When devaluation came, we had drawn the whole of the $1,350 million then available under the agreement.

Mr Callaghan has described these various arrangements as 'ad hoccery', and has cited the speed with which vast rescue operations have been mounted, from time to time, as evidence of the superb co-operation which exists among the world's central bankers. Their ability to conjure up hundreds of millions of pounds, seemingly out of thin air, certainly is impressive. But in the end, the pound was devalued all the same. And many people – including Sir Leslie O'Brien – were left wondering whether the readiness of others to make vast sums available were really such a blessing. If the Government had been unable to borrow, the pound would have been devalued in 1965, when the first crisis came. The country would have come to terms with reality there and then, and many unpopular decisions would have had to be taken. By postponing them, Britain ended up with debts which will take years to repay – and which, inevitably, will continue to put us under 'multilateral surveillance'. The bankers meant well, and so did the Labour Government, which was anxious to avoid measures which would inevitably have meant higher unemployment. The emotional charge of 'bankers' ramp' seems, in the circumstances, quite unjustified. But one could argue that Britain might have been better off *without* their kindness.

9 A Privilege or a Handicap?

Mr Reginald Maudling said in 1967 that, when he was Chancellor, he could never make up his mind how far sterling's world role was, as he put it, 'a privilege rather than a handicap'. Many backbench Labour MP's, having never been exposed to the persuasive arguments of the Governor of the Bank of England and top Treasury officials, had no such difficulty. As far as they were concerned, running a world reserve currency was just another pretentious relic from the imperial past. It was kept up, they alleged, so that the City could become richer still. For the rest of us the price was heavy: it put us at the mercy of foreign bankers and limited the Government's ability to improve our standard of living. When Mr Callaghan took over as Chancellor he was urged 'to do something about it'.

The Chancellor was willing enough to do so, but his advisers patiently explained to him 'the facts of financial life'. Mr Callaghan did his best to pass the message on. 'It is true', he told me in a television interview early in 1966, 'that because we are a world banker there are certain limitations on our policies. But there are advantages too. You should not put it all on one side'. Britain had not created sterling's world role: it had evolved from our success as a trading and banking nation. It was useful to us that people should want to settle a lot of their debts 'not in dinars or pesos or whatever it may be, but in sterling'. It helped us a great deal in our invisible exports (earnings from banking, shipping, insurance and other services) as well as in other ways. Mr Callaghan did however, concede that in time of balance of payments stress the world role could become a burden. 'I would say', he explained, 'It is a yoke, in the sense that when you put a yoke round your shoulders it may be a burden if one pail is empty, but not when you have them equally balanced.'

The trouble is that, throughout the three years leading to devaluation, one of the pails was awfully light. We had run up an uncomfortable large balance of payments deficit, and our gold reserves looked small in relation to our trade, and our responsibilities. A world banker cannot afford to have people wondering about his credit-worthiness. For this reason, the Labour Government has undoubtedly found the role more of a handicap than a privilege.

At the same time, it would be very wrong to lay all the blame for our troubles at this particular door. The basic cause of the periodic pressure on sterling is the tendency of the British economy to run into payments deficit. There *have* been a few occasions when we had to take protective action, even though we were in surplus, because we were affected by massive monetary tides. In 1957, for example, Bank Rate was raised to 7% (the highest for forty years) because traders and bankers overseas were withdrawing money from London in the hope of making fat profits on a rumoured up-valuation of the German mark. But the 1964–67 crisis can be largely explained in terms of the deficit. This deficit, as Mr Wilson never tires of pointing out, was resulted from Mr Maudling's deliberate attempt to break away from stop-go by vigorously stimulating economic growth. The experiment was abruptly terminated by the change of Government, and we shall never know whether it could have been continued if the Tories had remained in power. We do know, however, that everything Ministers tried to do between 1964 and 1967 was overshadowed by the plain fact that our national balance sheet was substantially in the red. Sterling's world role was not the cause of our problems. But it undoubtedly added to them.

General de Gaulle and others have made much of the balances deposited in London by countries in the sterling area. These are the core of the pound's reserve currency role. When Britain went off the gold standard in 1931, a number of countries which had strong financial ties with us decided to link the exchange value of their currencies to sterling rather than to the dollar. They included the present Commonwealth countries (except Canada and South Africa) the Scandinavian states, and various others such as Egypt and Portugal. When war broke out this sterling bloc, as it was known, was formally linked with us in our exchange control regulations to become the sterling area. From the start, it operated on simple principles. Members agreed to conduct their trade with each other in sterling, and to ensure that trade and payments among them were relatively unrestricted. They also agreed to turn the bulk of their foreign exchange earnings into pounds, which they left in London; these sterling balances formed the bulk of the reserves backing their own currencies. When they needed gold or non-sterling currencies, members bought them for pounds in the London foreign exchange market.

Inevitably, the past twenty years have seen substantial changes. The proportion of world trade in which sterling area countries participate has steadily fallen. So has the share of trade which member countries do with one another. Freedom in trade and payments has also declined. The non-sterling world now supplies our partners with three or four times as much capital as we do. The general 'pool' in London no longer provides the mutual insurance which used to be one of its best features. Indeed, it has sometimes tended to work to our disadvantage. In 1963–64 a rise in Australia's sterling balances helped to finance a growing UK deficit on current account. This lured the British Government into a false sense of security, and action was left until much too late. On other occasions, our fellow members have drawn on the pool at a time when we were losing reserves on our own account, and, of course, servicing the balance is an expensive business at a time of high interest rates. On the face of it, therefore, the sterling area system long ago became of questionable value. Mr Wilson's passionate declaration, in 1965, that 'to turn our backs on the sterling area would be a body blow to the Commonwealth and all it stands for' was the kind of emotional statement which confuses important issues. It is true, at the same time, that we have never been pushed into a crisis because of our sterling area obligations alone. If Britain had managed her domestic affairs more skilfully over the last decade, there would have been little or no embarrassment.

Given the general uneasiness about the pound, which never quite disappeared during the 1964–67 period, it was not surprising that the financial world frequently speculated about the stability of the sterling balances. General de Gaulle did his best to help this along when Britain decided, against his wishes, to apply for membership of the Common Market. How long would it be, people asked, before Australia or Malaysia grew tired of Britain's ineptitude and switched part of their deposit into gold or dollars? Could one expect them to sit back, and do nothing, while we were moving inexorably towards devaluation – an event which would cost them a great deal of money?

These questions seemed reasonable enough. But, as it happened, most of our sterling area partners remained calm throughout the long crisis period. 'We do not intend to rock the boat', Australia's Treasurer declared during the 1965 crisis. Nor did he. The British Government was able to boast that, apart from short-term fluctuations, the balances had remained 'pretty stable' for more than twenty years, and to claim that General de Gaulle was talking nonsense when he said that they represented 'a major threat'.

There is little doubt, however, that the very existence of the balances served to heighten the nervousness during the worst parts of our successive crises. Moments like these invariably see a plethora of wild rumours. Some arise from fear, others from a desire to cash in on the general panic. In that kind of atmosphere, it is comparatively easy to spread reports that, say, Australia is about to pull £200 million out of London and leave sterling at the mercy of speculators. The fact that such a move would clearly be against Australia's own interest tends to get overlooked in the general excitement; panicky people seldom stop to consider logic. In the summer of 1967, moreover, speculators got something to bite on. The Israelis went to war with the Arabs, who promptly accused Britain and the United States of plotting against them.

Almost at once the sterling balances – which General de Gaulle had talked about in such grave tones a few weeks ago – became big news. The Middle East, it was noted, had more than £350 million here. Withdrawal of even half this sum could cause considerable embarrassment. The pound, which had been making an excellent recovery in the early months of the year, came under new pressure. As always, wild rumours began to circulate. Officials at the Treasury and the Bank of England dismissed them as absurd, and insisted that co-operation between the world's central banks were strong enough to cope with any problems which might arise. They were not, however, prepared to give any figures. Speculators were, therefore, free to invent their own – and they did not hesitate to do so. News of sterling's new 'weakness' was well-publicized in Cairo, Moscow and elsewhere. Cairo Radio also made much of Sudan's decision actually to move its sterling holdings to Switzerland. The fact that Sudan had less than £20 million in London was not mentioned.

The idea, of course, was to unnerve Britain by fanning fears about the Middle East balances and particularly those held by Kuwait. The Arabs were in a vindictive mood – who could say what would happen next?

As it turned out, most of the money stayed where it was. The Sheiks of Kuwait and other rulers paid lip service to Arab unity, but kept their heads. One simple reason, of course, was that they would not easily find a profitable new home for such large funds. Beirut had become a discredited financial centre. Other countries either maintained strict exchange control regulations, which had the effect of locking money in, or paid too little interest. The United States was thought to be another hated backer of the Israelis, and therefore not a worthy recipient. Switzerland, the traditional haven, was already handling more foreign funds than it thought desirable. It was causing considerable distortions in its own economic affairs. So where could the Arab balances go? In the end, some did go to Switzerland. The Arabs soon discovered, however, that the Swiss were promptly re-depositing much of it in London – and, naturally, making a profit in the process. The Swiss National Bank quietly arranged to return some £10 million, and later three leading Swiss commercial banks openly offered the British Government a loan of £37½ million, which Mr Callaghan accepted with 'appreciation'. The millions mostly represented money which Kuwait and others had withdrawn from the City, where it was earning interest of around 5½%. The Swiss had agreed to take it, on the condition that they would pay the Arabs an average of around 3%. It was then returned to London, to earn 5½% for the smart Gnomes. The money-conscious sheiks got the message – and they still have not forgotten the lesson.

The Middle East episode showed that, although the sterling balances were less volatile than many people had feared, they *did* represent a potential threat in times when Britain was coping with financial troubles of her own.

This applied particularly to *private* balances, owned by banks, international companies and commodity dealers who keep sterling because they need it in their business or use London markets and the British banking network. Sterling reserves could be kept reasonably stable by agreement between Governments; private balances could be kept stable only by maintaining confidence in the pound. The weeks of rumours and speculation during the Middle East crisis – like earlier bouts of jitters – undoubtedly played an important part in the events leading up to our forced devaluation in November 1967.

A suggestion that the balances should be funded by a large low-interest loan from other industrialized countries was first made as long ago in 1945. Britain's reserves had been depleted by the war effort, and large balances had been accumulated by countries like India and Egypt, because of their provision of supplies, services and currency to British troops. The Americans pressed us to do something there and then, and a proposal for the liquidation of the sterling balances was made in the original White plan for Bretton Woods. But Britain would have none of it – partly because both the Bank of England and the Foreign Office argued that we had a moral obligation to continue as we were, and partly because the Board of Trade felt that the sterling balances provided an important reserve of purchasing power for British exports in the anticipated post-war slump. Only about 1% of the balances were written off (a voluntary goodwill gesture by Australia and New Zealand) and part of the rest was 'blocked' until conditions improved. Sundry schemes for 'getting rid of the balances' have been aired at regular intervals ever since. But theorizing is one thing, and raising the necessary cash quite another. At the IMF's 1966 conference, M Pierre-Paul Schweitzer told me that the chances of getting an agreement on such a massive operation were slim. Germany's Dr Otmar Emminger, one of the leading figures in the discussions on monetary reform which have been going on in recent years, also said that 'raising a loan to repay the sterling balances is not feasible in the amounts which would be required'. The pound, he added, could not avoid or escape continuing the role, 'because no one has yet found a means of relieving it from this particular responsibility'. The British Government, at this time, gave the impression that it was not even looking. Ministers indicated that all the theorizing was uncalled for and unnecessary. But Mr Callaghan gradually changed his tone, especially after General de Gaulle made it look as if the sterling balances were the only barrier to British membership of the Common Market. He announced that he had no patriotic attachment to sterling, and that he would be willing to listen to 'any sensible suggestions'. At the IMF's Rio conference in September 1967, he was closely questioned about his intentions.

He said that, looking a long way ahead, he expected eventually to see the development of a common currency in Europe. If anyone thought he wanted to keep sterling away from that, they were mistaken. In the short run, unless someone had any offers to release us from our liabilities, he had no plans for ending sterling's world role. Reports of offers to deal with the sterling balances had appeared only in the press, and had no substance. None had ever been made to him in any of the discussions or negotiations he had been involved in. 'If any of you know of any offers that are on the way', he told journalists from all over the world, 'I will be glad if you keep me informed.'

Mr Callaghan rejected the French view that it was Britain's job to put forward ideas for others to discuss. 'There are always two parties involved', he said. 'It is not just a question of what Britain is willing to do. It also matters what others want to do. Every country has its own problems – the Americans, the Germans, and the French. It is not for me to propose that those who put their reserves with us should find them farmed out to someone else. That is not the proper attitude for me to take'.

A few weeks later he returned to the theme at a bankers' dinner in the City. With whom, he asked, were we supposed to share our present role as world banker? There were various possibilities. For instance, should the dollar area be extended to take over sterling's role. Or should the International Monetary Fund take over some sterling balances if they were willing to do so, in return for claims on the fund? Or, in the context of our entry into the Common Market, should there be some development in which the community played an enlarged role?

These questions, Mr Callaghan added, could not be answered overnight. The new special drawing rights scheme had taken four years to work out, and was still not in its final form. Was it likely that a further evolution of the monetary system affecting sterling would take place any more quickly?

The UK's net liabilities to the sterling area countries totalled £2,237 million at the end of 1967. They had been 'inherited' by

Mr Wilson, along with the £800 million balance of payments deficit, and they clearly could not be ignored.

Here is a breakdown, provided by the Bank of England:

	£m
Malaysia, Singapore, Hong Kong and other Far East	694
Australia, New Zealand, South Africa	452
Middle East	399
East, Central and West Africa	339
Caribbean	228
India, Pakistan and Ceylon	114
Other	538
Total Sterling Area liabilities	2,764
Total Sterling Area claims	527
Net liabilities to Sterling Area	2,237
Net sterling liabilities to the rest of the world	1,327
Total net sterling liabilities to countries	3,564

In theory, all this could be switched out of sterling and into gold, dollars, francs, marks and other currencies. Devaluation had been, as one banker put it, 'an act of betrayal' (though Treasury officials were quick to point out that the high interest rates paid on the balances for years more than made up for the 14·3% loss.) It released our sterling area partners from any moral obligation to Britain, and it made private holders – whose holdings are not included in the table – reluctant to stay with sterling. How could they be sure that Mr Wilson would not devalue again in a year or so? The reduction in our military commitments and the continuation of the 'voluntary and temporary curbs on investment in the developed countries of the sterling area' which Mr Callaghan introduced in 1966, gave further offence. So, of course, did our attempt to join the Common Market. The sterling balances became something of a political issue in Commonwealth countries. Ministers were urged to 'diversify' – meaning a gradual process of achieving a better 'mix' in the reserves, either by swapping some of their pounds for dollars or gold, or by putting new funds into currencies other than sterling. This, it was claimed, would have become necessary even without devaluation because of the changed pattern of trade. Most of the sterling area countries recognized, of course, that as long as the pound remained suspect any wholesale attempt to switch would almost certainly backfire. Australia's Treasurer told me in Sydney early in 1968 that his Government would not embarrass Mr Wilson by making any large and sudden switches out of sterling, or running down balances deliberately to a low level. At the Reserve Bank of Australia, however, it was made clear to me that the existing spread of reserves was not regarded as 'appropriate' and that the process of diversification would be accelerated once confidence in sterling and the dollar was fully restored. Hong Kong, a British colony, decided it could not be quite that generous. It made a deal with London under which the Treasury guaranteed up to half its official sterling reserves. Malaysia promptly announced that it would seek a similar deal. Kuwait, meanwhile, indicated that it would make use of its long-standing special rights of conversion into dollars and showed considerable enthusiasm for gold.

The sterling area was obviously on the move. So were private holders of sterling: devaluation had touched off the biggest post-war movement away from sterling as an international trading currency. Mr Maudling, with more than three years' experience as a merchant banker under his belt, was no longer in doubt about the 'privilege or handicap' question. He joined the many MP's who were urging the new Chancellor, Mr Roy Jenkins, to 'do something'. Jenkins needed no prompting. 'This', he told me early in 1968, 'is an urgent problem. I do not regard it as something which can be tackled on a three to five years basis'.

The Bank of England was asked to 'put a ferret in the hole' and find out how the other central bankers felt about a funding operation. This was done without fuss, because officials rightly felt that it would be unwise to advertise their anxiety all over Europe. At a banquet in the City of London, however, the Governor of the Bank of Italy, Dr Guido Carli, indicated that something was afoot. He revived, in a speech, an idea which had been advanced by his Finance Minister three years earlier. It was, roughly, that the European central banks, together with the United States Federal Reserve, should act as a sort of buffer between holders of sterling balance and the Bank of England.

The reserve banks of countries like Australia and Kuwait could then be free to exchange their sterling reserves for new obligations on the consortium, which, in turn, would redeposit the sterling with the Bank of England, and have a claim on the Bank to convert these deposits into dollars or gold at some date in the future. This would effectively eliminate any danger to the pound for as long as the consortium held together.

Dr Carli was one of the most respected bankers in Europe, and his hint was well taken. An interim arrangement of sorts had already been introduced the year before, when Britain was given a large credit for the specific purpose of offsetting fluctuations in the sterling balances. But this was strictly a short-term credit, renewable every few months, and by the spring of 1968 it had been largely exhausted. Dr Carli was thinking of a more permanent arrangement. So was the Bank of England. Their idea was that Britain should get a loan of up to £800 million, and that it would be available for at least five years. The Government would not be able to use it to finance a continued balance of payments deficit, but the loan would cover the volatile part of the sterling balances – about a fifth of the total. Treasury officials would then be able to conduct separate deals with each of the sterling area countries. Discussions took place in the 'Basle club' of bankers for several months, and opinion was far from unanimous. France, which had run up against financial trouble of her own as a result of the student riots in May, declined to take part and Germany suggested that Britain might like to float a loan on the private German capital market instead. But the central bankers knew that, if they failed to shield sterling from possible diversification moves, the whole monetary system might be in still bigger peril.

In July 1968, after meeting in Basle, they announced that agreement had been reached in principle on a ten-year standby credit to cushion sterling's exposure to pressures arising from its world role. Mr Jenkins told the Commons that this was not a loan as such, and that it would not increase indebtedness. The central bankers had simply decided to provide new means for offsetting fluctuations in the sterling balances. Shortly afterwards, teams from the Treasury and the Bank of England went off to see our sterling area partners. The hope was that, if they could be given some form of guarantee against any further devaluation, they would resist the temptation to indulge in further wholesale switching. London, it was stressed, still offers a wide range of opportunities for investing money, or putting it on deposit, and we pay an attractive rate of interest. Sterling, moreover, is still a useful trading currency. Why switch out of a guarantee currency into gold – which earns no interest – or into currencies which do not carry a guarantee? Given a good response, ministers felt, Britain might not actually have to draw on the new credit. But even if she did, we would merely be exchanging one debt for another.

It is easy to say that sterling's world role should have been tackled more vigorously in 1964 and 1967. It was always a potential source of trouble. It meant that we were more exposed to international events than Italy or Japan, and that interest rates had to be kept higher than would otherwise have been necessary (servicing the sterling balances cost £200 million a year). It provided General de Gaulle with an excuse to keep us out of the Common Market – though, if the balances had not existed, he would have found another – and it deprived us of the exchange rate of flexibility which is such an important weapon in a country's armoury. The arguments for devaluing voluntarily in 1964 or 1965 would have been much more persuasive if sterling had not been a reserve currency. But in fairness to Mr Callaghan, it has to be accepted that this is one of the legacies which the Labour Government could not have shed at the stroke of a pen, even if it had wanted to do so. It has also acknowledged that Treasury and Bank of England officials told him very firmly that the practice of invoicing trade in sterling brought to London banks, insurance firms, and commodity dealers a lot of business which they might not otherwise get. (The weakness of this argument was not exposed until the Committee on Invisible Exports published its report in 1967.) It seemed to him, rightly, that the best solution lay in securing an impressive balance of payments surplus rather than in hastily off-loading balances held on behalf of someone else.

Devaluation marked the beginning of the end for sterling's world role, and we may well be better off as a result of it. Many people will regret the passing of this controversial reminder of the days when sterling (meaning 'first class') ruled the world alongside the Queen's Navy. But even more will see it as a long-overdue release from bondage.

10 Export or Die

BRITAIN HAS HAD a trade gap in all but seven of the past 176 years. In the second half of the last century – generally regarded as our apogee – we did not have a single export surplus. Never, though, have the British people been made to feel as guilty about it as they have been in the last decade. They have been nagged endlessly about the need to export more, and urged on with a succession of slogans. 'Export or die' and 'exporting is fun' are two of the more absurd examples. The monthly trade figures have hit the headlines with a boring regularity, and the politicians have studied them as anxiously as a hospital patient confronted with his latest temperature chart. The Labour Government, whose needs have been particularly desperate, has elevated exporting to one of the highest human virtues.

Writers, painters, scientists and humanitarians have to be content with second place in the Honours lists. The man who sells power drills to the Germans, booze to the Americans, fertilizers to the French, and textiles to the Arabs is prized above all. By the same token failure to export or inadequate performance in overseas markets has become one of the greatest evils. Thousands cringed (or, at least, were meant to) when Prince Philip delivered one of his 'this isn't good enough' speeches in February 1967. 'I am', he thundered, 'sick and tired of making excuses for Britain'.

In other countries, this intense pre-occupation with the mundane business of persuading people to buy our wares has always been observed with incredulous amusement. It seems astonishing to many people that a great nation can look upon itself as a failure – or at least give the impression of doing so – because its export sales fall short of expectations. How did we get ourselves into this state?

Britain is popularly seen as a small, heavily populated country which has to import its food and raw materials, and pays for them by exports of coal and manufactures. If it sells more to others than it buys from them, the economy is healthy. If not, the country is in trouble. Generations of politicians have churned out this simple message. Mr Callaghan told the nation shortly after he took office, that 'we are still left with some disconcerting features – in particular the failure of our exports to continue to rise and close the gap between what we buy and sell . . .'

The truth, however, is that we have never depended on this basic, Micawber-type formula. If we had done, we would not have been able to build ourselves into a financial and military world power. Britain has been a net importing country for centuries. The gap has been filled by currency income from other sectors – principally the service trades, shipping brokerage, merchanting, commission agenting, together with banking, insurance and other financial services, and earnings from overseas investments. The performance of a British play on Broadway, the shipping of foreign goods by a British ship, advice given to foreign clients, royalties paid to the Beatles and other pop groups, buying of British industrial 'know-how' by a foreign firm – all these things earn money which is no less important to our overall balance of payments position than exports of washing machines or bicycles.

Our real strength has always come from our financial skill, and from our vast investments in other parts of the world. This century's two world wars, unfortunately made quite a dent in our profit-making assets. The 1914–18 conflict is estimated to have cost Britain at least £1,000 million of the £4,000 million worth of foreign investments accumulated up to that point. By the second world war foreign assets were back to a nominal value of £4,000 millions, but the same process was promptly repeated. Our earnings from the remaining nest-egg have continued to advance. The increase, however, has not been sufficient to counter *both* the gap on visible trade and the very considerable rise in Government spending abroad. This is the crux of our post-war balance of payments problem.

Politicians have gone on spending on a huge scale, and have done their best to divert attention from this fact by nagging ordinary citizens about the trade gap. Britain, they have insisted, could easily afford to keep up a world military role if only exporters worked a bit harder. Ministers have never acknowledged responsibility for the balance of payments deficits which this policy has produced at regular intervals. Their answer, invariably, has been to 'force' industry to export more by depressing the home market, and to reduce the payments deficit by resorting to exchange controls. Mr Wilson's Government has clamped down heavily on new overseas investment, in spite of industry's fierce objections. Sterling's troubles, Ministers explained each time, left no other choice. The CBI, the Bank of England and others have countered that 'eating the seed corn' is a short-sighted policy. By restricting overseas investment, in order to permit Government spending, which brings no return of any kind, the country will eventually end up in a position where the historical gap on visible trade can no longer be covered by earnings from 'invisibles'.

The Banker magazine published a table in December 1967 which showed that, for many years the private sector has been producing a combined surplus while the public sector has been producing a deficit. (Only in 1955 did the private sector slip, marginally, into deficit.) The public sector, moreover, has shown persistent growth. Here are the figures for the ten years 1956 to 1966: (£ millions)

	Total current balance	Total private trade balance (visible and invisible)	Total Government spending overseas
1956	+208	+383	−175
1957	+223	+367	−144
1958	+336	+555	−219
1959	+136	+363	−227
1960	−275	+ 8	−283
1961	− 5	+328	−333
1962	+101	+462	−361
1963	+107	+490	−383
1964	−395	+ 38	−433
1965	−118	+328	−446
1966	− 59	+398	−457

This clearly adds up to a powerful argument for restraint in Government spending, and Ministers have given some tangible recognition of the fact since devaluation. But one cannot entirely ignore the point that, by boosting exports, Britain could afford to play a significant role in the world.

There is strong evidence that, over the years, British industry has suffered from failing competitiveness. Our share of world trade has been steadily declining, and each successive reflationary exercise (to 'go' part of the stop-go cycle) since the mid-fifties has opened up a wider gap between exports and imports. In self-defence, exporters have pointed out that Britain still sells a higher percentage of output abroad than almost any other nation – a record which could hardly have been achieved if they were as bad as all that. They have also made the valid point that for a long time Britain's exports have gone largely to the Commonwealth and other countries with slow growth rather than to continental Europe. They have added that the pattern of trade has been changed by tariff barriers and other hurdles: instead of exporting directly, many firms have set up manufacturing units inside a market and sent the earnings back to Britain in the form of 'invisibles'. The Government has never quite accepted these 'excuses'. Nor was it willing to acknowledge, until November 1967, that the lack of profitability of export sales represented a serious handicap. As the Prime Minister saw it, all our problems would be solved if industry could be made more competitive and more 'export-conscious'. Some ministers, however, have at least been willing to concede that there are two sides to the trade gap problem.

If Britain's import bill could be cut down, it would make just as effective a contribution towards eliminating the balance of payments deficit as an increase in exports could do.

As a manufacturing nation, we need to import industrial raw materials, many of which find their way out again as part of completed products. The 'import content' of our exports has been estimated at 18%. There is less need, however, to buy vast quantities of foreign goods, and the staggering increase in imports of such goods since quotas were removed in 1948 has cost us dearly. Figures published early in 1968 showed that, between 1958 and 1967 the total rose by more than £1,500 million to £2,500 million.

Before he won power, Mr Wilson had talked a great deal about import substitution. People were going to be encouraged to buy British products, and the Government was going to see that these were at least as good as those made by foreigners. It was wrong to spend £300 million a year on imports of timber, paper and pulp, even though modern spruce for softwood was known to grow in a much shorter time, and at much lower cost, in the West of the British Isles than in Scandinavia or North America. There was also scope for huge import saving throughout our main manufacturing industries, provided that we specialized on those products where our success is greatest and took steps to boost efficiency. Once in office, Mr Wilson and his colleagues tried to put their ideas into practice – but they had to acknowledge that the process was bound to take a long time. To deal with the more immediate problem, they introduced the import surcharge.

Economists will be debating the merits of this controversial weapon for many years to come. I would have preferred to see quotas instead, and I still believe that the rejection of quotas in 1964 was one of Mr Wilson's biggest mistakes. Statisticians have calculated that the surcharge may have saved us up to £200 million in the two years of its existence. But this is the roughest sort of estimate, and it is wide open to argument. It is reasonable to say that sterling would have come under even bigger pressure without it – but how much did we lose through the ill-will created by the Government's arrogant recourse to an untried measure?

The fierce reaction of other countries, and particularly of our partners in the European Free Trade Association, certainly came as a surprise to Ministers. At the EFTA meeting shortly after the surcharge was announced, Douglas Jay and Gordon Walker were forced to sit up until dawn defending themselves against bitter verbal attacks. During the night, they telephoned Mr Wilson in London. It was essential, they informed him, that Britain should give a public assurance that the process of 'reducing and eliminating' the surcharge would begin 'within a matter of months'. Without this, Britain would probably lose her existing tariff preferences in the EFTA countries. Mr Wilson had no alternative but to agree.

EFTA Ministers were as angry about the way the surcharge had been introduced as about the measure itself. The British

Government had acted without consulting its partners first. It was an open snub, and no politician worth his votes takes snubs without vigorous protest. Mr Brown, to his credit, made great efforts in the months that followed to correct the earlier mistake. He established personal contact with all the EFTA Ministers and tried hard to win their sympathy and understanding. Private, unpublicized meetings were held when he visited the Continent (ostensibly to attend Socialist rallies) and when EFTA Ministers visited London. By the time the next EFTA Conference fell due in May, 1965, a much better relationship had been established. As a goodwill gesture Mr Brown had privately informed our partners of his intention to announce a 5% cut in the surcharge, and the meeting itself turned out to be a pure formality. Twelve months later Mr Callaghan announced in his post-Election Budget that the surcharge would be abolished altogether on November 30. The EFTA crisis was over, but the Government had prematurely dropped one of its key measures. The hoped for balance of payments surplus still seemed a long way off, Ministers appeared ready to allow imports to rise again. This was, I believe, an important factor in the events which led up to the summer 1966 sterling crisis, and which forced Mr Wilson to introduce a stiff deflationary package in July.

The surcharge went against international trading rules, and EFTA countries had every right to complain about it. Import quotas, on the other hand, were perfectly permissible. Under Article 12 of GATT (The General Agreement on Tariffs and Trade) a nation threatened with a 'serious decline in its monetary reserves' was entitled to use temporary import quotas as long as the need lasted. Others were not, in these circumstances, allowed to retaliate. Mr Douglas Jay, who strongly favoured quotas right from the start, continued to urge them on his Cabinet colleagues until he was sacked in 1967. But Mr Wilson's wish prevailed, and the unhappy surcharge experiment won over most of the other ministers. Mr Wilson's case was, of course, a good one. A large and complex machinery would have to be set up to issue licences, check abuses, and generally administer a quota system. Then, quotas would protect the lazier element in British industry, a development which the Government was anxious to avoid. They would involve steep cuts in the sections where retaliation was most likely, and they would probably make it more difficult for Britain to enter the Common Market. As a young President of the Board of Trade, years earlier, Mr Wilson had made a bonfire of the last quota system. It was one of the proudest moments of his life, and he had long resolved not to go back on it. Nothing would change his mind. And since neither Mr Jay nor any other Minister was prepared to make a resignation issue out of it, quotas stayed on the shelf.

The rejection of quotas, and the premature abolition of the surcharge, inevitably made it more important still to boost exports. With devaluation also ruled out, this was a formidable task. Ministers worked hard to create 'export awareness' and to improve the machinery. The Tories had tried this in earlier years, but the Labour Government gave more attention to this whole subject than it had ever had before. The three years 1964–67 saw ceaseless activity. British weeks were held in major cities abroad, subsidized trade missions were dispatched to all parts of the world, export credit facilities were greatly improved, embassies were strengthened by the appointment of officials with business experience, and innumerable committees were set up to study overseas markets. Every conceivable idea for boosting exports was carefully examined – and, in many cases, put into effect. Mr Wilson also made some highly publicized attempts to boost trade with the Iron Curtain countries, notably the Soviet Union. We have long had an unfavourable balance of trade with the Russians, and the Prime Minister talked enthusiastically about the market's great potential. In fact, however, Anglo-Soviet trade is comparatively small. Like all the frantic effort at home, it helped the export drive, but it was not enough to secure the massive 'breakthrough' which the Government so desperately needed.

The pound, Mr Wilson insisted right up to November 1967, was not overvalued. Our internal price structures were not out of line with price structures elsewhere. Costs had risen, but the same was true of our main competitors. Other people, including many prominent economists, were not so sure. They argued that Mr Wilson would only get his breakthrough if the pound was devalued by 15% or 20%. If he would not do this, heavy deflation and strict wage control was the only answer. And it would have to be accompanied by a vigorous attack on some of our basic shortcomings: inadequate investment in new plant, old fashioned marketing techniques, poor after sales service, and inability to honour delivery dates. The Government countered with declarations of faith in the prices and incomes policy, and in the work of the various new organizations. But as wage statistics poured in, Mr Callaghan grew more and more sceptical about the incomes policy. So did the gnomes of Zurich, and in July 1966 the Government was forced to introduce its fierce deflationary package – combined with a wage freeze which, in effect, amounted to a modest hidden, devaluation.

Many people believed that the moment of truth would have come a lot earlier if world trade had not been reasonably buoyant. They may be right. Exports did well for quite some time because world trade in manufactured goods grew rapidly between 1963 and 1966. In virtually every country imports of manufactures were rising faster than home output for the home market. Thus increasing their share of total consumption. When world trade turned down in 1967, however, British exports were affected fairly quickly. And although our terms of trade continued to be favourable, Mr Wilson's prayed-for 'breakthrough' became as elusive as ever.

The Prime Minister still maintains that we would probably have pulled through, and met the next upturn in trade 'leaner and fitter' than before, if it had not been for the dock strikes. Like the seamen's strike the year before, these long and bitter disputes certainly did a great deal of damage. They disrupted shipments for considerable periods of time and cast doubt on our willingness and ability to get out of the red. On each occasion, most of the arrears were made good afterwards. But we also suffered quite substantial once-for-all losses, and at moments when we could least afford them. The psychological harm was probably greater still: many customers were made to feel that they simply could not rely on any sort of guarantee. Even so, it will not do to heap all the blame for Britain's failure to secure an export boom in 1966 and 1967 on the broad shoulders of the seamen and the dockers. They made the situation worse than it was, by highlighting our basic weaknesses, but it is highly doubtful whether we could have performed our hoped-for miracle if they had not missed a single day's work.

We failed because of a combination of factors. Some were outside our control (there is little we can do about the state of the

American or German economies) and some were given inadequate attention by people who should have known better. The Government underrated the importance of the profit motive in exports, dragged its feet over restrictive practices on both sides of industry, and made insufficient allowances for the fact that companies will only invest in new capacity if they have confidence in the way ministers run the economy. Union leaders were reluctant to acknowledge that exports meant full employment, and that no-one owes us a living. Businessmen paid generous lip service to exports, but all too often stayed at home.

Mr Wilson says that devaluation has given Britain a new opportunity 'to break out of our strait-jacket'. Most economists agree. But devaluation does not guarantee greater efficiency, or improve delivery dates. And the success of the operation is still dependent on what happens to world trade generally. This is why the expensively bought lessons of the past three years must not be forgotten.

11 The General Says Non

One of the moves which was, of course, meant to give exports a big boost was Britain's entry into the Common Market. It was going to give Britain easier access to a large and prosperous market right on her doorstep – a market which had been making rather a nuisance of itself by erecting formidable tariff barriers against the outside world. It was going to enable British and Continental industrialists to pool their resources, and fight the powerful competition from America's giants with a new vigour. It was going to give industrial investment – once described by Mr Wilson as the key to Britain's economic future – a major boost. The Americans, in particular, were going to spend hundreds of millions on new plant and equipment here because, as the CBI's John Davies put it, 'this is the country in which the Americans like to invest'. Not least, it was going to present British industry with an 'invigorating challenge' that would 'blow away the cob-webs'. Even Sir Leslie O'Brien, the cautious Governor of the Bank of England, was moved to declare that 'entry into the European Economic Community is the best way to greater prosperity for Britain'.

It all sounded very exciting, and most of the business and financial world responded with enthusiasm. There was only one snag. General de Gaulle was still determined not to let us in. And at the end of 1967, the British Government conceded that there was 'no chance of entry in the near future'. Privately, ministers said that, although the application remained on the table, it would not be re-activated so long as de Gaulle was in charge of French affairs.

The Common Market episode was yet another example of a fire-cracker that burnt itself out too quickly, and left the country with a sense of anti-climax and disillusionment. It was billed as a way out of Britain's continuing economic dilemma, and Ministers had made confident pronouncements about our chances of being accepted. Lord Chalfont, the Minister in charge of negotiations, had repeatedly said that, according to his information, France would not veto Britain's application. Mr George Brown had repeatedly declared that 'we expect to get in'. In the end, however, the affair came to be regarded as one more piece of evidence of the Labour Government's inability to 'get the country moving again'. And there is no doubt that the war of nerves between Paris and London which led up to the General's second veto played an important part in the 1967 sterling crisis which culminated in a forced devaluation.

The Prime Minister's conversion to the Common Market cause, in the late summer and autumn of 1966, took many Labour Party people by surprise. Mr Wilson, after all, had for years made very eloquent speeches *against* British membership on the kind of terms which were likely to be available. In 1962, a deflated Edward Heath had cringed under his merciless attacks in the Commons. He had expressed deep concern about the effects of entry on the Commonwealth, on our partners in the European Free Trade Association, on economic planning, on the sterling balances, on public ownership, on agriculture and a dozen other issues. 'In any future negotiations in Europe', he had declared in February 1963, 'we cannot allow ourselves again to get into the posture of supplicants. It was in that posture that the six regarded us, even if we did not so regard ourselves'. All this still seemed to apply. So did a statement he made in Bristol just a few months before announcing his own Government's 'European probe' on November 10, 1966: 'The Common Market is no cure-all for our economic problems. There are strong industrial problems. There are strong industrial arguments for being in Europe, particularly the extension of the market for sophisticated science-based products, and the resulting economies of scale. But we should not accept so easily that the cold wind of competitive imports will, of itself, make British industry more efficient.'

Why, then, the change of mind? The key lies in the July sterling crisis, and in the severe deflationary package which had to be introduced to end it. The crisis severely shook Mr Wilson's faith in his ability to control events, and dealt a blow to industrial confidence. He was wide open to the suggestion that Common Market membership would provide a fresh impetus. And many influential people were determined to exploit his mood. George Brown, who had moved to the Foreign Office, after the July 1966 crisis was a particularly strong advocate of the theory that nothing could be lost – and a good deal gained – by making an approach to the Community. He was supported by Roy Jenkins, Tony Crosland, Ray Gunter and other senior colleagues. Almost every leading industrialist Mr Wilson came into contact with urged him to go ahead. So did the Americans; Washington was keen to see Britain enter the Common Market and perhaps wrest the political leadership from the French. Not least, Britain's partners in the European Free Trade Association were urging him to get a move on. It all added up to very powerful pressure. Mr Wilson still had serious doubts about the terms we could get, at a time of financial weakness, but he was persuaded that the July 1966 package – which the French Finance Minister had praised as 'very courageous' – had dealt with most of the serious Common Market objections.

The Government, he declared early in 1967, was taking its decision 'after two and a half years of policies which have secured for Britain a position of economic viability and independence, a position of economic viability and independence, a position from which we can now look the world in the face'. It was a premature claim, to say the least. Mr Wilson also convinced himself that he had left his options open. A probe was not the same as an application, and the application itself could be made heavily conditional. 'We ask no favours', he told the Parliamentary Labour Party, 'we crook no knee. Our negotiations will be based not on what we need so much as on what we can contribute'. He stuck to this throughout the extraordinary tour of Europe which he and Mr Brown undertook in order to conduct their 'probing' at the highest level. His attitude is said to have made a bad impression on the French, but it is doubtful if the General himself would have opened the gates even if Mr Wilson had been more humble. George Brown did his best to make up for what he considered to be an unduly cautious attitude. He had set his heart on getting Britain into Europe, and he was impatient with the Prime Minister's attitude. As far as he was concerned, Britain's application had to be unqualified by any doubts or uncertainties.

At the cabinet meetings which followed the probing, he made generous use of the weapon his colleagues had become so familiar with: he threatened to resign. With a comfortable parliamentary majority under his belt, Mr Wilson may well have felt tempted to accept the resignation. But other Cabinet members backed the Foreign Secretary's call for an unconditional application (the notable exceptions were Douglas Jay, Denis Healey, and Barbara Castle) and the Prime Minister decided to placate George – as he had done so often before.

When the Commons got down to debating the Government's decision to go ahead, the Foreign Secretary was able to tell MP's that 'we now intend to put in a clear, clean, and uncluttered application'. There would be no 'ifs' and 'buts', no conditions or stipulations. 'We shall apply to join'. Manny Shinwell and several other implacable opponents of the Common Market roared their disapproval. The Government, said the peppery Mr Shinwell, seemed determined to lead Britain into Europe 'at almost any price'. But the Foreign Secretary remained undaunted. He hurled himself into a lengthy, passionate speech in which he outlined the visionary concept that had inspired his enthusiasm. Ever since the war, he declared, there had been in Britain a steady and growing awareness that the country's future was closely linked with that of her neighbours in Europe. This had come about, too, because people sensed Britain's changed position in the world. The development of the world meant that there was no longer a place for imperial powers. But Britain, a European country, still had a crucial and influential role to play in the world. Our first concern, politically, had to be for the security of our own country. Historically, our security was centred on Western Europe. Today, if we joined the community, the rivalries within Western Europe, which led to two world wars, would finally be silenced. 'A seal', Mr Brown went on, 'will be put upon the reconciliation of deeply felt antagonisms by including as partners in a single entity, the principal Western European combatants of those two wars'.

Some MP's silently wondered whether history could be changed at the stroke of a pen, and whether it was really necessary to join what after all was still a predominantly economic grouping in order to prevent another world war. But Mr Brown sailed on. The Government had always recognized, he said, that joining the

EEC was not the only course open to Britain. We could look to some as yet unformulated Atlantic grouping, or we could go it alone. 'Going it alone', he went on, 'sounds very well. It has a good British ring to it. At first sight it appears to have much to commend it. We could retain our EFTA partnership and our Commonwealth trade, and we would not have to face any of the changes or balance of payments problems which joining the community might entail'.

But, Mr Brown warned, the reality would be very different. 'EFTA has been a great success. But its members have always had in mind that it was only one step along the road to the larger European market which all its members want. If we turn our backs on the EEC now, then others would not follow suit just to oblige us'. Commonwealth trade was highly important to us, and whatever happened we should make every effort to preserve it. But here also changes were taking place. 'The world', Mr Brown declared, 'does not stand still. If we try to go it alone, we cannot count on our traditional trade just going on along in its present lines'. Many believed that the most compelling argument against going it alone was the question of technological development. We were an industrial country, living by our brains and selling what we invented and made. But brains, know-how, and technological skills were not enough. We needed scale and specialization 'if the prizes are not to go the United States and the Soviet Union'.

As a précis of the basic reasons for applying, this was fair enough. The Tories had said much the same six years earlier – and Edward Heath had been repeating it ever since. But many MP's felt that Mr Brown either had no idea of the practical difficulties involved in joining the Common Market at this particular time, or deliberately chose to ignore them. Mr Michael Stewart, who had succeeded George Brown at the Department of Economic Affairs, attempted to deal with this, but succeeded only in boring the House. A continuous drone of conversation formed the background to his speech, and the Speaker had to request that MP's should be more polite. Mr Stewart's message was that, in spite of the Foreign Secretary's bold words, the Government had 'made no attempt to minimize the very real and serious problems that face us'. It is, he said, 'a tough thicket of difficulties through which we must make our way. We must not make the mistake of taking too short-term a view of what is involved.'

It was a neat admonishment, delivered in Mr Stewart's best headmaster manner, but it totally failed to make an impact. And there were open yawns when Mr Stewart remarked, somewhat lamely, that 'one of the things to which special attention will have to be given, if we enter, will be the improvement of communications between development areas and the ports of the South and East coasts'. MP's understandably felt that this was the least of their worries: it was a problem which had to be tackled whether we went into the Common Market or not, and in any case it seemed to have little to do with the basic decision on which they were asked to vote.

The debate ended, on the night of May 9, 1967, with a Government majority of 426 – the biggest since the Attlee Government had called for emergency powers in 1949. Brother George, it seemed, was on his way. But a few days later, General de Gaulle reminded him – and the rest of the world – that the fulfilment of some ambitions requires more than a Commons majority. He said there had 'never been any question of a veto', but described the obstacles to British entry as 'formidable'. Britain, he added, must first undergo a 'deep economic and political transformation'.

The General went on to list the reasons for his scepticism, and it seemed to me and many other journalists covering the conference that – whatever his motives – he had made out a case which Mr Wilson and his colleagues would not be able to brush aside. He was, after all, voicing the same doubts which had troubled the international financial community – and most financial editors – for quite some time. The General did not stoop to quote Mr Wilson's own 1962 speeches, but he selected Britain's weak spots with an unerring touch. We looked forward to seeing Downing Street's reactions, and we were not disappointed. Yes, it was conceded, General de Gaulle's response to Britain's application had been chilly. But he had not ruled out the possibility of negotiations, had he? He was trying to get into the best bargaining position, that was all. In any case, we could be sure that France's five Common Market partners would make it very difficult for her to prevent the start of negotiations. For good measure, we were informed that the General's observation about sterling were 'naïve'. France had entered the Common Market at a time when her own currency was one of the most unstable in the world, and the British Government saw no reason to give up the world role of sterling.

I wrote at the time that Mr Wilson and Mr Brown were indulging in their old habit of believing what they wanted to believe, and therefore underrating what they were up against. Mr Brown has since claimed that he had, at all stages, a realistic view of what the outcome would be, but that he felt he could not allow 'the slightest quiver of doubt ever to pass across my face'. If this is true, one cannot help feeling that it would have been better to treat the General's comments with a good deal more respect than they got at the time.

The Government's optimistic interpretation of the situation was accepted, at face value, by all the other Common Market enthusiasts. Mr John Davies, Director General of the CBI, said that de Gaulle had expressed no new objections, and that British ministers had 'answered and refuted' everything the General had said before. Surprisingly few people pointed out that de Gaulle held most of the aces, that the British Government's timing was bad, and that he had the means to block British entry if his strategy was not, as Mr Wilson claimed, simply designed to wring the maximum number of concessions from Britain. Mr Davies might have been satisfied with Mr Wilson's arguments, but there was no reason to expect that General de Gaulle would share the widespread admiration of the Prime Minister's eloquence.

During the weeks that followed, the French calmly set about the task of giving Britain the brush-off. Mr Wilson had gambled on the possibility that France's five Common Market partners would force her to start negotiations, and that General de Gaulle would not dare to use an actual veto for a second time.

The Benelux countries and Italy had made it plain that they favoured British entry, and although the Germans had given Mr Wilson an unexpectedly cool reception during his 'probing', he believed that Germany would also press France to get down to negotiations. On May 25, Downing Street announced that Mr Wilson had accepted an invitation to meet President de Gaulle near Paris in June for a private chat. The talks were to last 'a full day', but Mr Wilson and his wife were to stay one night, or perhaps two, as the General's guests. Hopes rose. Mr Wilson let it be known that he would 'play tough' at the Paris meeting.

Meanwhile, Mr Brown would meet the Foreign Ministers of the Six at the Hague and explain once more what Europe could gain from British membership. Five main arguments were to be used. One, British membership would help Europe to assert its 'political personality' and give it a stronger voice in the world – a point calculated to appeal to General de Gaulle. Two, the EEC countries are dynamic not static, and should therefore be able to take new members in their stride, in spite of France's 'philosophical' doubts about enlarging the Community. Three, an enlarged EEC would mean a 'wider Europe', because it could bring about a reconciliation between Western Europe and the Communist countries. Four, a united Europe would be more 'outward-looking' in that it would be able to give more aid to developing countries than the EEC did in the past. Five, the Common Market debate in Parliament had shown that the three parties were overwhelmingly in favour of British entry.

On the eve of his departure for the Paris *tête-a-tête*, Mr Wilson added a sixth point. He said that 'the addition of our scientific, technological, and industrial resources to those of the present members could have a decisive effect upon the ability of Europe to face the future.' Without such co-operation, Europe would find itself relying on the United States and, perhaps, Russia for the advanced technological products of the 1970's and 1980's. This had long been Mr Wilson's favourite theme, and he clearly hoped it would have a major impact. General de Gaulle, however, remained unimpressed by all the arguments when the two leaders talked for five hours at the Trianon Palace. As Mr Wilson told the Commons on his return: 'I would not want to suggest that the President is more enthusiastic about British entry than he has been at any other time'. Asked whether the General's answer would be 'Yes' or 'No' or 'Perhaps', the Prime Minister replied he thought there were other possible alternatives going through his mind, including 'yes, but . . .'

George Brown reported a little more success – most of the Foreign Ministers at the Hague had supported British entry – but he admitted that they might be unwilling to risk a breakdown of the Common Market if France decided to remain stubborn.

M Couve de Murville, the French Foreign Minister, soon made clear what his Government's strategy would be. Discussions among the six themselves on a reply to Britain's application, he said, were bound to be 'complicated and prolonged'. The French wanted detailed consideration of the 'formidable problems' which it had presented. Britain protested, in vain, that these problems were by no means insoluble, and that they could be hammered out during actual negotiations. Mr Callaghan announced that he had 'an open mind' on sterling's world role, and was willing to consider any workable schemes for dealing with the sterling balances. But the French refused to budge. They intended to delay the whole question of British membership for as long as possible – and meantime, to pound away at those 'formidable problems'. They knew that the other five shared France's concern about Britain's financial and economic situation, and that the Middle East crisis had helped to show that, whatever Mr Wilson might say, the sterling balances *were* a major handicap.

The French tactics were eminently successful. Five months after Mr Wilson's chat with General de Gaulle the British Government was still waiting to start negotiations. And it had been forced to devalue, by a sterling crisis which France's persistent harping on Britain's financial weakness had helped to bring about.

A week after devaluation, General de Gaulle held one of his olympian press conferences – the sixteenth since he returned to power in 1958. Great Britain, he began, had pressed its case with 'an insistence and an extraordinary fury, some of the reasons for which may have been made clear by recent monetary events'. He went on to repeat his familiar case for keeping Britain out, and warned France's Common Market partners that the very existence of the Community was at stake. Then came the punch-line: 'France cannot at present enter any negotiations with Britain and its associates which would lead to the destruction of the Community to which it (France) belongs.' By way of consolation, he suggested that Britain might like to try for associate status – a course which Mr Wilson had earlier rejected as out of the question.

General de Gaulle's pronouncement, which amounted to a categoric veto, was followed by some frantic coming and going among the other five. Messages of sympathy and promises of support flooded into London. All the five said Britain was right to keep in her application, and everyone forecast a 'rough ride' for France at the December meeting of the Council of Ministers, which was to give formal consideration to the request. Dr Joseph Luns, the Dutch Prime Minister, denounced General de Gaulle's 'negotiations by press conference' and warned that 'the moment of truth' would come in Brussels. Mr Wilson chipped in his with a nineteen point reply to de Gaulle, 'to put his points in truer perspective.' But when the moment of truth arrived, on December 19, the answer remained 'no'. It came in lengthy diplomatic verbiage, which recorded the feelings of five members that negotiations should begin at once, and of one who believed that Britain's economic recovery had to come first. Germany's Professor Karl Schiller, the outgoing president of the Council, said the door remained open, and the Foreign Office in London immediately responded by saying that 'the application stays in'. But it was clear that General de Gaulle had won the day.

Whatever one thinks of his motives, or of the wisdom of his actions, one has to respect General de Gaulle's strength as an opponent. The British Government thought it could beat him, and set out to try. The prime mover in this was George Brown, whose enthusiasm had often before clouded his judgment, but Harold Wilson also underrated the skill and determination of the man they were up against. In retrospect, it seems incredible that neither of them realized what would happen when they first talked to the General – and to the German Government in Bonn – during their famous 'probe'. If they had decided, at that point, that the General's obvious intransigence made it futile to go ahead, a great deal of trouble could have been avoided. A lot of people would have protested that the Government was giving in too easily – but a strong Prime Minister can take that sort of criticism in his stride.

It is generally assumed, of course, that the setback was only temporary. Britain is expected to have another go when General de Gaulle has gone, and it is reckoned that a decade from now she will be firmly established as a leading member of the Common Market. This is certainly the view held by Mr Wilson, and Mr Heath is such an enthusiastic European that there can be little doubt about the Tories' attitude if they should return to power. By the seventies', it is pointed out, Britain should have regained her economic and financial health, and should be able to bargain from a position of strength. She has demonstrated her willingness to be European, and should be able to draw on a considerable store of goodwill when the time comes. The 1966–1967 episode will, therefore, have been altogether in vain.

This line of argument obviously has considerable merit, though I think it may be a mistake to imagine that France will welcome Britain with open arms the moment General de Gaulle is no longer at the Elysée Palace. Meantime, however, it is as well to recognize that British industry has to struggle against EEC tariff barriers, and to accept that the Commonwealth countries are developing close links with industrial nations like the United States and Japan. It makes it all the more essential to deal with Britain's many structural problems.

Some people, of course, argue that the Government should not keep waiting outside Europe's door. They point out that Mr Wilson himself advocated a more positive course in the carefree days when he was leader of the Opposition. 'When we have all had time to get over the shock', he said in the 1962 Commons debate, 'why not have the same negotiations with the United States with, perhaps, a different shaped table; with the United States, Britain, the Commonwealth and Latin America and the EFTA countries on one side, and the six on the other?' He also suggested that if the Brussels negotiations conducted by Mr Heath broke down, the Government could call 'a Commonwealth trade conference'. Both these ideas have been brought up again since de Gaulle's second veto, though not by Mr Wilson.

Douglas Jay, who was sacked from the Cabinet because he opposed the Prime Minister's Common Market line, has enthusiastically advocated the idea of an Atlantic Free Trade Area. Such an area, he and his supporters maintain would bring substantial benefits to the British economy in terms of extra trade – greater than could be achieved by joining Europe. It would mean free entry into a market which, by 1977, may have a gross national product more than three times that of the Common Market. The 'dynamic effect' of intensified competition would be bigger, and Britain would not have to bear the heavy burden of the EEC's agricultural policy. We would be able to maintain the principle of buying food in the cheapest world markets, and retain in some form our economic links with the Commonwealth. There would, moreover, be no obligation for eventual political federation or union. It would be a purely commercial arrangement.

These arguments were, in fact, considered in some detail by

George Brown and other ministers before they decided on the 1967 Common Market application. But the proposal was firmly rejected. The Cabinet took note of several points made by opponents of the scheme, including the argument that it would involve Britain becoming a virtual economic colony of the United States, with her industries taken over and an accelerated 'brain drain' of scientists and technologists to America, where all advanced technology would be based.

The issue was really clinched, however, by two key considerations. First, it was agreed that Britain is so much a part of Europe historically and geographically that she must try to get into the Common Market before looking at anything else. Unlike the North Atlantic free trade area scheme, EEC membership offered a chance of political leadership. Secondly, Washington had made it clear that President Johnson's Administration simply wasn't interested in the proposal. General de Gaulle's second veto, and the departure of George Brown from the Cabinet, have not changed the situation. If the next American President decided to take the initiative, Harold Wilson and Roy Jenkins would be prepared to listen. But their basic assessment is unchanged: Britain's place is in Europe.

12 Antics on a Tightrope

On Friday, November 17, 1967, Lord Chalfont, Britain's special envoy to the Common Market, addressed a capacity luncheon meeting of French luminaries. Twice he insisted that the British Government had no plans for changing the exchange rate of the pound. 'Nowhere in our thinking', he declared, 'is devaluation included . . . we do not regard devaluation as the best solution for the United Kingdom or for the world's economic problems'.

His Lordship was talking nonsense. The Cabinet had unanimously decided 24 hours earlier to devalue by 14·3%. No-one seems to have thought fit to inform Lord Chalfont. But his audience did not believe him anyway. Most Continental bankers and economists were convinced that the weekend would bring official news of devaluation; the only uncertainty was over the percentage change in the parity. Friday had seen the biggest ever scramble to get out of sterling. The curtain was about to come down on the last act of the three-year-long drama entitled 'Saving the Pound', and starring Harold Wilson and Jim Callaghan.

As Mr Callaghan tells the story, his thoughts had first turned to devaluation three or four weeks earlier. As in July 1966, he was told by his advisers that if nothing was done, the balance of payments wouldn't come right in the current year or next year either. Instead of the surplus he had confidently predicted for 1967–68, Britain was likely to end up with a deficit of £300 million–£400 million. World trade could be expected to pick up, but not fast enough to put us into surplus during 1968. Partly because of the reflationary measures introduced in the summer, and partly because wages were rising again at a disturbing rate, the economy was heading for a dangerous boom. This was almost certain to push us into another sterling crisis some time during 1968. Failure to act now, the Chancellor realized, would merely be postponing the evil day. It was a bitter disappointment to him.

Only five months before, it had looked as if everything was going to work out fine. The tough deflationary package introduced in July 1966 had been effective. The Treasury was predicting a 1967 surplus of around £200 millions, and the independent National Institute of Economic and Social Research put the likely basic surplus at £175 millions. The Bank of England had repaid all its short-term debts, and unwound its forward commitments. A substantial debt repayment had been made to the International Monetary Fund. Mr Wilson, still smarting from the barrage of criticism levelled against him the previous summer, had proudly announced that Britain was 'paying her way'.

Instead of worrying about the gnomes of Zurich, it seemed possible for the Chancellor to turn his attention to some of the less desirable effects which the July package had been having on the domestic scene. The unions were restless about the comparatively high level of unemployment (it had topped 600,000 in January), and so were backbench MP's. All the forecasters seemed to agree that on unchanged policies there would be little to prevent a continuous rise in unemployment until well into 1968. The experience of 1962 was a recent reminder of the dangers of delaying reflationary action for too long; the delays in that year had allowed unemployment to reach a winter peak (admittedly aided by severe weather) of 878,000 by February 1963. Some union leaders were gloomily predicting that this time the total might pass the million mark. Neither Mr Wilson nor Mr Callaghan needed to be warned about the political consequences of such a black milestone. The rank and file of the Labour Party, they knew, would never have forgiven them.

During March, some of Whitehall's leading economists had suggested, privately, that the moment had come to 'devalue from strength'. Inflation had been brought under control, and devaluation would probably produce a big enough upswing in exports to take care of the unemployment problem. It was an attractive argument, but the Government rejected it. I have a letter from Mr Callaghan, written in January 1968, in which he lists the reasons. It has never been made public, but it deserves to be quoted in full.

'First the reactions of a number of Governments and institutions would not have been as understanding in the spring of 1967 as they were in the autumn. At that time the official forecasts on which so much (and some would say too much) weight is placed, were not showing a situation that would have enabled us to justify devaluation to other observers. In addition the trading figures in the last quarter of 1966 had been good, and in the first quarter of 1967 certainly did not justify the extreme act of devaluation. Secondly, it would have placed in jeopardy the special drawing rights scheme for a number of reasons which I will not go into here. Thirdly, with the developing recession in the German and United States economies we would not have experienced any immediate boost in our exports. As it is, we have a good chance of a substantial increase in our exports now, floating them off on the expected higher level of world trade in 1968. Fourthly, if we had devalued in the spring we would still have had the Middle East war ahead of us. A devaluation in the spring would certainly not have prevented the shock to confidence that occurred at the outbreak of war; still less would it have stopped the political withdrawals from sterling that were made by the Middle East countries. Indeed, a spring devaluation might have accelerated such withdrawals, so we would have been in a situation last summer where to the shock caused by devaluation would have been added the political disturbances of the world money markets caused by the Middle East war. All this would have been placed against the background of poor trade figures because the consequences of devaluation would not have been successful by then. My considered conclusion is that all this might even have culminated in a second forced devaluation last autumn for the wrong reasons, and where would we be now if that had happened?'

Having ruled out a spring devaluation (with the warm approval of the Prime Minister) the Chancellor had concentrated on the difficult question of how soon and how far he could dare to reflate. After two and a half years at the Treasury, he fully realized that one must never take anything for granted. Sterling was still convalescing, and the balance of payments surplus remained a hope rather than a reality. Failure to achieve it would have serious repercussions. Some £292 million had to be repaid to the International Monetary Fund by the end of the year, and a further £544 million had to be repaid by early 1971. Premature reflation might well jeopardize the hard-won financial recovery – and if that happened, he could hardly slam on the brakes again. The shot had already been fired.

One fortunate development late in 1966 and early 1967 had been a general agreement among leading nations that the world-wide interest rates 'war', which had done a lot of damage to sterling in 1966, should be brought to an end. Mr Callaghan organized a 'disarmament' conference of finance ministers at Chequers, and shortly afterwards announced a cut in Bank Rate. Two other reductions, bringing Bank Rate down to 5½%, were made during the next eight weeks. It was a modest degree of reflation in monetary policy, made possible by the help of the Americans, the Germans, the French, and several other nations. Mr Callaghan felt that, for the time being, this was all he could do. The Budget, early in April, was strictly neutral. Trade union leaders and Labour MP's were dissatisfied, and said so. Jim Callaghan was called 'The Iron Chancellor', and there were suggestions that he should be replaced by someone with a little more feeling for the plight of the working-class. Shortly after the Bank of England had told him that its short-term debts were settled, and after the Treasury had made a substantial repayment to the International Monetary Fund, Mr Callaghan relented. He announced early in June that 'the period of standstill in the economy is finished', and that we were about to start 'a period of controlled growth and expansion'. To mark the occasion he relaxed the terms of hire purchase agreements – a quick-acting weapon. The newspapers, always quick to forget, promptly dubbed him 'Sunny Jim'.

The Chancellor knew that he had taken a gamble. He thought it had a reasonable chance of coming off, but he was painfully aware of how much this depended on events which were totally outside the Government's control. The Middle East war had started two days before he made his announcement, and the Suez Canal had been closed. This meant that our import bill – already swollen by the rebound in purchases which followed the removal of the temporary surcharge in November 1966 – would have to bear an additional burden. It also meant that the Arab countries might switch some of the sterling balances to Zurich or other centres –

or at least, that foreign exchange markets would worry about the possibility of such a switch. The Treasury was doing its best to play down the likely impact of all this, but the Chancellor knew that it represented an extra handicap which he had not really counted on when he and Mr Wilson decided that something must be done to prevent unemployment reaching an 'unacceptable level'. He also knew that, with the phase of 'severe restraint' in incomes policy about to end, earnings were likely to rise quite sharply. He was, in his own phrase, 'walking on an economic tightrope'. His main consolation lay in those cheerful balance of payments forecasts, and in the substantial international credits which the Government could draw on if sterling should come under new attack.

To me, the tightrope act never seemed justified – and I was astonished when, in August, Mr Wilson appointed himself economic overlord and celebrated the occasion by relaxing HP controls still further. I fully sympathized with the Govermnent's concern for the unemployed, but I thought (and said so in my *Guardian* column) that it should have given itself more room for manœuvre by making some pretty drastic cuts in overseas spending, introducing import quotas, or even launching a scheme for the voluntary acquisition of at least part of the very substantial privately held dollar portfolio. It did none of these things – nor, it seemed to me, did it retain sufficiently strong powers to curb incomes.

Other observers again brought up the subject of devaluation. The case for it was given a thorough airing, both in the newspapers and in private. It infuriated Mr Wilson and Mr Callaghan, as it had done in the year before. Financial journalists were asked to be 'patriotic', and not to make devaluation inevitable by talking about it. Foreigners, it was pointed out, were reading their comments, and they might well start to protect themselves. One minister after another issued authoritative denials that devaluation was even the remotest possibility. Even Mr Herbert Bowden, the Secretary for Commonwealth Affairs, got in on the act. A great deal of nonsense, he declared on July 23, was being talked in some papers about the value of devaluing the pound, as if it would be the cure for every possible problem that this or any other country has. It was not – and the Government 'completely rejected talk of devaluation'. Mr Callaghan added his own authoritative voice a day later. 'Devaluation', he told the Commons, 'is a flight from reality'. It would mean a reduction in the living standard of every man, woman, and child in Britain. The Government 'rejected the notion that our economic strategy should include the exchange rate of the pound'.

The newspapers hit back by casting grave doubts on Mr Callaghan's ability to get through 1967 on his existing policies, and pointing out that the gnomes of Zurich did not need to have a map drawn for them – they were perfectly capable of doing their own sums, and drawing their own conclusion. So they were. As the Bank of England has since revealed, sterling came under persistent pressure from May onwards. Foreign bankers, traders and others who held sterling were simply not prepared to join Mr Callaghan in his tightrope act.

The Middle East war was short-lived, but it did considerable damage. And as the year went on, Mr Callaghan found himself faced with other handicaps, the significance of which he either failed to recognize or deliberately underrated. One of the most important of these arose from Britain's decision, early in May, to go ahead with an application to join the Common Market. General de Gaulle was determined to keep us out, and he knew exactly where we were most vulnerable. His Ministers began to hammer away at 'the problem of sterling' with untiring zeal. French newspapers dutifully backed the campaign, and Fleet Street obliged by reporting every word. It was most effective propaganda warfare. M Debre, the French Finance Minister, and M Couve de Murville, the Foreign Minister, concentrated their attention on the sterling balances. But questions were also asked about Britain's ability to cope with the substantial extra burden which would arise from entry into the Common Market. Perhaps the most damaging development, from Britain's point of view, was the publication of a report by the Commission of the EEC, commenting on British entry. The section dealing with sterling was drafted by a Frenchman, M Raymond Barre, and its main conclusions were leaked to the French newspapers several days before the date of official publication. They left a widespread impression that the Six regarded devaluation as the price of entry, and that General de Gaulle's fears about the sterling balances were shared by his partners. 'The present distribution of these balances,' the report noted, 'is of a nature to provoke fears of substantial withdrawals'. Mr Wilson and Mr Callaghan must have found all this embarrassing, but they gave no public indication that they were concerned. Stiff upper lips were the order of the day.

Mr Callaghan was, at this time, somewhat pre-occupied with a subject which had fascinated him for many months – monetary reform. He was the sole authority in the Cabinet on the complex questions which had been hotly debated in various international forums since 1963. These had finally come down to a compromise plan for the creation of 'special drawing rights', which could be added to a country's first line reserves and used in times of trouble. (The details are more fully discussed in chapter nine.) The plan had obvious attractions for Britain, which was short of reserves, and the Chancellor pushed it for all he was worth. In July, his efforts were finally rewarded with success. Under his chairmanship, the ministers in the so-called 'Group of Ten' rich countries agreed to give the green light to the scheme. It was approved at the full meeting of IMF governors in Rio de Janeiro in September. At this stage, however, it was no more than an outline. The details had still to be worked out, and the legislative bodies of all 107 IMF member countries had to ratify the final version. This was not expected to be completed until mid-1969, and even then 'activation' depended very much on how far the United States and Britain had managed to reduce their balance of payments deficit. The French had insisted on strong provisos, and the other Common Market countries had gone along with them. The 'special drawing rights' could not, therefore, be regarded as being in any sense an answer to Britain's immediate financial problems. They had a useful psychological effect for a while – and Mr Callaghan was understandably pleased that something had gone right for a change. But they did not make his tightrope act more safe.

Meanwhile, the dockers in London and Liverpool had decided to come out on strike. They were not concerned with sterling, the Common Market, or anything else. What bothered them was the Government's decasualization scheme. Like the seamen in the previous year, they were prepared to endure considerable personal hardships in order to win their point. General de Gaulle must have blessed his luck. He had a powerful new ally.

The vision of the lofty French General conspiring with a pint-sized Communist docker from Stepney to topple the mother of the

British Empire seems utterly absurd. But in September and October 1967, General de Gaulle and Jack Dash were widely seen as the common foe. Jack Dash protested, in vain, that he wasn't trying to bring sterling down. He was simply challenging the capitalists who employed him and his fellow-dockers. Mr Wilson and his Chancellor lashed out at the 'wreckers', as they had done a year earlier. But the dockers stood their ground. Exports piled up in the ports, and the dispute – coming at a time when Britain's economy was under close scrutiny – was given considerable publicity on the Continent. This not only hurt the pound, but left a permanent impression in many foreigners' minds that Britain was constantly bedevilled by industrial turmoil, and that our firms could not be trusted to keep delivery promises. Mr Wilson's repeated boast about 'the determination and resolve of the British people' seemed to them totally unjustified.

In the middle of this the gnomes of Zurich – of all people – decided to help Mr Callaghan get through what was obviously a trying time. A consortium of commercial banks offered Britain a £37·5 million loan. As explained earlier, this largely represented money which had been switched from London to Zurich during the Middle East crisis by irate Arab sheiks, and the gnomes were going to make a useful profit on the deal. But the Chancellor publicly expressed his gratitude. Zurich was showing faith in sterling, while British subjects did nothing but question his ability to maintain the 2·80 dollar parity! The fact that the gnomes had made the loan conditional on repayment in dollars, and were therefore safeguarded against any possible devaluation of sterling, either escaped his notice or was deemed unworthy of acknowledgment.

At the end of October, the Liverpool dockers returned to work, but 6,000 London dockers remained out. Some £150 million worth of exports were piled up in Liverpool alone, and overtime was promptly introduced in an attempt to catch up. But a good many orders were permanently lost, and it was calculated that a trade deficit of £300 million had accumulated in the first ten months of the year. In addition to the dock strike, overseas sales had been helped back by the slower-than-expected recovery in the German and United States economies – two vital markets. And the year's import bill looked like being a good deal bigger than Mr Callaghan had allowed for when he launched his 'period of controlled growth and expansion'. The Suez Canal remained closed, and was likely to stay out of action for quite some time to come. On top of this, the Chancellor had found to his dismay that international interest rates were going up again. His brave attempt, at the Rio conference, to secure another round of 'disarmament' had failed. Everyone was willing enough to acknowledge that interest rates *ought* to be kept down, but no-one wanted actually to *do* something. This particularly went for the Americans, who were again fretting about inflationary pressures and found Congress unwilling to exercise control by a tax increase. The Treasury's stark new balance of payments forecast, at the beginning of November, simply confirmed something which Mr Callaghan had guessed already. Wearily, he re-examined possible ways out of the dilemma. A new wage freeze was turned down as impracticable, and import controls were rejected on the grounds that they would involve steep cuts in the sections where retaliation was most likely. Other ideas were eliminated on the grounds that they were insufficiently potent to achieve what was required. This left the possibility that Washington, and the Continental central bankers, would once again rally round with a massive loan to tide Britain over until exports picked up.

Having spent a good deal of time with key men like Pierre-Paul Schweitzer, Kark Schiller, and Henry Fowler, Mr Callaghan knew that their patience was wearing thin. They were willing to acknowledge that Britain had run up against special problems, which were likely to be of a temporary nature, but they had become increasingly doubtful whether we were ever likely to get anywhere. We had already borrowed more than any previous British Government, and there was no guarantee that another loan would solve anything. Sir Leslie O'Brien, the Governor of the Bank of England, confirmed that the central bankers who made up the 'Basle club' had much the same misgivings. The Americans, who remained firmly opposed to devaluation because of the unsettling effect it would have on the dollar, would probably be prepared to help if their arms were twisted hard enough. And having made a repayment to the IMF earlier in the year, we had reconstituted at least some of our drawing rights. Under the IMF rules, Mr Callaghan was perfectly entitled to draw on this if he wanted to. M Schweitzer, the IMF's managing director, was also willing to discuss a programme for rephasing our huge outstanding debt. The cupboard, therefore, was not entirely bare.

But Mr Callaghan had come round to sharing the misgivings of other finance ministers, central bankers, and Whitehall economists. 'I decided', he told me after devaluation had become an accomplished fact, 'that it would have been irresponsible to go on borrowing'. His mind was more or less made up by November 6, and he went into a long huddle with the Prime Minister. Mr Wilson, who was fully aware of the gravity of the situation, still fervently disliked the idea of devaluing. His basic objections, which had led him to reject such a step for three years, remained as strong as ever. And he was enough of a political realist to know that devaluation would deal a severe blow to his personal standing in the country. He told Mr Callaghan that he wanted time to think it over. Meanwhile, he agreed that Bank Rate should be raised on November 9 to 6½%. It failed to make any significant impact on foreign exchange markets. Bank Rate only acts as a magnet when foreigners have confidence in the continued stability of a currency; half a per cent more or less interest does not make up for the loss of 10% or more of one's capital in case of devaluation.

A day or two later Mr Wilson reluctantly conceded that the fight to preserve the 2·80 dollar parity had gone on long enough. The complicated process of preparing for devaluation was set in motion. The key question, of course, was by how much Britain should devalue. A top Treasury official, Mr Wynne Godley, was given the task of calculating the likely economic effects of certain percentage changes. Sir Denis Ricket, the Second Secretary of the Treasury, and Sir Leslie O'Brien, the Governor of the Bank of England, agreed to sound out international opinion. It was vital to discover what sort of change could be made without inviting massive retaliation. If other leading trading nations were going to follow Britain's lead, and devalue their own currencies, the whole operation would be virtually worthless. Indeed, the damage such a chain reaction would inevitably do to the world's monetary system might severely handicap our export effort.

Sir Leslie was going to Basle at the weekend, for the usual monthly meeting of the Bank for International Settlements, and Sir Denis was due to attend a meeting of the influential OECD

'Working party 3' in Paris a few days later. Both men, therefore, had a useful opportunity to assess what was likely to happen. They could not, of course, actually announce that the British Government intended to devalue. The meetings were private, but bombshell news of this kind would have leaked out in a matter of hours. They had to make their soundings on a purely hypothetical basis, and without giving the impression that Mr Wilson and Mr Callaghan had already made up their minds. It was an extremely delicate task, and it was not made any easier by the fact that foreign exchange markets were buzzing with rumours. Sterling had been under heavy pressure for some time, and it was fairly clear that this could not be allowed to continue for much longer. *Something* had to be done. Some reports suggested that Sir Leslie would spend the weekend fixing up a large new loan, or at least attempting to secure a fresh statement of support from the central bankers. Others hinted that the weekend might bring devaluation; some Paris hotels refused to accept sterling from British customers.

It was a dangerous atmosphere. In Basle that Saturday and Sunday, reporters from dozens of British and Continental newspapers were desperately trying to find out what was happening. Back home, their news editors were clamouring for copy. With the central bankers maintaining their usual strict secrecy, seemingly oblivious of the feverish air of speculation outside their conference room, the reporters had to augment their guesswork with the few scraps of information they could gather from aides – or each other.

On Monday morning, November 13, some papers reported that Britain had been granted a loan of $250 million (£90 million). This was correct, but it was a purely technical facility – Britain had to repay this sum to the IMF in December in various European currencies, but she only had dollars available. It was not intended to save sterling; the amount was, in any case, far too small for that. Many people jumped to the conclusion, however, that £90 million was all Sir Leslie had been able to secure after two days of pleading with his hard-hearted colleagues. The result was predictable: sterling was sold on a large scale. The Treasury and the Bank of England made things worse by refusing to confirm that we had been granted even £90 million. It was a pointless decision, and it cost the country dearly. When Sir Leslie arrived back at London airport, he was surrounded by reporters. He said very little, but what he said – combined with his gloomy expression – made headlines. Had he managed to secure new support for the pound? 'I always get their moral support'. Could he say anything about the safety of the pound in the next few weeks or months? 'Nothing at all'. What about the October trade figures, due to be published the following day? 'I am not looking forward to them'. It was hardly a performance to reassure jittery financial markets.

Sir Leslie's mood was understandable. His fellow bankers had been tough. They had discussed various alternatives, including the possibility of a modest devaluation backed by a standby credit, but had given him very little reason to believe that a last-minute rescue operation of a sufficient size to avoid the need for devaluation was likely to be forthcoming. The IMF, some of them had suggested, might be prepared to make a special loan – but after consultation with Pierre-Paul Schweitzer in Washington, even this idea had been more or less shelved. Sir Leslie, who disliked devaluation and had half hoped that it was not too late to prevent it, had come back virtually empty-handed. He could not even produce a statement of solidarity with sterling. All he was able to tell the Prime Minister was that, if he devalued, the central bankers would do their best to protect the world's monetary system from the shock waves, and to organize a new credit line to underpin sterling at its new parity until the beneficial effects of devaluation started to show up in published returns.

That evening, Mr Wilson made a speech at a bankers' banquet in the City. It was an annual affair, and it had been arranged months before. The Prime Minister tried to use the occasion to take the sting out of the next day's trade figures by a forewarning that, because of the dock strikes, they would be 'meaningless'. But the bankers were much more struck by his omission of the customary promise to defend the parity of the pound. Mr Wilson had never before failed to condemn the 'doubters' and the 'faint-hearted', and to issue a categorical declaration that the Government intended to maintain the value of the pound. Why leave it out this time, knowing that the Bank of England was having a hard time in foreign exchange markets? It seemed to the bankers that there could be only one possible explanation: Britain was about to devalue.

The October trade figures, published at noon on Tuesday, were every bit as bad as expected. At £107 million, the trade gap – the difference between what we buy and sell overseas – was the highest in history. They were, as the Prime Minister had pointed out, 'distorted'. But explanations and excuses tend to count for less in foreign exchange markets than hard facts. Coming in a week like this, the figures merely underlined the fact that Britain was not going to get out of the red in 1967. By the end of the day, the Bank of England was reported almost to have lost the equivalent of that £90 million loan in defending the 2·80 dollar parity.

The centre of attention now shifted to Paris, where representatives from most of the world's key financial institutions had gathered for what was officially billed as a series of routine meetings within the ambit of the Organization for Economic Co-operation. Everyone knew that the occasion would be far from routine, and the Chateau de la Muette – headquarters of the OECD – was alive with newspapermen and television reporters. Speculation among them was even more intense than it had been at Basle. At the formal meetings, officials went through the items put on the agenda weeks before – but the real activity went on behind the scenes, in private meetings attended by the heads of delegations and a few top aides.

Security was strict, but it was not difficult to guess what they were discussing. The situation had reached a point where only two possible solutions really made sense: devaluation, plus stand-by credit, or a massive loan to help Britain maintain the existing parity. Mr Frederick Deming, America's Under-Secretary in charge of Monetary Affairs, was in favour of a loan. He indicated that Washington would be willing to pitch in with $500 million, provided the European countries made proportionate contribution. In theory, the British Government could still have stopped the devaluation procedure at this point, but it was clear that the alternative would involve conditions which would be politically unacceptable. Sir Denis Ricket therefore concentrated on the job he had been given the week before: assessing what the reaction would be to a modest devaluation, and a request for a new stand-by credit. He concluded, later that evening, that retaliation could be avoided providing the parity was not changed by more than 15%.

In London, meanwhile, there was a development which – in view of the keen interest in the Paris talks – could hardly have been unexpected, but which was nevertheless embarrassing. BBC Television led its main news bulletin that evening with a report that the British delegation was negotiating for a $1,000 million loan. Graham Turner, the BBC's Economics Correspondent, had put the story out after getting a telephone call 'from a Paris source'. It was not exactly new. *The Times* and *The Guardian*, among others, had indicated earlier in the week that a loan of this size was a strong possibility. But the BBC report was so unequivocal that it made a major impact – and this was strengthened further when the story was repeated in subsequent news bulletins.

Fleet Street editors, who were putting their first editions 'to bed', responded at once to the BBC 'scoop'. They contacted their financial editors, and their reporters in Paris, and requested a 'follow-up'. This was easier said than done, but some frantic telephoning took place. No-one, of course, succeeded in getting confirmation from Sir Denis Ricket himself, or from the Treasury. But everyone who was contacted thought the story 'rang true'. My own reaction was one of scepticism: I went and told my Editor that, even if such a loan were possible, it was unlikely to be granted without really severe 'strings'. I doubted whether Mr Wilson would be willing to agree to the sort of terms which the lenders would almost certainly impose. The paper could not, however, afford to ignore the BBC story – so I wrote a piece which mentioned the report from Paris, and which expressed my reservations. Some of my colleagues decided to be much more emphatic (as often happens with 'follow-ups' to someone else's scoop) and the following morning black headlines proclaimed that the pound was about to be rescued.

When the London foreign exchange market opened, sterling improved sharply against all other currencies. The early editions of the London evening papers gleefully reported that speculators were 'running for cover'. But Labour MP's found it difficult to join the cheering. They were deeply troubled by the prospect of even stronger foreign influence over British economic policy. With the Treasury and the Bank of England still refusing either to confirm or deny that loan negotiations were, in fact, taking place, two backbenchers put down private notice questions to the Prime Minister and the Chancellor about the loan reports. This was communicated to the news agencies. Both Mr Wilson and Mr Callaghan, however, believed that they would not have to answer the questions. At their request, the Speaker, Dr Horace King, was asked to disallow them on the grounds that they arose from unsubstantiated press stories. The speaker decided, however, to allow one of the questions – put by Mr Robert Sheldon, a right-wing Labour MP and a keen devaluationist.

Downing Street found itself in a dilemma. The Cabinet had, that morning, unanimously agreed at a three-hour meeting, that the pound should be devalued by 14·3% and that this should be accompanied by various deflationary measures. It *was* negotiating a stand-by credit, but the proceedings were still at a highly delicate stage. An announcement was planned for the weekend, when all the world's money markets would be closed. To reveal this on Thursday afternoon, in a casual answer to a backbencher's anxious inquiry, was out of the question. Yet to say there was no loan could have quite a disastrous effect on keyed-up foreign exchange markets. The easiest solution, one might have thought, was to take either the Speaker or Mr Sheldon into the Government's confidence – and to appeal to their patriotic spirit. They would surely have understood that a false step, at this late stage, could cost the country hundreds of millions of pounds. Such a move was, in fact, briefly considered. But it raised various constitutional issues, and it was decided that the formalities of Parliament should be observed as they would be on any routine occasion. The intention was, however, to make the answer as short, and as non-committal, as possible.

Just before the question was due, sterling reached its highest level since early September. The press gallery was packed as Mr Sheldon rose to address the Prime Minister. But the Chancellor replied instead. What followed must surely go down as the most expensive piece of repartee in Parliament's entire history. Here is how Hansard recorded it the next morning:

> MR SHELDON (BY PRIVATE NOTICE) asked the Prime Minister if he will make a statement on the $1,000 million loan being negotiated with foreign banks.
>
> THE CHANCELLOR OF THE EXCHEQUER (MR JAMES CALLAGHAN): I have been asked to reply.
>
> MR RIDSDALE: On a point of order. Is not the Prime Minister

in charge of the economy? Could he not answer this Question?

MR SPEAKER: No point of order arises at this moment. The Chancellor of the Exchequer.

MR CALLAGHAN rose –

SIR HARMAR NICHOLLS: On a point of order –

MR SPEAKER: Order. I understand what the Hon Member for Peterborough (Sir Harmar Nicholls) is trying to do, but I have ruled that no point of order can arise about one Minister answering a Question addressed to another Minister.

SIR HARMAR NICHOLLS: On that point of order, Mr Speaker. While it is common form and generally accepted, as it has been for years, that a Minister may ask another Minister to answer for him in his absence, is it proper, normally, or acceptable that someone else should answer when the Minister concerned is actually present?

MR SPEAKER: I am sorry that the hon Member did not understand the Ruling I gave. The Chancellor of the Exchequer.

MR CALLAGHAN: I understood that the question was transferred to me.

The reply is, No, Sir. It would clearly be wrong for the Government either to confirm or to deny a press rumour of this kind.

MR SHELDON: Is my right hon Friend aware that almost the entire press, if not the entire press, has carried this story? Is he aware that what is particularly concerning hon Members is the conditions likely to be attached to this loan, since, as *The Financial Times* put it, a loan of this size and duration is unlikely to be given without considerable conditions whatever may be said for the record and that if this leads to unemployment and lower levels of consumption and a lower standard of living and a wage freeze this measure will be totally unacceptable?

MR CALLAGHAN: I have been long enough in this House not to believe everything that I read in the press, and I would advise my hon Friend accordingly. So far as Her Majesty's Government is concerned, we shall take what decisions are appropriate in the light of our understanding of the needs of the British economy and no one else's. That, at this stage, certainly does not include the creation of any additional unemployment.

MR IAIN MACLEOD: Would not the right hon Gentleman agree the continued uncertainty in this matter is the worst of all worlds? Subject to that, until these matters are finalized one way or another, when we would expect to have a full statement immediately in the House by the Government, is he aware that if negotiations are in progress I would not wish to comment?

MR CALLAGHAN: I am obliged to the right hon Member for not wishing to press on a loan the conditions about which I have not said any discussion is at the moment taking place. I quite agree that uncertainty and rumour are bad for the exchanges and I hope that some of the speculators get their fingers burned. I did not start the rumours and I do not propose to comment on them. The press must take full responsibility for anything it prints.

MR DICKENS: Is the Chancellor aware that many hon Members on this side of the House – (Interruption).

MR SPEAKER: Order. The House always wants to hear both sides.

MR DICKENS: Is the Chancellor aware that some of us, at any rate, are totally opposed to – (An hon Member: 'Everything'.) – this country having further money from foreign bankers?

MR CALLAGHAN: Yes, I understand my hon Friend's point of view. I have no further comment to make.

MR THORPE: Whether or not there are negotiations under way, could the Chancellor say for how much longer the Government will rely upon borrowing to maintain confidence in the pound? Is he aware that there is a general feeling that to sacrifice full employment and economic expansion for the sacred cow of sterling is something to which many people are opposed?

MR CALLAGHAN: That does not arise out of my original Answer.

MR SHINWELL: Does my right hon Friend understand what all the fuss is about? Have we not been living on borrowed money for the last twenty years?

MR CALLAGHAN: Yes, but quite recently we have been transferring from one form of obligation into another form.

SIR C OSBORNE: Will the Chancellor take the earliest opportunity available to confirm or to deny this rumour? Secondly, will he bear in mind that it would probably be better for the country if we borrowed no more money from abroad but decided to live on our own income?

MR CALLAGHAN: I understand that it is a long-standing practice of the House that ministers are not expected to confirm or deny press statements and hon Members should not rely on them when putting their questions.

MR ORME: Would my right hon Friend agree that if the difference is between a reduction in public expenditure at home, a wage freeze and the introduction of a regulator and devaluation, devaluation is preferable to those three things?

MR CALLAGHAN: I have nothing to add or to subtract to anything I have said on previous occasions on the subject of devaluation, and, in any case, it does not arise from my original Answer.

MR STRATTON MILLS: The Chancellor's original Answer is quite incredible. Will he clear up whether negotiations are or are not progressing? When he makes his statement, will he give full details of all the outstanding short-term loans which this country has incurred and which have not been revealed to the public?

MR CALLAGHAN: I have nothing to add to my original Answer.

The result of this extraordinary performance was entirely predictable. Sterling was sold on a massive scale, both by speculators and commercial interests. Dealings were chaotic. The Bank of England, still committed to propping up an exchange rate which its Governor knew was already doomed, was the only buyer in the market. Never before had there been such a run on the pound – and Bank officials were to spend many months afterwards clearing up the mess. By November 19, the Bank had drawn the whole of the £1,350 million credit available under the Federal Reserve reciprocal 'swap' arrangement and had also more or less exhausted other credit lines. It's forward commitments had soared to an estimated $4,000 million.

At 9.30 on Saturday evening, November 18, as the nation was settling down to watch 'The First Freedom', an account of a Moscow Trial on BBC Television, and the star spots in the Royal Variety Performance on the other channel, devaluation was announced in a statement from No 10 Downing Street.

The first editions of the Sunday papers had already gone to press, and there was a feverish scramble to remake the front pages. The new sterling exchange rate against the dollar was 2·40 to the pound. Bank Rate was going up to 8% and banks were asked to limit advances except to priority borrowers, especially exporters. Hire purchase controls were being tightened, and the rate of corporation tax was going up to 42½%. Defence expenditure was being cut by more than £100 million in the coming year. Except in development areas, the Selective Employment Tax premium was being withdrawn. Other public expenditure, including the nationalized industries' capital spending, was being reduced by £100 million. A formal application was being made to the International Monetary Fund for an immediate standby of $1,400 million. Together with additional arrangements already made with central banks, this would provide new resources of around $3,000 million.

Jim Callaghan had fallen off his tightrope.

PART 3 INQUEST ON A DEFEAT

Out of the Strait-Jacket

FRANCE, PREDICTABLY, SAID that a 14·3% devaluation was not enough. Germany praised 'Britain's courage' and President Johnson said he understood 'the powerful reasons that made devaluation necessary under the circumstances'. Moscow declared that it appeared to be an attempt to 'preserve the high profit of the monopolies at the expense of worsening the position of the working classes'. Denmark, Israel, Ireland, Spain, Ceylon, Trinidad, Hong Kong, New Zealand, Iceland and a number of other countries announced that they were also devaluing. The Australian Government, caught off guard in the middle of its campaign for Senate Elections, held a special Cabinet meeting and decided not to follow Britain – a move bitterly criticized by Mr John McEwen, the Trade Minister, who was abroad and heard the news too late.

In London, the Director General of the CBI gloomily told ministers that devaluation was 'a further damaging blow at industrial prospects' and that industry would be 'out of pocket on the whole deal'.

A large crowd had gathered in Downing Street on the Sunday morning after the devaluation news, and there were shouts of 'Wilson out, Labour in' as financial editors and lobby correspondents trooped into No 10 for a briefing by the Prime Minister and the Chancellor. Mr Wilson, in green country tweeds, was his usual bouncy self. Mr Callaghan, in marked contrast, looked crestfallen. The authoritative manner he had displayed for three years had gone. He explained at once that the decision to devalue had been his and that he was assuming full responsibility for what had happened. The amount – 14·3% – had been decided upon because 10% would have been too small to be credible, and because anything over 15% would probably have compelled most of our competitors to follow. It represented, statistically, an eventual increase of about 3% in the cost of food in Britain, but it would give British exporters a telling advantage in world markets. He requested correspondents – 'as patriots' – not to speculate about the possibility of a second devaluation at some time in the future, 'because that would be the surest way of bringing it about'.

Mr Wilson, who allowed the Chancellor's manful acceptance of all the blame to stand without comment, said that devaluation would allow Britain 'to get out of the strait-jacket of sterling speculation'. The Prime Minister has a remarkable facility for seeing the bright side of life, once an unpleasant decision has been taken, and he was behaving true to form. (Frank Cousins has since told me that, just before the devaluation news was officially announced, Wilson had told him that, 'you'll be hearing something that will please you'. Cousins thought the Government was about to announce the cancellation of its F–111 order, and was shattered that Wilson should consider devaluation pleasant news.) It was clear, on that post-devaluation Sunday morning, that the Prime Minister was determined to make the best of a bad job. The Government had struggled long and hard to defend the 2·80 parity, and he clearly felt this called for praise and understanding. Telegrams, we were told, had poured in from all over the world thanking him for holding out for so long and conveying best wishes for the future. Whitehall economists were predicting a great export breakthrough, and he saw no reason to doubt their forecasts. Devaluation was a springboard, not a slide.

This, it transpired, was the theme of the address he dictated afterwards to his secretary for a 6 pm television broadcast to the nation. As *The Times* reported the next day, 'the father figure looked stern and purposeful, though scarcely grim or foreboding, and the voice was strong and commanding, though quiet. Even those whose long memories go back to Mr Wilson's speeches as Opposition leader in 1963 and 1964 would have needed an extremely sharp ear to catch any hint of embarrassment as he explained why the Government were now doing what until last month they regarded as heresy'.

Looking back on the Government's three years of power, Mr Wilson said that they had needed time to restructure and modernize British industries, to build up British trade, and to cut down overseas defence commitments. 'This time was denied to us', he added. 'Whenever Britain ran into short-term difficulties there were some who sold sterling in a panic, and there were others who gambled against us in the hope of a quick gain – and all this even though our basic position was showing a steady improvement'. Britain was a major trading country whose financial position depended on how much she sold to others, but because Britain was an international bank, with sterling as an international currency, she was 'subject to speculative attacks for short-run reasons which have nothing to do with Britain's trading position'. He said the decision to devalue 'attacks our problem at the root', and ended with a call to national pride: 'This is a proud nation . . . we have the chance now to break out from the strait-jacket of these past years. We're on our own now. It means putting Britain first'.

Listening to this, most viewers must have wondered why, if devaluation presented us with such a splendid opportunity, Mr Wilson had opposed it so vigorously from the day he took office. Not once in his TV speech did he concede that devaluation was a defeat. The general impression one was left with was that, as Mr Wilson saw it, we had been freed from slavery and were about to embark on an exciting new era. The many professional economists who had long advocated devaluation would have agreed with that assessment – but coming from Mr Wilson, in this form and at this time, it inevitably widened the credibility gap. And the situation was made worse by a slip which the wily Harold of old would never have committed. Trying to explain what devaluation was about, he said that 'it does not, of course, mean that the pound here in Britain, in your pocket or purse or in your bank has been devalued'. It gave Lord Cromer, his old Bank of England adversary, a splendid opening to say on a television news programme that Mr Wilson was talking nonsense. There was a 2s 10d in the pound reduction and it would not only affect the pound in the pocket, but also the savings.

Mr Wilson afterwards privately admitted that he had, perhaps, been a bit too bouncy. He acknowledged, too, that the reference to 'the pound in your pocket' was a mistake. It was the only sentence he had taken from the brief supplied to him by the Treasury. Technically, it was correct. Devaluation means altering the exchange rate in terms of other people's currencies. But he ought to have been shrewd enough to recognize the propaganda value of the piece of ammunition he had handed to the Opposition. The pre-1964 Wilson would have pounced on it with glee; it was inevitable that the 1967 Edward Heath would do the same.

Interviewed on commercial television later in the week, Mr Wilson looked and sounded much more subdued. He admitted that hopes of an increased standard of living in 1968 would have to be deferred. In 1969, however, the people would get the benefit of devaluation. He considered the first benefit would be seen in full employment. The Government had been elected to maintain full employment. It would carry on, and he believed the nation would respond to the challenge.

Looking tired, and at times searching for words, Mr Wilson admitted devaluation was 'a defeat'. The past two weeks had been the worst that either the Chancellor or himself had known. 'It has been hell'.

The question that seemed to throw him more off balance than any other was what had been his biggest mistake. After emphasizing that he did not regard decisions not to devalue earlier as mistakes, the Prime Minister said his biggest mistake was that he had underrated the power of speculators at home and abroad who put the pound in jeopardy and forced the Government into short-term measures injurious to the country. They had learned that lesson now. He went on to reject suggestions that there should be a change at the top of the Government to give the administration fresh credibility. The Government as a whole, he said, would stand or fall on the new policy. He defended the position of Mr Callaghan, saying that 'the Chancellor has been through enough with all this hounding'.

In the Commons debate on devaluation, Mr Wilson made a determined effort to hammer home his point that speculators were to blame for everything. Lashing into his critics, he said that 'a great deal of speculation has emanated from this country, from the City'. Foreign exchange dealers had felt it would be wrong to devalue, but all the time there had been 'the insidious spread of political gossip persuading them'. Mr Wilson went on to quote a press interview with a Swiss banker, which said that the most persistent rumours about the pound seemed to originate from London rather than the foreign centres. 'The gnomes of Zurich ask why it is that the people in the City sell sterling short', he added.

Going off on a tangent, Mr Wilson said the Labour Party had

supported sterling when in opposition, even during Suez. Pointing at Mr Macleod, he thundered: 'He hated Suez, but he had not got the guts to resign. That is his morality. And of his leader, who cajoled and bullied his backbenchers into supporting an action which was not only immoral but which was solved on a basis which was totally removed from the truth'.

Speaking at Mr Heath, he said: 'What we do not know is whether he himself was deceived or whether he was a party to deception. Some day will tell us'.

Mr Duncan Sandys interrupted to say that these were irrelevant debating points.

Mr Wilson retorted: 'I thought he (Mr Sandys) was in competition for the Leader of the Opposition's job, not the Chief Whip's job when he got up. We are not taking from him, who was a member of the Suez Cabinet, any rebukes.'

Mr Wilson went on to say that it was a fifteen-year situation, not a three-year situation, with which last Saturday represented a decisive break.

Three years ago, when it took office, Labour had faced the biggest deficit in the country's trading history. It had three choices. It found three contingency plans ready to be put into operation. There were import controls and quotas, import surcharges and finally devaluation.

'Our decision of October, 1964, not to devalue, but to take other measures, was a conscious and deliberate decision. I believe it was the right to fight to maintain parity'.

The conditions which applied now, Mr Wilson went on, did not apply then. There was no spare capacity in the economy and there was then no general international acceptance of the case for devaluation, 'such as clearly emerged last Saturday'.

The Labour Government had set out in 1964 to 'break clear from the dilemma of more than a decade, by a policy of reconstructing industry, cutting out waste in prestige aviation projects and tackling the basic problems of shipbuilding, coal, steel and electrical engineering'. It also set out 'to make two nations one, by bringing the depressed areas of the country into one economy'.

It carried out other far-reaching reforms in taxation aimed at ensuring that national savings would be concentrated more and more on investment in British industry as opposed to investment abroad.

'All this', Mr Wilson said, 'meant increasing taxation, and at every point we were opposed by a party which promised to increase every sector of public spending, and at the same time decrease taxation. All that we were seeking to do during this period required time, and it was becoming quite clear that this was to be denied us – that was why we took the decision of last Saturday'. But all the measures taken would now stand in good stead. There would be opportunities for both industry and agriculture, and more challenges.

Mr Wilson went on: 'The reorganization of shipbuilding and steel has put us in a position where we are not only competitive, but we are able to take the offensive. A few more weeks of Tory rule, and the British computer industry would have sold out to the Americans. Now it is one of the most powerful industries in Europe. Our technological development has increased greatly in the past three years, particularly our nuclear power development, which will get a great boost, from devaluation.

'All this illustrates the advantages of our new competitive situation.

'Even before last Saturday's decision we were facing an increase in production which we have not seen for a number of years. Now we must ensure that the expansion into which we are moving is controlled to avoid inflation. The measures we have chosen, harsh though they may be, are directly relevant to our objectives'.

From the other side of the House Mr John Boyd Carpenter, a former Treasury Minister, said he had 'never heard a speech so unworthy both of the occasion and of the great office of the Queen's First Minister as that which the Prime Minister treated us to this afternoon. When he is in a corner with a thoroughly bad case he lashes out with personally offensive references, wholly irrelevant historical allusions and does everything to distract attention from the main issue'. It was a fair charge, but it was also a fair summing up of the kind of game politicians have played with each other since the breed was first invented.

Jim Callaghan's speech represented a complete contrast. He did not protest against the harshness of an attack he plainly expected. Indeed, he brought cheers from the Labour back-benchers when he told the House – as he had told reporters a few days earlier – that the full responsibility for the course taken on sterling – right from the beginning – had been his. The Cabinet had acted all along on his recommendations. He wanted no alibi, he said. A Tory backbencher jumped up to demand to know why Mr Callaghan was reserving the pillory for himself, and clamouring Opposition backbenchers left no doubt that much more than Mr Callaghan's head they wanted that of Mr Wilson – who sat with folded arms throughout these exchanges, poker-faced in the uproar. Callaghan, grim but determined, went on to explain that devaluation offered an opportunity, but that it could easily be 'frittered away if delivery dates are not kept'. Labour backbenchers, including left-wingers who had so often harried the Government on its economic policy, began to jump to his defence. As *The Guardian*'s Political Correspondent put it the next day: 'The Government's decision to devalue the pound appeared last night to have united the Parliamentary Labour Party as it has not been united since October 1964. From extreme left to extreme right, the reaction was to swallow detailed reservations in relief that something definite has been done at last'.

This 'relief', in fact, developed into a general mood of euphoria among Labour MP's that fully matched Mr Wilson's own cheerful performance on devaluation day. It was partly due to an understandable desire to hit back at a cock-a-hoop Opposition, and partly to an equally understandable desire to clutch at straws. The majority of economic commentators supported and encouraged this. Professor Alan Day said in *The Observer* that 'the decision to devalue the pound by 14·3% is the best news the British public has received for months'. Roger Opie, writing in *The New Statesman* said that 'On October 16, 1964 the Labour Government won office. On November 18, 1967, it won power'. And most astonishing of all, the *Statesman*'s main leader claimed that 'no Socialist need weep tears over the events of the past week'.

The only Labour MP who, it seemed, was prepared to take his leader's stirring words over the three previous years seriously enough to resign the party whip was Mr Richard Crawshaw – and he changed his mind in less than 48 hours. Callaghan found himself cast in the role of honest and upright Jim – an overburdened, misunderstood politician who had always meant well. It was a rather sickening spectacle, and it prompted me to write an angry column. Here is part of it:

Is the fact that, to use Mr Callaghan's words of last July, 'devaluation will cut real wage standards of every working man in the country', something for socialists – or indeed, the public as a whole – to cheer about? Does it fill every Labour MP with glee that thousands of old age pensioners and others living on fixed income will find prices of food, and other essential items, rising sharply against them?

Cannot a single socialist spare a tear for the fact that in industries which don't benefit from devaluation – such as building – men are going to be out of a job as a result of Mr Wilson's about-turn? Is it wrong to feel pity for the army of small shopkeepers and business men who are struggling to maintain their independence in an age of giant organizations – and who find themselves faced with a new credit squeeze, high interest rates, and other deflationary measures?

It's easy enough for economists to rejoice, ghoulishly, over the failure of the Government's previous policies – and to pronounce, at the stroke of a pen, that we can 'shift £800 millions' worth of resources into the export field'. Economists have a habit of forgetting that their inexact science exists to serve men, and not the other way round.

But Labour MP's have no excuse for cheering a Prime Minister who consistently rejected import quotas, which would have been perfectly permissible under GATT rules, and dragged his feet over cuts in overseas defence spending and other measures which, if taken in time, could have allowed us to break out of our straitjacket without devaluation. Jim Callaghan lashed out at the wrong people when he attacked Sir Paul Chambers and his chums in this week's debate. The business world may have a monopoly on many things, but it certainly has no monopoly on cynicism.'

Callaghan himself, to be fair, took no part in the general jubilation. He made it clear, throughout, that he regretted the need for devaluation. A few hours before the news was announced, he had sat down at his desk to compose a letter of resignation. Wilson asked him to think about it for a few days, and on the Sunday morning after devaluation Callaghan held a family conference. He told them what he had done, and added: 'I can't really think straight at the moment. Do you think I did the right thing?' The concensus of opinion, it appears, was that he had.

His intention was to 'have a rest on the back benches', but a few days later George Thomson and several other parliamentary friends came to see him and urged that he should change his mind. Callaghan dithered. He told Wilson that if he was to stay at the Treasury, he would have to get down to work on the 1968 Budget. Wilson had, however, decided that Roy Jenkins should get the job. Callaghan got the impression, during their talk, that the Prime Minister was planning to reshuffle the Cabinet in January, and that he would be given the Foreign Office. But things came to a head sooner, partly because news of his resignation letter had leaked out to the press. A straight swap with Jenkins, then Home Secretary, was arranged eleven days after devaluation, and Downing Street released the text of the letter. It read:

My Dear Harold,

Last Thursday I felt it necessary to recommend the Cabinet to devalue the pound, and they accepted my advice.

When I did so, I was very conscious that I was going back on pledges that I had given in good faith to a number of overseas countries about the value of their sterling holdings.

No Chancellor of the Exchequer can escape this dilemma. But I do not think it right that I should continue in the office, and so with the deepest regret I must ask you to accept my resignation.

We agree that it would not be right for this to be announced until matters have settled down a little, and I am ready to carry on for a short time before the resignation is made public.

I shall continue to hope and work for the success that you and the Government deserve.

We have lived through great days together in the last three years and I have no regrets.

I believe that under your leadership the Government have laid the foundations for future success for the British people and I am glad that the Labour movement in this country has thrown up a Government of men and women with the courage to do what is necessary and the idealism to carry them through our difficulties and troubles.

I believe there are brighter days ahead.

With thanks and warmest personal good wishes.

Yours sincerely,

Jim Callaghan

14 The Price of Optimism

The Economist said in its obituary on Callaghan's Treasury career that he had been a 'disastrous' Chancellor. *The Financial Times*, on the other hand, noted that there would be 'widespread regret' at his departure. The Exchequer, it added, had been the graveyard of political reputations during the past decade.

'Disastrous' is not a term I personally would use in summing up Mr Callaghan's three years hard labour at the Treasury. He took a difficult situation, and he was often badly advised. The statistics and forecasts on which he had to base his decisions were hopelessly inadequate. Callaghan did, however, have one basic characteristic which was to prove highly dangerous. He was an optimist. The same is true of the majority of human beings, but in the circumstances which ruled during the Labour Government's first three years it was an expensive luxury. Callaghan preferred, always, to look on the bright side of life and he desperately wanted to be popular with all sections of his party. Given two sets of forecasts, he invariably chose the more cheerful one. On several important occasions, he refused to acknowledge unfavourable developments until it was too late. Besides being an optimist, he was also a basically nice man. In 1964, he had set out with many hopes and ambitions. Sterling's troubles, and constant contact with hard-headed Treasury officials, had quickly shown him the wide gap between a politician's dream – and promises – and the harsh realities of government. Friends had taunted him, after a while, that he was becoming too much of an 'establishment' man. Trade Union leaders had urged him to remember that he was a socialist. Pulled this way and that way, he had tried to be all things to all men – and had come unstuck.

The same, unfortunately, has also been true of George Brown and Harold Wilson. They inherited an inadequate industrial structure, and a huge balance of payments deficit. They recognized that this represented a very formidable handicap. But having made the right diagnosis, they could not bring themselves to apply the proper cure. Despite Mr Wilson's repeated assurance that they would govern, regardless of political popularity, they used drugs where surgery was needed – and hoped that, somehow, everything would turn out alright. As a result, they were constantly forced to fight a rearguard action. They were over optimistic about the incomes policy, and about the balance of payments. They under-estimated the time it would take for an 'industrial revolution' to produce results, and made insufficient allowance for adverse developments in the rest of the world. They confused words with action – and, as Harold Wilson eventually acknowledged, they underrated the power of the speculator.

Looking back one still appreciates what they were trying to do, and feels sorry for their bad luck. They were not to blame for the deficit run up by the Tories, and for our thin gold reserves. It was not their fault, either, that the Arabs decided in 1967 to make war against the Israelis or that the Americans got themselves entangled in a war which put tremendous strains on the world's monetary system. In its report for 1967, published in June 1968, the Bank for International Settlements – the 'Basle club' of central bankers – put much of the blame for sterling's troubles on post-war Conservative Governments. 'It is likely', the report said, 'that sterling was an overvalued currency by the beginning of the 1960's. As this decade progressed, the situation was aggravated by a substantial increase in Government expenditure at home and abroad. Given the prospective balance of payments situation,' the report added, 'there was no room for such an increase'. To hold the currency in the 1960's 'a realistic priority in policy on the balance of payments was a necessity; and to enforce this priority without unreasonable sacrifice of economic growth or full use of resources, demanded strict discipline over wage increases and no pressure from excess demand. In the event, once the experiment with reflation was launched in 1963, there was neither. Heavy borrowing from abroad delayed the second (1967) devaluation; it could not prevent it. The basic situation had been too much weakened and confidence worn so thin by years of indecisive action.'

The main charge which can fairly be made against Mr Wilson's Government is that it made a bad situation worse. There were too many headlines, followed by too many anti-climaxes. Mr Wilson's decision not to devalue the pound will always be controversial. Many economists feel that, if he had devalued there and then, in 1964 the Government's efforts to tackle Britain's structural faults would not have been constantly bedevilled by sterling crises. The National Plan would not have become a joke, and the Government would never have faced the disillusionment which set in after Mr Wilson won his second term of office.

Personally I think this is an over-simplification. The basic arguments which dissuaded Wilson and his colleagues from devaluing in 1964 were quite sound. Devaluation would not have solved our basic problems – and, since we could not have devalued by more than 15% without causing havoc throughout the world, it is possible that, as in 1949, the benefits would have been dissipated within a few years. By 1968, the Government might have found itself faced with new speculative attacks on the pound. But, having decided against devaluation, Mr Wilson did commit a fundamental error. He failed to build himself a proper financial base through drastic cuts in Government spending abroad, and through import quotas.

British Governments, as the BIS report pointed out, have been over-spending for years. Mr Wilson used to make vigorous speeches about it when Labour was in Opposition, and his party was firmly committed to prune expenditure when he took office. It was always clear that, for a socialist government, it would be easier to cut back on defence than on domestic programmes. Many people therefore expected that Mr Wilson would abandon Britain's military role. It would take time to unwind our commitments, but bankers (who are good at doing their sums) would have acknowledged our determination and the actual benefits would certainly have started to show up in a big way by 1967. As things turned out, however, it was not until after the pound was finally devalued in 1967 that the Government gave up Britain's presence East of Suez, cancelled a huge order for American planes, and announced that 'we are no longer, and have not been for some time, a super power'. Mr Jenkins, the new Chancellor, gave his own verdict on Mr Wilson's earlier strategy when he said that 'the changes are no more than a recognition, some would say a belated recognition, of basic currents in the tide of history'.

In a review published by the monthly magazine *The Banker* early in 1968, Richard Fry noted that between 1957 and 1967 the British Government's net current expenditure overseas had trebled – from £147 million to £449 million. If one went back to 1952, when the net figure was only £54 million, the increase was eight-fold. That, Mr Fry commented, is an astonishing trend. The 'main period of retreat from Empire and the subsidence of cold war' had, in effect, been accompanied by a doubling of the number of servicemen and many more bases and commitments abroad.'

Mr Wilson did make cuts in 1964, and again in 1965 and 1966, but they were not equal to the occasion. Greater emphasis was put on cutting back private overseas investment – which, unlike defence expenditure, was producing a useful return. We stayed East of Suez, and continued to spend vast sums on playing police-man in other parts of the globe. Mr Denis Healey, the Defence Minister, shares a large part of the responsibility for this. But Mr Wilson was also subjected to considerable pressure from Washington. President Johnson's administration offered to prop up the pound, in return for continued British presence in the world's trouble spots. Mr Wilson gratefully accepted. In 1966, we were still spending more than $1,000 million abroad. No other European country incurred a similar burden, the next highest figure was a miniscule $46 million. Germany, the financial strong man of Europe, actually benefited from other people's overseas defence expenditure to the tune of over $300 million net. Mr Wilson's one act of rebellion, during the three years leading to devaluation, was to refuse President Johnson's request for a token force of British soldiers to fight in Vietnam. He was only too well aware that his party would never have gone along with British involvement in that sorry war.

Domestic spending, too, should have been curbed much more drastically. Mr Wilson and his colleagues chipped away here and there, and Mr Callaghan never stopped lecturing the Cabinet on the dangers inherent in the obvious lack of balance between the public and private sectors. Successive Governors of the Bank of England, adding their influential voices, warned many times that failure to curb Government spending was likely to trip us up. 'This year's increase', the Governor said at a City banquet just a month before devaluation, 'has only proved manageable because of the severe restraints previously imposed on the private sector. What will happen when the private sector regains its confidence and begins again to expand? When business investment, exports, and stockbuilding all turn up, consumption will not lag far behind. If together they come to a head-on clash with rising Government spending, the economy will be in danger of boiling over again. This would inevitably set back all the good work recently done in the field of productivity and jeopardize our improving balance of payments'. Sir Leslie's fears proved to be well justified – then, as in earlier years.

Mr Wilson, an economist himself, knew this perfectly well from the moment he took over, and Mr Callaghan was soon educated by his advisers. But their attempts to deal with the situation were never very convincing. Weighed down by commitments and good intentions, ministers found it difficult to swing the axe. As with defence spending, it was not until the pound succumbed that they decided to check the cost of social services by re-introducing prescription charges, and to announce other restraints. All this was duly noted by bankers and 'the gnomes of Zurich', and played a considerable part in undermining foreign confidence in sterling.

I am convinced that if Mr Wilson had been more ruthless in the first few months after taking office, he would not have been forced eighteen months later to pin his faith on the discredited stop-start routines. Because he failed to be really bold, his Government's many productive efforts in the industrial field were constantly overshadowed by sterling's recurring troubles. Kept on the defensive, Mr Wilson borrowed more and more money – and went on television to tell the nation why he could not deliver the goods. This worked for quite some time, but he must have known that people's patience would not last forever. They voted him into power because he promised vigorous action. They expected to be hurt, and were prepared to suffer – as long as it would get them out of a rut. By pulling his punches, Mr Wilson forfeited an awful lot of goodwill. Like Churchill, he promised blood, sweat, and tears. Unlike Churchill, he found the Governor of the Bank of England telling an interviewer three years later: 'Look around you. Who can you say is really suffering?'

15 Whose Finger on the Headline?

THERE ARE, CLEARLY, many lessons to be learned from Mr Wilson's first three years of power and one would like to think that having paid such a high price, we shall not forget them. Mr George Brown said once that the British people, not the Government were on trial. Predictably, it produced a storm of protest. But in a way, he was right. Governments can only do so much; the rest is up to the men and women who elect them. Their role does not begin and end in the polling booth. Economic miracles can happen only if everyone feels involved. Company directors, civil servants, shop stewards, economists, journalists – they all played a part in Labour's hopeful experiment. Mr Wilson may have provided disappointing leadership, but that does not automatically absolve everyone else from responsibility.

'Industrial revolutions' inevitably produce outcries from vested interests, and there is a tendency for people to 'squeal before they are hurt' (Mr Wilson's phrase). Both sides of industry must ask themselves whether their record is as unblemished as they like to pretend. Some ministers feel that they were let down by the trade unions, and there have indeed been occasions when, like the City, trade union leaders have been 'less than helpful'. Fleet Street too, could do with a bit of soul-searching. The press is not immune from criticism; 'power without responsibility' is a privilege which can easily go to the head of an extrovert profession.

In 1966 the *Neue Zurcher Zeitung* bitterly criticized British newspapers. It said that their reports were rarely constructive, sometimes plucked out of the air, and often sensational. They were, the paper said, constantly adding to the general unrest. The Swiss were not alone in thinking this. Harold Wilson complained, around the same time, about the 'moaning minnies' in the newspaper world and their 'wet editorials'. Many other ministers, including Jim Callaghan, were sharply critical in private. They still believe that national newspapers – and journalists working in radio and television – added to the Government's problems by irresponsible behaviour. Mr Wilson, in particular, feels that the British press, which is predominantly Tory-orientated, went out of its way to highlight sterling's difficulties in order to cause his Government embarrassment. It is a charge which deserves to be examined.

From the day the Labour Government took office, financial journalists were faced with two nagging questions. How much attention should be focused on the ups and downs of sterling? And how far can one go in discussing devaluation?

The pound was news. Mr Wilson himself had made sure of this in the election campaign by harping on Britain's financial weakness. Fleet Street news editors, who until then had little interest in putting daily movements in the foreign exchange markets on page one, began to demand that their City offices kept them constantly in the picture. They were right to do so, and they were right to insist that the specialists in the City should write their stories in page one style. Unfortunately, bad news of any kind is usually more dramatic than good news. Fleet Street, therefore, tended to highlight the downs rather than the ups. So did radio and television. This is a legitimate criticism. At the same time, though, journalists were justified in arguing that it was the Government's job to protect sterling, and that ministers were wrong to try to shift the blame. The financial crisis had been created by the politicians, not by the journalists, and it was Fleet Street's duty to report the consequences.

Personally, I never felt this gave my profession *carte blanche*. It did not really matter who was to blame; the important thing was to avoid making the situation even worse.

Financial journalists are, by and large, very conscious that they have a dual responsibility. One is to their newspapers. They must report the news, in whatever manner is acceptable to the editor, and they must comment on events. But they must also recognize that their words can have quite an important influence on the course of financial events. During the great share boom of the fifties, City Editors concentrated on tips – and moved the market. Small investors acted on their advice, and one was very conscious that if the tip turned out to be wrong some widow in Bournemouth or Hastings might find part of her savings gone. From 1964 onwards, there was much more emphasis on the economy. Business people read the pundits, and were influenced by their comments. They recognized that governments and foreign exchange markets could turn their calculations upside down.

Financial journalists did their best to keep events in perspective, but this was not always easy. A phone call to half-a-dozen foreign exchange dealers might produce as many different answers. Which one should one believe? A trip to Zurich (I went there at least a dozen times between 1964 and 1967) could be equally confusing. Was the banker one interviewed telling the truth, or merely 'talking their book' because he was speculating against sterling? There were other problems, mostly of a technical nature. Space might be short, especially on popular newspapers, and the style of the newspapers might call for dramatic treatment. City offices, moreover, had no control over page one headlines or even the final shape of their pieces. This was a matter for the page one sub-editor, who generally regarded it as his main duty to make the story justify its place. A 'filler story', requested on a Sunday night because there was not much else around, could be built up a truly terrifying tale during periods when the business world was already nervous and jittery. Sub-editors love words like 'crisis' and 'drama', because they are arresting and short enough to fit into a big headline. It rarely occurs to them that their efforts may have other effects besides helping to sell papers. While, therefore, the press could not be blamed for Britain's financial problems, it is quite possible to argue that Fleet Street generally did not always realize its potential impact on personal and national finances.

This argument, however, hardly applied to the financial commentators who believed that the pound should have been devalued in 1964, and kept up their campaign until Mr Wilson finally conceded the point. They knew exactly what the impact of their words would be. Few of them were motivated by political considerations; they genuinely believed that devaluation would be in the national interest, and that they had a duty to convince the Government of this.

Ministers pleaded with them (and indeed, with all financial editors) to stay off the subject. They pointed out that, in a battle to maintain confidence in a currency, persistent devaluation talk is Government's worst enemy. The gnomes of Zurich were entitled to say what they pleased – but no true British patriot ought to let the side down by mentioning the unmentionable. I thought this was a foolish line of argument when I first heard it from the Chancellor, and I have not changed my mind. The Government's decision to defend the existing parity was the cornerstone of its entire economic policy. Everything that happened on the financial front resulted directly from it. To say that economic commentators, MP's or anyone else with a close interest in the way the country was run must never question this decision was patently absurd. One could not ignore the academic case for devaluation, or the fact that the people one met in the financial world were openly talking about it. In my view, however, the Government was entitled to ask that any public discussion on the subject should be approached with some caution, and that it should not be one-sided. Its own reasons for not devaluing were good enough to be treated with respect. A leading article or City column which presented devaluation as an easy answer to Britain's problems, without paying the slightest attention to the snags, deserved to be called 'irresponsible'. And, let's face it, there were many of those between 1964 and November 1967.

There was also a tendency, among leader writers, political correspondents, and columnists to harp on Britain's shortcomings to quite an extraordinary degree. The self-denigration which the whole nation went in for after 1964, was a phenomenon which never ceased to astonish people in other countries. Words like chaos, crisis, and mess were hardly ever out of the headlines. The foreign visitors who picked up a British newspaper looked in vain for cheerful news. Britain's achievements were largely ignored, and so were her strong points. We were a nation which appeared to have completely lost its self-confidence. London correspondents of foreign newspapers reflected this mood in their despatches, and we quickly became known as 'poor old Britain'.

Ministers and their advisers, of course, were often just as bad. Mr Wilson himself had played pied piper to the 'knockers' when in opposition, and he and his colleagues continued to highlight Britain's weakness when they gained office. Their aim was to prod exporters, trade unions and others into action, but they inevitably undermined foreign confidence in Britain in the process.

With opposition leaders also taking every opportunity to stress that Britain was on the brink of disaster, it is hardly surprising that many foreign holders of sterling decided that they had better play safe. As Sir Leslie O'Brien, the Governor of the Bank of England, put it: 'We all too thoroughly provided the raw material for a bearish view of sterling and have no right to complain because it was increasingly taken both at home and abroad – and not only by speculators.'

Amateurish public relations work in Whitehall was another source of trouble. The country paid heavily for some of the blunders committed by people in charge of dispensing information. There is a tradition in Britain that civil servants should not be held to public account for mistakes. But there is also a tradition that ministers should not fire key men they regard as incompetent. As a result, slipshod work tends to go unpunished – and more often than not, is repeated.

Journalists collect their information from many sources, but one of the closest – inevitably – is the Whitehall machine. Ministers regularly meet specialist writers for 'off the record' briefings, either together or individually. These contacts are valued by both sides, and confidences are treated as such. Without mutual trust, the system would quickly break down. The same applies to the relationship established between Fleet Street and press officers at the various ministries. But most of the people in charge of public relations at, say, the Treasury, have never worked in journalism themselves and frequently show scant regard and understanding for the journalist's needs and problems. The reporter working for a popular newspaper, or for radio and TV, often asks questions that appear rather naïve to the civil servant at the other end of the telephone. He may, therefore, find himself treated to a condescending lecture, or to haughty stone-walling. Press officers who have spent their whole career in the civil service often have little time for the mass communications medium: *The Times* and *The Guardian* may find them helpful, but the man from the *Mirror* or Independent Television News does not. The London correspondent of an overseas newspaper may also have difficulty in getting what he wants. There is a huge foreign press corps in London, and our economic difficulties are reported in great detail.

The Japanese have three dozen or more reporters here, and there are as many Australians and Americans. One would think that this merited the appointment of a special Government public relations officer for each group, whose task it would be to liaise between correspondents and Government departments. The outlay would be well worthwhile. Senior Embassy officials in Tokyo and Australia have told me they consider 'expenditure at source' far more useful than the maintenance of costly information departments abroad. 'Whenever a knocking story appears in a paper here,' I was told in both countries, 'we get a cable from Whitehall asking us to put it right. Sometimes we can do this. But one cannot keep ringing up an editor and ask him to correct a story sent by his man in London. The proper answer is to look after him at home – to see that he can get to the right people, and that he gets the right information.'

Public relations has never been one of Whitehall's strong points, but it is rather odd that there should have been so much ineptitude under the Wilson Government. Mr Wilson, after all, was reckoned to be a master of the art. During his Opposition days, and in the early stages of power, he was the darling of the press. His personal public relations work was faultless. His television technique was acknowledged to be superb. Mr Wilson, it seemed, needed no lessons in how to handle the Government's image. It was inevitable, of course, that Fleet Street's enthusiasm would wane a little once it dawned on journalists that there is a considerable gap between words and action, and that overnight miracles simply do not happen. It was inevitable, too, that Tory writers should be increasingly successful in finding chinks in Mr Wilson's armour. But this does not explain why the Government made so many mistakes, both in detailed handling of public relations and in general strategy. Both Mr Wilson and Mr Callaghan, for example, frequently fell into the trap of making firm forecasts on the basis of guesswork. Mr Wilson was forever promising an 'export breakthrough' by such and such a date, and boasting that we were 'out of the red'. Mr Callaghan was forever telling the bankers that Britain would have a balance of payments surplus by the end of the year.

These kind of statements may have helped sterling at the time, but in the end they opened a yawning credibility gap. Less definite commitments would have saved a lot of trouble. The gap was widened further by Mr Wilson's fondness of grand gestures – notably at times when he had run into difficulties over something else. No-one was better than he at thinking up new schemes – National Productivity Councils, technological deals with France, high-powered study groups – or at putting them across. But when, as invariably happened, performance failed to live up to the excitement originally generated, the Tory charge of 'gimmickry' looked more than justified.

As I see it, the most regrettable public relations failure of all has been in the field of incomes policy. The Government had the widest ever mass communications system at its command, but never really managed to get across to ordinary people what it was trying to do with its wonder weapon. Having got closely involved with the world of high finance, ministers lost touch with ordinary people. The incomes policy (there was always too little emphasis on the words 'prices and productivity') was presented as something which existed to please the bankers in Zurich and Washington, instead of being 'sold' on TV and elsewhere as a means of keeping down unemployment and protecting the purchasing power of the money in people's pockets. There was too much talk about 'activating part four' and 'early warning on dividends', and not enough plain speaking in language that housewives could understand. There were foolish attempts to pretend that governments could freeze price increases, and idle threats which ministers knew perfectly well could not be made good.

One would like to think that this is one field where the lessons of the past three years will be put to good use. It would also be useful, surely, to initiate a comprehensive review of the whole Whitehall public relations machine. Whatever the expense, it would be insignificant compared with the cost of some of the blunders we have seen. Should the civil service team be augmented by top-class public relations consultants? Could official papers – such as the Vote on Account and the quarterly balance of payments – be couched in simpler language? Would senior Treasury men benefit from more frequent contact with foreign exchange dealers and bankers in leading financial centres? Are ministers kept as fully informed of everything that happens, and of the views held by businessmen at home and abroad, as they ought to be? These are the sort of questions which deserve closer examination.

Some Whitehall officials have long argued that the outside world gets not too little, but too much information. The masses, they maintain, don't understand these things and one should not confuse them with facts and figures. Why publish monthly trade returns? Why disclose the Treasury's economic forecasts – or for that matter, the latest unemployment figures? All these statistics are open to misinterpretation – and, so the argument runs, the publicity given to them is against the national interest.

The most frequently cited examples are the trade figures and gold reserves statement. Mr Crosland, the President of the Board of Trade, has said that he would be happier if the trade figures were published quarterly instead of monthly. Mr Jack Diamond, the chief secretary of the Treasury, announced early in 1968 that he was prepared to consider switching to quarterly publication of the gold reserves. There is a case for doing both, but the argument seems to me to miss the point. The strong need not to be afraid to tell the truth. If the financial and economic situation is sound, no-one will be in the slightest bit bothered by temporary ups and downs. If it is not, secrecy simply leaves the door wide open to rumours and guesswork. And experience suggests that speculators are only too eager to invent their own tales of disaster.

Cooking the books did not prevent devaluation. On the contrary, some people maintain that it helped to make it inevitable. Instead of dropping monthly publications, Whitehall ought to re-examine its methods of presentation. We have, in the past, tended to understate our full resources. No mention has ever been made of our vast overseas assets or even of the huge credit lines available – in addition to the gold reserves themselves – for the defence of the pound. The Treasury has simply been content with issuing a single sentence statement, giving the latest reserve total. Occasionally, it has added that we have had 'recourse' to credit facilities, but there has never been any indication of the amounts involved. Bank of England and Treasury officials defend this on the grounds that it pays to keep speculators guessing. But it also allows people to invent their own figures, and gives men like Cecil King the opening to say – as he did early in 1968 – that the Government is telling lies about the state of Britain's reserves. The aim, surely, should be to become more, not less, open as time goes on. Mr Jenkins has indicated that he shares this view. He feels, rightly, that people should have a chance to consider his actions against the same sort of background that he faces himself. He decided, in his first Budget, to publish the Treasury's economic forecasts for the first time. This is an adult approach, and it merits the full co-operation of the Press.

16 Too Many Cooks

IF YOU LAID all the studies, surveys, reports and documents written by economists in the past three years end-to-end, you would probably find yourself with a mile of highly confusing expertise.

Economics may have become increasingly sophisticated, but it remains an inexact science. Professional practitioners of this modern form of witchcraft are, therefore, free to offer a dazzling range of solutions to a nation's economic ills.

Britain has been an ideal patient for many years, and Mr Wilson (an Oxford economics don at 21) an ideal sponsor. The Labour Government has employed more economists than any previous government, and more attention has been paid to them than ever before. It is tempting, but unfair, to say that this explains why we have ended up in such a mess. Public disillusionment with Mr Wilson, however, has rubbed off on economists to some extent, and it is not altogether surprising that the profession itself has been conducting a debate on its role in Government.

Professor Michael Postan wrote early in 1968 that 'on any impartial allocation of blame, a share must attach to the economic experts'. What may have gone wrong, he thought, 'may well be that the very quality of post-war economics, the greater sophistication of its theoretical constructions, its much refined statistical and econometric methods have put it out of touch with real economic situations'.

The professor went on to say that all economists were nowadays Keynesians, manipulating aggregates like savings, investments and exports. As a result, their policies, whether to inflate or to deflate, whether to reduce comparative costs by devaluation or by universal wage freeze . . . were posed and debated as if they affect in equal measure and in the same way all and every branch of the economy. 'Britain's economy', he concluded, 'would have been healthier and Britain a healthier country to live in had its economists been less influential than they are'.

Fighting words – and, of course, they produced some angry reactions. Roger Opie, for example, jumped to the defence of fellow Keynesians with the characteristic statement that 'if this is meant seriously, it is simply rubbish'. But Professor Postan was not short of supporters, either.

An Oxford Professor, John Jewkes, for example, said that economists had failed 'because they were pretending to knowledge which they did not possess and because their masters were not hard-headed enough to allow for the vulnerability of the expert, and thereby stumbled into clumsy and disruptive interventions in the economic system'.

One of Professor Postan's Cambridge colleagues, Dr Graham Hallett, made some equally forceful criticisms a year earlier in the May 1967 issue of the Westminster Bank *Review*. 'As an academic economist myself', he wrote, 'I am convinced of the usefulness of my subject for practical policy. It does no service, however, either to the economic profession or to the country, to blink the fact that the experience with academic economists as Government advisers in the past two years has been rather disastrous'. Dr Hallet went on to make a number of constructive points. The greater reliance placed on outside advisers, he argued, had succeeded in introducing new ideas into British economic policies but it had also been shown to have some grave defects.

'It is not enough in economic policy to have a good idea; the practical problems of implementing it must be carefully thought out if it is in practice to do more good than harm and this has not been done'.

There was, Dr Hallett felt, 'a need to alter the status in the machinery of government which university economists have been given in the past two years. The need is not to reduce the amount of outside advice available to ministers, but to ensure that any proposals from this source are filtered through the Civil Service, and fully discussed with non-governmental bodies, before being adopted as official policy'.

This, one would have thought, is common sense. The method employed in introducing the controversial Selective Employment Tax, however, suggests that common sense often tends to be in short supply. Invented by the Chancellor's favourite outside adviser, Nicholas Kaldor, it was hurriedly taken off the shelf because Harold Wilson and Jim Callaghan wanted to deflate without being accused of breaking their 1966 election promise. Kaldor was recalled from holiday, and the new tax was launched with the minimum of thought about the practical implications.

Like Professor Postan, Dr Hallett felt that academic economics had tended to become 'increasingly remote from practical problems'. He also thought that many economists tend to be more definite in their prognoses than the available facts warrant.

For many important questions underlying economic policy, he pointed out, the available information is insufficient to yield a definite answer, and an economist has to rely on his judgment. But many economists seem to think it below the dignity of their science to say that 'I think that – although I may be wrong'. And so they say, 'it is clear that . . .' Under the circumstances, Dr Hallett added, 'economists would be well-advised to present their conclusions with more humility than some are in the habit of doing'.

This, again, could be looked upon as commonsense. The widely conflicting views and forecasts we have had from some of our most eminent economists in the past three years certainly suggest that the profession often tends to make bricks without straw. But humility may be too much to ask for.

I hope the debate continues. There has been too much tendency to leave economic advisers alone – to argue that any criticism is constitutionally improper, since they hold Civil Service appointments. But I agree with Dr Hallett that the position of university economists who accept a temporary advisory post under a government of one political persuasion cannot be equated with that of permanent civil servants who, during their whole career, avoid participation in political controversy and are ready to serve under whatever government is in power. Economic advisers to the Government exercise a semi-political function, and will have to accept being treated in a semi-political way.

Some of their ideas, at least, ought to be submitted to public discussion and debate before they are implemented in a parliamentary bill to which political reputations are irreparably attached and to which no really fundamental adjustments can subsequently be made. The Selective Employment Tax is a particularly good example. Some attempt ought also to be made to put economic forecasting in better perspective. Forecasting is a tricky business at the best of times, and there is no doubt that ministers have frequently been misled by the crystal-gazing of their advisers. The Treasury's record under Jim Callaghan left much to be desired. It more than once misjudged the amount of deflation required, and it was over-optimistic in the balance of payments estimates handed to the Chancellor in, for example, early 1967.

This does not add up to a condemnation of Sir William Armstrong, Mr Callaghan's top Treasury man, or Sir Lac Cairncross, who headed the economic team. The inadequacy of statistics was a major handicap – and, of course, no-one could be expected to predict the sudden closing of the Suez Canal. What it does add up, however, is an argument for taking the mystery out of the whole business. First, the key forecasts ought to be published, so that we can all see the reason for the Government's economic strategy. Mr Roy Jenkins made a start on this in his first Budget, and one hopes he will continue publication.

Secondly, there ought to be a thorough re-appraisal of the way in which forecasts are used. Sam Brittan has suggested (*Financial Times*, February 19, 1968) that the central estimate, on which Chancellors tend to pin their faith, should be done away with altogether and that forecasts should instead be presented in terms of a range of figures. There would then be two sets of figures both for the domestic economy and the balance of payments giving the likely out-turn on both pessimistic and optimistic assumptions. The arguments for both outcomes should be stated as persuasively as possible, leaving the Minister to make his choice. Brittan also feels that there ought to be 'more contingency planning against eventualities which are a normal part of twentieth century life'. Such planning, he acknowledges, does take place – 'but in a secret backroom unrelated to normal policy considerations'. This seems a bit harsh on the Treasury team, but there is much to be said for making fuller allowance for possible disturbances on the world scene. Economic policies ought not to be based on assessments which leave little or no margin for unexpected developments in the world at large.

This brings one, inevitably, to the question of whether it was right to have a National Plan, and whether the experiment should be repeated. Economists disagree about this, as they do about everything else. Professor John Jewkes is among those who think that George Brown's 1966 effort did positive harm, and that there should be no return to it. The promulgation of a plan for a 4% annual rate of increase, he argues, meant that wage and salary earners naturally expected and demanded a roughly corresponding increase in incomes and, since the 4% proved to be too high, the Plan constituted a built-in inflationary pressure. Similarly, since it is a well-established British dogma that public expenditure can always safely increase at least as fast as national income, the fixing of the number at 4%, made for an escalation of public expenditure at the expense of private expenditure.

National plans, Professor Jewkes adds, also weaken competition. The planners conceive of them as a substitute, in whole or part, for the free market. They have a distaste for the free market because it renders planning more difficult and frustrating. They feel that the competitive spirit within industry is inimical to the prolonged 'dialogues' and collective action between businessmen called for by planning. These are fair criticisms, but they do not – in my view – represent a convincing case against economic 'blueprints'. This case is based on the fact that one cannot make intelligent decisions, whether about the short-term regulation of the economy, the growth of public expenditure, the investment plans of the nationalized industries or the proper movement of wages and prices without having some view about the future course of the economy as a whole, at least over the next five years.

Some such view is implied by every decision; it is as well that the same view should lie behind them all. Fred Catherwood, the Director General of Neddy, has put it in another way. 'The merit of a published plan at a national level', he wrote in *The Times* on February 14, 1968, 'is that it puts those responsible for national economic policy through the severe discipline of working out in numbers – numbers of people, numbers of skills, volume of investment, volume of exports, volume of imports, terms of trade and so on – the most likely consequence of their policies. Of course, what they predict cannot be precisely accurate. But if, for example, their policies require, for their success, a sharp upward turn in exports without any plausible means to produce that turn, then the process of planning puts on a red light which might not otherwise be visible – and the fact that someone drives through a red light the first time it is put on is no reason for abolishing red lights'.

The chief reason why someone 'drove through a red light' in 1966 was, of course, bad luck with the balance of payments – and a resulting sterling crisis. Ministers also made a mistake in choosing a growth rate which they should have recognized as unrealistically high. There were other defects in their plan, and the lessons taught by the experiment should not be forgotten. One, clearly, is that national plans cannot, and should not, be presented as a fixed long-term programme to be enforced by government and industrial action. The uncertainties are far too large for that. (The possibility of Britain's entry into the Common Market at some point in the future, for example, makes it impossible to plan on the basis of one single set of assumptions.) They are at best a general framework – an indicator of aspirations which sets out a range of possibilities, assesses the risks of alternative decisions, and gives government policy a sense of direction. As long as this is clearly understood, they surely have a useful role to play in the modern economy.

17 Great Britain Limited?

SOME PEOPLE MAINTAIN that, instead of bringing in so many economists, Mr Wilson should have recruited more administrative talent from industry. It has even been suggested that Britain would be better off if it were run like a company – a kind of Great Britain Limited, with a Board of directors composed of men like Lord Robens and Arnold Weinstock.

Mr Cecil King, who was sacked from the chairmanship of the International Publishing Corporation after calling for Mr Wilson's removal early in 1968, argues that government is 'mainly administration' and that the Labour Government is bad at it. 'This', he says, 'has proved to be the fatal flaw'. I do not go along with this. It is true that, when Mr Wilson and his colleagues came to power, none had any experience of running anything. But the 'fatal flaw' lay in areas of high policy where administrative skill had very little scope. The key decisions which set the course for the economy, and for sterling, were largely political.

Should we stay East of Suez? Should we cut spending on the social services? Should we devalue? Should we have a voluntary or a compulsory incomes policy? How high should unemployment be allowed to go? Questions such as these cannot be guided purely by administrative considerations. Unless we want radically to change our whole system, they must be decided by ministers who are responsible to Parliament – and who can, at intervals of not more than five years, be held to account by the electorate.

It is possible to argue, however, that Mr Wilson should have picked his team with more of an eye on administrative ability and understanding of industrial affairs than on parliamentary skill and position in the Labour Party. Switching men like Michael Stewart from the Foreign Office to the Department of Economic Affairs, simply because it had become necessary to find a different slot for George Brown, was not the sort of move which could be expected to improve understanding between Government and industry.

The appointment of Harold Lever, an able and wealthy businessman with a wide range of contacts, as one of the DEA's junior ministers and his subsequent switch to the Treasury was a much more successful experiment.

It could also be argued that a greater effort should have been made to improve the quality of the advice and assistance ministers were getting from the Civil Service. Mr Brown and others did take on some men with practical industrial experience, and both Mr Wilson and Mr Callaghan took considerable trouble to keep in touch with industrialists. They would reject the claim that 'ministers are as clay in the hands of high officials'. But politicians do have to rely heavily on their civil service aides, and there are countless occasions when key decisions are effectively made by 'the faceless men of Whitehall'. (A good deal, obviously, depends on the character of the individual Minister.) In the main, these decisions were made by men whose academic life had been devoted to history or the arts, and whose first-hand knowledge of the business world was minimal. The poor handling of public relations at the Treasury, mentioned earlier, is a good example of the problems this can produce. The Bristol Siddeley affair (which originated before Labour won power) is frequently given as another. Millions of pounds of excess profit were made on defence contracts because of innocent bungling by ministry officials. Mr Wilson and his colleagues were aware that the Civil Service needed to be brought up-to-date – but as with trade union reform, it was decided that action ought to await the report of a Committee of Inquiry. The Fulton Committee was appointed in February 1966, but its recommendations were not published until the summer of 1968.

If and when they are implemented, the ministers should be better served. The evidence given by various interested parties during the Committee's three years of labour does, however, throw some interesting light on the difficulties which arose from the traditional Civil service methods of recruitment and operation during a period when, as a result of the Labour Government's policies, Whitehall gained more power than ever before in peace-time. The Confederation of British Industry, for example, claimed that many civil servants, especially at lower levels, were unable to understand what was involved in industrial problems and decisions, to think positively about them, and be willing to study them at first hand. By the nature of his work, they went on, the civil servant looks for principles and for general solutions based on them. Enterprise and constructive initiatives 'do not readily flourish in this soil'. There were many government activities which called for attitudes and skills similar to those required of management and the business sense, and the Civil Service should 'watch for the man who shows a managerial bent, help him to develop the necessary skills, and see that successful performance is rewarded appropriately'. The fact that civil servants have almost complete security of tenure was regretted: 'It cannot', said the CBI, 'be good for effectiveness or for morale. There should be greater rewards for success and initiative and greater penalties for failure'.

The CBI went on to deal, at some length, with 'the experience of industry as a user of the Civil Service'. One of the reasons for some of the needlessly complicated legislation, it claimed, was the absence of detailed consultation in advance. There was sometimes 'an over-rigid interpretation of the convention that Parliament must see the Bill first, and the consequent reluctance of some of the civil servants to discuss the practicalities in advance'. A further handicap was 'the reluctance of the Civil Service to acknowledge, let alone display, interdepartmental differences of opinion to anyone outside'. This could result in consultation being postponed until interdepartmental differences had been resolved, by which time it was too late to influence the essential argument.

Whitehall officials, predictably, reacted with indignation at some of these charges and countered, in private conversation, with equally vigorous comments on the shortcomings of industrialists. But ministers rightly took the view that constructive criticism of this kind was extremely useful. Civil servants are shielded from public attack by the doctrine of ministerial responsibility, but this does not mean that their qualifications and attitudes should be allowed to go unchallenged.

18 How Much Unemployment?

WHETHER WE LIKE it or not, it seems inevitable that we shall be stuck with an incomes policy for a long time to come – if not for ever. It may change, but it is unlikely to disappear. One question which is bound to go on bothering people, however, is how much of a 'margin of unused manpower and resources' we should keep until we have proved that it can work. Sir Leslie O'Brien was bitterly attacked by the left-wing of the Labour Party when he suggested, in a speech made in Buenos Aires just before the pound was devalued, that we needed a 'rather larger' margin than in the past. MP's and trade unionists immediately jumped to the conclusion that their old enemy, the Governor of the Bank of England, was using his position to force the Government into throwing people out of work. The storm subsided, but the question which Sir Leslie had raised thousands of miles away remained.

The Labour Party is understandably emotional about unemployment. The right to work is one of its most cherished principles, and the idea that a Labour Government should, by a deliberate act of policy, create a pool of half a million or so unemployed workers is anathema to most of its members And yet, from an economic point of view, one could certainly argue that the Government's stubborn insistence on maintaining overfull employment for as long as possible did a great deal of harm. If the incomes policy had been a great success, it might not have mattered. But it was not – and one of the reasons why it was not, of course, was the very existence of overfull employment. Mr Callaghan, if not Mr Brown, came to recognize this during the three years he was in charge of economic policy.

Economists have no inhibitions when it comes to discussing unemployment. To them, it is a purely abstract thing – a factor in economic management which has nothing to do with moral rights and wrongs. The physical capacity of an economy is fully utilized if all machines, plant and men are fully employed. There will always be some temporary unemployment, partly because some people are unemployable on personal grounds and partly because of changes in occupation or position. So it has long been assumed that in Britain the economy reaches its peak at a level of unemployment of between 0·75% and 1%. At this point, it is argued, bottlenecks appear and dissatisfied customers turn to foreign suppliers. Export deliveries lengthen and the trade figures become steadily worse. At the same time, firms seeking to expand find they must pay more to attract the necessary labour. This raises overheads, and in turn leads to higher prices.

The quality of investment, too, deteriorates in the less competitive climate because an inefficient firm can make profits and survive without becoming efficient. Some firms tend to postpone needed improvements and re-equipment because of their fear of losing business while production is interrupted. Mobility of resources – redeployment from the less efficient to more efficient and more productive activities – gets obstructed if demand is too high. Labour hoarding, with its inevitable consequence of declining productivity of labour for the country as a whole, brings the level of output below what it could be if expanding and efficient firms were to get hold of the resources they need. Sir Leslie O'Brien and others maintain that, because of this, the output apparently foregone by maintaining a small margin of spare capacity is not really foregone. The possibility of securing that extra output, and sustaining the higher level of capital utilization in the longer term is, in their view, illusory. 'This', Sir Leslie said in 1967, 'is one of the hard permanent facts of life, not simply a temporary phenomenon'.

Post-war economic history tends to support all this. Between 1951 and 1968 there were five periods of low unemployment – 1951, 1955, 1960, 1964 and 1966. In each of these periods Britain developed problems on the external front, and inflation became a serious worry. There is no reason to believe that Socialist planning has, so far, succeeded in changing this. Professor Frank Paish, whose lack of faith in the incomes policy was well-publicized from the day Mr Wilson took over, still insists that to prevent another balance of payments crisis Britain must accept permanent unemployment of some 500,000, or rather more than 2% of the work force. Half a million unemployed, he suggests, would be reduced to rather more than 300,000 if those on the register not able effectively to compete for vacancies available could be excluded. Few of these 300,000, Professor Paish argues, would be unemployed for long. As their number would equal that of vacancies, they would be a continually changing population in transition from one job to another. 'Attention could then be concentrated on alleviating hardship', he adds, 'and on reducing the average period out of work by increasing mobility'.

Much the same reasoning can be heard from most Whitehall economists. If devaluation succeeds, unemployment is bound to fall and could be down to 1½% or even less by the end of 1969. As before, this could make the incomes policy difficult to operate, and bottlenecks would develop. The advantages gained by devaluation would be whittled away.

Roy Jenkins and Tony Crosland both know their economics well enough to be worried about this. But they are politicians, as well as economists, and they are well aware of the depth of feeling about this subject in the Labour Party. Mr Wilson told the 1967 Labour Party Conference that the Government's whole policy was 'to secure full employment and to maintain it on a permanent basis'. He indignantly rejected 'the creation of a permanent pool of unemployed as an instrument of economic policy'. The many trade union MP's sitting on the Labour benches in the Commons will keep a careful watch for any sign that this pledge is being broken. Mr Callaghan told the 1967 Labour Party Conference that the right way to overcome unemployment was to concentrate on specific measures of reflation in the development areas. There is, obviously, a lot in this. It is absurd to follow policies which produce a situation where there are eight vacancies for every unemployed man in the Midlands, and three or four unemployed men for every vacancy in the Highlands of Scotland. The regional employment premium and other measures should help to produce a better balance. In time, it should reduce the size of the 'margin' required. But it is essentially a long-term job.

The ideal state of affairs, of course, would be to have such unemployment as we must have made up more and more of people in the process of changing their jobs. For unemployment, in other words, read redeployment. Mr Wilson tried to present his July 1966 crisis package as a purposive measure, designed to produce just this. 'We need' he proclaimed 'a shake-out which will release the nation's manpower, and lead to a more purposeful use of labour for the sake of increasing exports and giving effect to other national priorities'. The exercise, however, turned out to be a flop – as every economist predicted it would be. It flopped because there was no economic growth to speak of, and no real prospect of it either. It flopped, too, because retraining facilities were totally inadequate to deal with the sudden 'shake-out' of a very large number of men.

Devaluation should lead to a resumption of growth, and the Government has done much to speed up the process of retraining. But for redeployment to succeed, it must also make sure that the retrained man will not be debarred from practising his newly acquired skill by the relevant trade union. This is a problem which Ministers failed to tackle properly in their first three years of power, and which the trade union movement largely ignored.

A great deal, obviously, depends on how successful Mrs Barbara Castle manages to be in her new job. She has to get it across to trade union leaders, and to the men on the factory floor, that the answer to the whole unemployment question lies to a large extent with them. The fact that this approach was tried by Mr Brown, and subsequently discredited by the 1966 deflationary package and the freeze, should not deter her from persisting with her efforts. Protesting at Government policies is not enough; real results can only be gained through co-operation.

19 Down with Anarchy

THE CONSERVATIVE PARTY has long argued that appeals for co-operation have to be backed up by thorough trade union reform, and is committed to push through tough legislation if and when it gets to power. The Labour Government, which naturally finds this a much more tricky subject, excused its reluctance to take action in the first three years largely on the grounds that a Royal Commission was making exhaustive inquiries into the whole business.

The Commission was appointed in 1965, under the chairmanship of Lord Donovan, and included men like Lord Robens and George Woodcock, the TUC's General Secretary. Its report, published seven months after the pound was devalued, ran to 145,000 words but was more notable for what it left out than for what it put in. The language it used was tough enough. Employers and unions were both condemned for allowing industrial relations to degenerate into 'indecision and anarchy'. Grave concern was expressed about the growing menace of unofficial strikes, which the Commission noted account for 95% of all industrial stoppages. But the report went on to explain at great length why most of the remedies proposed for this situation are inapplicable. In particular, it rejected the idea that the way to deal with unofficial strikes is to penalize strikers. Legal penalties, it claimed, would be often unjust; would probably do more harm than good; and would very likely prove unworkable. Its one concession to advocates of legal sanctions was to propose that the law should be changed to allow employers to sue workers who try to persuade their colleagues to strike unconstitutionally.

Britain, the Commission noted, has two conflicting systems of industrial relations. The first is the formal industry-wide agreement, like the one applied in engineering covering 4,500 firms and $3\frac{1}{2}$ million workers. The second is the informal 'tug of war' system where factory-floor bargains are struck between the managers of individual companies and shop stewards. According to the Commission, inefficient use of manpower, unofficial strikes, reluctance to change and the undermining of incomes policy all result from this situation. The solution proposed was that the informal workshop system should be developed into an effective and regulated method of bargaining to bring some order into the chaotic factory relations. This would be done by a new Act, forcing companies with 5,000 or more workers to register their agreements with the Department of Employment and Productivity. The Act would also apply to the nationalized industries and public services, but not the Civil Service. Initially it would cover about five million workers. A new Industrial Relations Commission would be set up to act as a kind of troubleshooter, ready to intervene in disputes at an early stage. 'Our proposals', the report claimed, 'would put in management's hands an instrument – the factory agreement – which, properly used, can contribute to much higher productivity'.

The reaction to this was mixed. Mr John Davies, the Director General of the Confederation of British Industry, said that 'the real problem of unofficial strikes has not been plumbed'. Mr George Woodcock said it was 'not the thorough-going, cool, reasoned, clear appraisal of trade unionism that I wanted it to be'. *The Economist* said that the Commission had 'picked up a very old hat, and proceeded to talk through it'. The real reform of trade union legislation, it suggested, was now likely to be left to the next Conservative Government'.

Closer study of the report revealed that the twelve-member Commission was, in fact, split on many issues, notably those dealing with legal penalties for unofficial strikers. To keep a united front and prevent the publication of a minority report signed by four or five of its members, it agreed on a compromise formula drawn up by Professor Otto Kahn-Freund. This said: 'We expect the reform of the collective bargaining system to lead to a very considerable reduction in unofficial strikes. This expectation may not be entirely fulfilled. If so, it may then be necessary to reconsider the desirability and practicability of giving some legal support to procedure agreements'.

If unofficial strikes continued to be a serious problem after a new Industrial Relations Act was enforced 'it will then be time to see what the law can do – but not until then'.

This, clearly, will take quite some time. It means, effectively, that both sides of industry are on trial – probably until after the country has decided whether to give the Labour Party another try or take a chance on Mr Edward Heath. Lord Donovan admitted, in his addendum to the report, that the introduction of satisfactory disputes procedures was likely to be a lengthy process and that he would have liked to find some interim remedy which would be both workable and just. He found it 'very elusive'. This is perhaps the kind of statement one would expect from an eminent lawyer; academic economists tend to be less fair-minded.

One can sympathize with his dilemma, but I fear that he and Professor Kahn-Freund overrate the likely impact of their measures. If, as the Commission argues cogently, the effective business in industrial relations is already done at factory level, we ought surely to have been able to avoid the alarming growth in unofficial strikes during the past few years. Statistics quoted in the report show that in the period 1964–66 there were an average of 2,171 unofficial strikes a year, involving 653,400 workers and causing 1,697,000 working days to be lost. Official stoppages average only 74 a year, involving 101,100 workers and 733,000 lost working days. The coalmining industry has easily the worst record, followed by the docks, shipbuilding, and motor manufacture. But, as the report stressed, 'the increase has been spread over the industrial field'.

It seems highly improbable that proposals which depend, as Mr Woodcock commented, on the British working man's sense of fair play, will drastically change this trend. On the contrary, the growing impatience with the Government's incomes policy may well lead to an even steeper rate of increase. Employers will continue to avoid seeking legal redress in the courts, because they know that it is likely to make industrial relations even worse, and I cannot see characters like Jack Dash bowing before an Industrial Relations Commission. I personally would have gone along with the idea, supported by Lord Robens and Sir George Pollock, that unofficial strikers should at least lose entitlement to things like redundancy pay. But I acknowledge that the whole business of unofficial strikes is highly emotional, and that tough legislation would probably cause more trouble – in the short-term – than we can really afford.

One interesting piece of evidence quoted in the Commission's report was that given by Sir Harold Emerson, a former head of the Ministry of Labour. It described what happened when an attempt was made to enforce the war-time ban on unofficial strikes. Four thousand men had gone on strike illegally at the Betteshanger Colliery, in Kent, in December 1941. There had been trouble at the colliery about allowances for work in a difficult seam where working conditions changed almost weekly. 'The prosecution of 4,000 men', Sir Harold told the Commission, 'seemed a tall order, but as the dispute had started with 1,000 underground workers we decided to concentrate on them. Then several Justices of the Peace had to be found willing to sign 1,000 forms in duplicate and extra police were drafted to serve them. If each man pleaded "not guilty" the proceedings might last for months. The unions were asked if they would instruct their members to plead guilty and accept a decision on a few test cases. The unions obligingly did so.

'The magistrates met in Canterbury. The news had spread to other coalfields and colliery bands decided to accompany the culprits. The Mines Department authorized the Regional Petroleum Officer to allow petrol for the journeys. Everything on the day was orderly and even festive.

'Three union officials were sent to prison. The branch secretary was sentenced to two months with hard labour; the local president and a member of the local executive each received one month with hard labour. 35 men were fined £3 or one month's imprisonment, and nearly 1,000 were fined £1, or 14 days.

'Protests came against the severity of the sentences, particularly against the imprisonment of three union officials. "Was this the way to treat good citizens?" There was talk of sympathetic strikes. But the real trouble was that the only men who could call off the strike were now in jail. The Secretary for Mines went down to Kent to see them accompanied by Mr Ebby Edwards, then the National President of the Miners' Union. Negotiations were reopened and five days after the hearing an agreement was signed in prison, between the colliery management and the Kent Miners' Union. Apart from some face-saving words, it gave the men what they wanted. Then the Secretary for Mines took a deputation to the Home Secretary asking for the immediate release of the three local officials. The men would not start work until their leaders were free. After eleven days in prison they were released. The mine reopened and in the first week the normal output of coal was nearly trebled.

'In the Ministry of Labour there was gloom and apprehension. Also what would be the effect on the men who had been fined? We were soon to know; for the Clerk to the Justices reported that of the men who had been fined only nine had paid. Before he went to the trouble of preparing nearly a thousand commitment warrants the Clerk asked whether it was proposed to recommend remission.

'The county jail could only accommodate a few at a time and it would take several years to work through the list. The company also wanted to avoid further trouble. They asked if they could pay the fines on behalf of the men, the cost to them would be so much less profits tax! They were told on no account to do this. The court was advised not to enforce the unpaid fines. Of course someone asked: "What about the nine men who paid their fines? should they have their money back?" But it was not until 1950 – eight years later – that the National Union of Mine-workers asked formally that the paid fines should be returned. The union was told, in appropriate official language, to forget it.'

Sir Harold's tale obviously impressed Lord Donovan's Commission. Whether the same sort of thing would happen today is debatable, but there is no doubt that prosecution of unofficial strikers is fraught with difficulty.

Industry, of course, is handicapped by other things besides strikes. Inefficient use of manpower is one of our biggest problems. The Royal Commission's central recommendation, on this, was that management should be encouraged and cajoled into tackling the unions on restrictive practices and inefficiency at the point where industrial deafness is least prevalent, the wage-bargaining table. The Commission claimed, hopefully, that its proposals for the reform of the collective bargaining system 'will get rid of assumptions and attitudes to collective bargaining which have allowed restrictive labour practices to grow and efficiency to languish'. One would like to think that this will turn out to be true. Experience suggests, however, that changing assumptions and attitudes is an uphill job.

20 Praying for Rain

'WE ARE A low investment industrial nation and we ought to be a high one. It is no exaggeration to say that the whole future of this nation rests on its becoming a high investment power'. That's how Mr Wilson summed up one of Britain's major weaknesses when he was still Leader of the Opposition, and of course he was right. Investment by industry in new equipment, especially in more advanced equipment, is one of the keys to industrial expansion, to faster modernization, to greater output, and to a stronger balance of payments. It was through rapid investment in the new industrial techniques of the nineteenth century that Britain became, for a time, the world's leading industrial nation. And it played a vital role in the post-war 'economic miracles' performed by Japan and Germany. Britain, the victor, lagged far behind. In a comprehensive survey of the British economy, published in 1968, the Brookings Institution noted that the absolute amount of investment made during the period 1947–1963 in the United Kingdom was less, per person employed in 1964, than in Belgium, Denmark, France, Germany, Holland, Norway and the United States. As a result, it said, the average British worker was supported by 'an exceptionally small amount of capital'.

Mr Wilson, of course, was not the first man to recognize the problem. In 1954 a Conservative Chancellor – R. A. Butler – introduced a system of 'investment allowances', under which 20% of the cost of all new investment in plant and machinery could be deducted from a firm's taxable income. Mr Butler urged industry to 'invest in success'. This slogan produced biting comment from Mr Wilson, and a far from enthusiastic reaction from industrialists. Investment did increase considerably in 1955, but that summer a burst of speculation against sterling forced Mr Butler to introduce a July package of restrictions, including cuts in the investment programmes of nationalized industries. Mr Wilson as usual, had a lot of fun with this. The Government, he said, had panicked and run away the moment industry responded to its slogan. It reminded him of the old story of the Scottish country preacher who was praying for rain and found his prayers suddenly answered with a cloud-burst. It burst with a deafening noise over the tin roof of his little church and he exclaimed: 'Lord, I was praying for rain, but this is becoming ridiculous'. 'That,' Mr Wilson went on, 'was the Government's attitude to the increase in investment.' They prayed for it for many years. That was all they could do, having no control. When their prayers were answered, they said: 'This is becoming ridiculous, and it must stop'.

When the Labour Party won power in October 1964, Mr Wilson invariably included the subject in speeches on his favourite theme – 'the wasted thirteen years'. Britain's net fixed investment, he told the Economic Club in New York, had for some time averaged only 8% of the nation's gross product – hardly more than half that of Germany and, apart from Belgium, the lowest of all the industrial countries. This could not go on. The Labour Government, he declared, was making 'an all-out effort to increase the rate of national investment, especially in productivity'.

The National Plan, published in September 1965, set ambitious targets. It showed that total investment, including both the public and private sectors, would need to increase by 38% between 1964 and 1970, compared with an increase of 25% in the national product. In the public sector (a combination of the central government, local authorities, the nationalized industries and other public corporations) the increase in gross fixed capital formation was expected to be around 35%. In the private sector, the Plan said, the most pressing need was to step up investment in manufacturing industry. We had to create sufficient capacity to enable us to achieve the necessary growth in our exports and to meet an expanding home demand without provoking an intolerable increase in imports. It was here, therefore, that an acceleration in productivity and in technical progress was most urgently needed if we were to improve our competitive position and our rate of growth. The plan therefore suggested that investment in manufacturing industry should increase at an average rate of 7% a year in real terms over the whole period 1964–1970.

To back up these hopeful projections, the Government took a

number of important steps. It switched to a corporation tax system, which would encourage firms to plough back more of their profits and discourage overseas investment. It reviewed the investment programmes of nationalized industries and other sections over which it had direct control. And in January 1966 a White Paper announced that the Conservative system of investment allowances would be replaced by a system of cash grants.

The Confederation of British Industry at first gave qualified approval to the switch, but changed its mind fairly quickly. Mr A. A. Shenfield, its economic director, said the arguments in favour were relatively minor, while those against it were relatively major. The discrimination between industries and types of investment was based on a crude assessment of the relative value of different investment activities, and did not survive examination. Transport, for instance, was considered no good, with the exception of hovercraft, and the same applied to office machinery, where computers were made the exception. Allowances, Mr Shenfield maintained, had the great merit that they were easy and inexpensive to administer. The new scheme was administratively complex. Other industrial organizations also criticized the switch, and the Conservative Party – predictably – claimed that it was calculated to reduce both the quantity and the quality of investment. Cash grants would be paid even where there was no likelihood of firms ever earning profits or paying tax, and the rules according to which they were given were so vague that, in effect, their allocation would depend upon the whims of officials.

As it happened, the investment grant scheme did not actually come into operation until a year after the first announcement. And by then, the Government's plans had been dealt a severe blow by the July package of deflationary measures. Stop-go has always been the greatest enemy of investment (as Mr Wilson stressed so forcefully during the years of opposition) and the abrupt change of course forced upon ministers by the July sterling crisis had a major psychological impact. Until then, many firms had been surprisingly willing to take a long-term view. The National Plan, and the activities of the Department of Economic Affairs, the Ministry of Technology, and 'Neddy' had persuaded them that the Government knew where it was going. The disillusionment, therefore, was all the greater. Mr Wilson and his ministers urged them to go on as before, on the principle that the best time to invest is when demand is comparatively slack, but the response was weak. 'Stop-go', one industrialist remarked bitterly, 'has been replaced by stop'. The National Plan targets were torpedoed. Investment in the public sector was maintained at a high level, but manufacturing investment actually went down. Here is a broad picture of investment between 1964 and 1967:

UK GROSS FIXED CAPITAL FORMATION, REVALUED AT 1958 PRICES

	Total £m.	Public authorities £m.	Manufacturing £m.
1964	5,363	1,182	1,092
1965	5,575	1,218	1,203
1966	5,658	1,295	1,233
1967	5,962	1,492	1,172

Source – National income and expenditure 1967 HMSO

The Government did its best to get things moving again. It speeded up the repayment of investment grants, and temporarily increased the rate. It applied for membership of the Common Market. And in 1967 Mr Callaghan launched his ill-fated 'period of controlled growth and expansion'. All these efforts, however, met with only limited success. Devaluation, accompanied by an 8% bank rate and other deflationary measures, was another event which made industrialists wonder whether they could confidently spend money on new factories and machinery when the Government was constantly being blown 'off course'. But Mr Wilson – and his new Chancellor – insisted that devaluation had strengthened the case for a higher rate of investment. It would, they argued, lead to an export-led boom which would soon place strain on existing capacity. If all went well, too, stop-go would be a thing of the past. Why not, they asked, look ahead five or ten years! The same message went across the Atlantic to the internationally-minded US corporations. Mr Wilson, who used to criticize Selwyn Lloyd and other Tory Chancellors for encouraging American take-over bids, had come to appreciate the dollar – and the know-how – which US giants had at their disposal.

The cut in public spending, announced a few months after devaluation, included some curbs on public sector investment. By itself this need not be a bad thing. Not all investment, after all, is productive. It is essential, moreover, to achieve a better balance between public and private investment. Too often, a 'hole' in the private sector has been simply filled up by increased spending in the public sector – with serious consequences once reflationary policies got under way. But the lesson of the three years 1964–67 (and indeed of the whole post-war period) is surely that industrialists cannot be forced or even cajoled into undertaking expensive new commitments. If the Government really wants them to take a long-term view, it must demonstrate convincingly that it has the ability – and the means – to do the same. The ideal climate for investment, as the Brookings report pointed out, is a booming, fast-growing economy. High profits encourage demand for capital goods, and strong demand presses upon physical capacity. The experience of countries like Germany and Japan suggests that this is a far more important factor than allowances or grants. (Which of the two is the better remains to be seen.) Nothing would act as a greater tonic than a period of strong growth, and relative freedom from the 'balance of payments constraint'.

It may be that we shall get this in the seventies. One can, perhaps, also draw some encouragement from the fact that the younger generation is more investment-minded than the older one. The growing influence of technical colleges and business schools, of management courses and industrial consultancy, is producing a welcome change in attitudes. Modern management is not content to make do with old equipment, or to accept low returns on new investment. But it is the job of government to create an environment in which the new attitudes can flourish.

Many people, of course, feel very strongly that the same applies to another form of investment – the purchase of plant and equipment, and of whole companies, in other countries. This has been a highly controversial subject in the last few years, and will continue to command attention. It deserves a closer look.

Long before Mr Wilson came to power, a lot of economists argued that Britain's high rate of foreign investment has been largely responsible for the slow rate of economic growth since the end of the Second World War. They included Mr Fred Catherwood and Mr Andrew Shonfield. Their case, very simply, was that this enthusiasm for overseas investment diverted resources from our own industries, and placed a considerable strain on the balance of payments into the bargain.

Mr Wilson's Government accepted this, without serious investigation, as soon as it won power. The urgent need to reduce the yawning deficit, and reassure foreign holders of sterling, acted as a powerful spur. But George Brown had also become genuinely convinced of the more fundamental arguments for curbing the outflow of direct investment. In 1965 and again in 1966 the Government took steps designed to bring about a marked change of trend. New and stiffer rules were applied to investment outside the sterling area, and in 1966 Mr Callaghan introduced a 'voluntary programme' to limit direct investment in developed sterling area countries like Australia. The switch to a corporation tax system was accompanied by other tax changes aimed at reducing the effective return on overseas investment to British investors. The CBI, predictably, bitterly complained that these moves were 'short sighted'. So did Lord Cromer, whose relationship with Mr Wilson had always been somewhat stormy. In his last public speech as Governor of the Bank of England, in March 1966, he said that the Government was 'restricting those very activities which contribute so much to our economic strength.' Earnings from overseas investments had been one of the few really sustained successes of the whole balance of payments struggle since 1954, and it was foolish to 'eat the seed-corn'. Mr Callaghan replied that he didn't need to be convinced of the benefits of many kinds of overseas investment, but refused to budge. The balance of payments situation gave him no choice, nor did George Brown. The CBI commissioned a Cambridge team of economists, under W. B. Reddaway, to make a thorough study of the whole subject in the hope that its findings would persuade the Government to take a more liberal long-term view. Mr Reddaway produced an interim report early in 1967, and the CBI claimed it proved that 'direct investment overseas is not wasteful of the country's resources and harmful to the economy'. The report also showed, however, that the average rate of return was, if anything, less than the after-tax rate of return on British domestic investment in manufacturing. If one allowed for the fact that taxes on UK profits earned abroad went to foreign Governments, while those on domestic earnings went to our own Exchequer, the national rate of return on home investment was substantially higher. Reddaway challenged several other popular assumptions, notably the view that direct overseas investment stimulates exports of capital goods and continuing exports of components and other intermediate products for British-owned plants abroad. This was enough for George Brown, Jim Callaghan and other colleagues. Reddaway went to work on the second half of this report (it was due at the end of 1968) and the CBI privately acknowledged that it had lost a round, if not the fight.

The argument is bound to be revived, of course, when Britain's balance of payments moves into surplus. I doubt if, even then, we will return to our former position as one of the world's largest exporters of capital. But an industrial country with a healthy balance sheet, and a useful growth rate, *should* be able to invest a fair amount of money abroad. It certainly makes more sense than, for example, spending £50 million a year on the Rhine Army. Overseas defence spending earns nothing – in our case not even prestige. Overseas investment, on the other hand, is an asset which produces growing amounts of foreign exchange. Mr Wilson's Government would have been in still deeper trouble, during its first three years, if income from past investment had not helped to bridge the persistent deficit on our visible trade.

One cannot ignore, either, the fact that tariff barriers and other hurdles have increasingly forced British companies to build factories on the spot. The Common Market, for example, is a large and prosperous area, with impressive growth prospects. But as external tariffs have risen it has also become more difficult for non-members to sell their products against local competition. When General de Gaulle first vetoed British entry, in 1961, many of our manufacturers decided to set up operations in the Common Market countries, including France itself. As a result, hundreds of British firms now have subsidiaries on the Continent – ranging from ICI's huge plants near Rotterdam to modest selling agencies. The process was repeated after the second 'non', but was obviously handicapped by the Government's tight restrictions. It may be that Britain will gain entry in the next few years. Meanwhile, however, the CBI might be well advised to concentrate on persuading ministers that, if a general relaxation is ruled out by our formidable debts, consideration should at least be given to a more helpful approach on this particular front.

21 How Vital are Incentives?

THE HEAD OF a New York firm not long ago put this message on its notice board:

> Some time between starting and quitting time, without infringing on lunch periods, coffee breaks, rest periods, story-telling, ticket-selling, holiday planning and the re-hashing of yesterday's TV programmes, we ask that each employee try to find some time for a work break. This may seem radical, but it might aid steady employment and assure regular pay checks.

Many British chairmen (the modern types, not the grouse-moor chaps) feel sorely tempted to do the same. They claim that we are getting much too leisure-conscious. Like all generalizations, this is open to debate – but we have it on the authority of Mr Jo Grimond, the former Liberal Party leader, that 'modern Britain doesn't exactly encourage hard work'. Is it true? And if so, what are we going to do about it? The Tory party, eagerly searching for a vote-winning formula at the last General Election, came up with a simple answer. We don't have enough incentives. Give people better financial rewards and – bingo! – all our problems will be solved. 'We would like', Shadow Chancellor Iain Macleod declared, 'to see encouragement and incentives, measures designed to give a sharp stimulus to saving and the use of the tax system to reward enterprise and initiative'. Mr Heath took up the battle cry, and has used it on every possible occasion since. It will, without doubt, be the Tory Party's chief slogan at the next general election.

The Labour Government, of course, has looked upon all this with considerable suspicion. It is not, in principle, opposed to incentives – and it certainly recognizes their political appeal. But it has different ideas about the form such incentives should take.

Labour, Mr Wilson used to explain with great passion, does not believe in a society where everyone grabs all he can. It rejects 'appeals to materialism, or selfish acquisitiveness, or competitive social emulation – keeping up with the Joneses – by either snobbery or its no less ugly partner, inverted snobbery'. A Labour Government should be dedicated to providing incentives which appeal to the community as a whole. This means 'more expenditure on social security for the under-privileged, a more comprehensive National Health Service, more expenditure on education, and a great drive to replace or modernize our generation's inheritance of ageing and sub-standard houses'.

Mr Wilson's critics charged, at the end of Labour's first three years, that he had failed in these noble objectives. It was an unfair charge; given the financial limitations imposed on his Government, its record is reasonably good. But the criticism made by the Tories – that Labour failed to make the economic progress it hoped for because it ignored the human desire for individual reward – is well worth closer consideration.

With few exceptions, people go to work to earn money. They have to keep their families, and they are naturally keen to improve their standard of living. From this, inevitably, arises pressure for bigger rewards – and for taxation policies that allows a man to retain a bigger slice of them. Hospitals, education and other facilities tend to be taken for granted after a while, and people readily listen to politicians who tell them that 'it should be up to you, not the Government, to decide how your money is spent'. The working man is, as a rule, interested in equality only if others tend to be more equal than he is. He does not want to work overtime so that Mr Wilson can be more generous to the under-privileged. He works overtime so that he and his family can have a bit more to spend. If a large chunk of the extra earnings are taken away from him in the form of taxation, he doesn't bother to go on exerting himself. 'Working for nothing' is, for him, a mug's game. The Labour Party may disapprove of this kind of attitude, but a Labour *Government* can hardly afford to ignore it.

The incomes policy launched soon after it took office, and maintained ever since, made it harder to secure fatter pay packets. And Britain's financial problems forced the Government to raise taxes, rather than reduce them. It was not much consolation to the chap on the factory floor that Mr Callaghan was bashing expense accounts and capital gains. Tough handling of the bosses could not buy him a car or a washing machine.

The same applied to middle-class executives, scientists, and small businessmen. They were working to make money they could keep, and there was no law compelling them to make extra efforts if they considered the net reward to be insufficiently worthwhile. There was no law, either, that said they had to stay in Britain and put up with Mr Wilson's policies. They could and did secure jobs in countries where the approach to mammon seemed more realistic. The brain drain to the United States was a direct reflection of discontent with Britain's tax systems.

Higher up, other motives came increasingly into play. Power, influence, prestige, honour and personal satisfaction kept wealthy businessmen going even though they could have retired to the South of France years earlier. The Labour Government took the view, right from the start, that this was the section of the community which could most easily dispense with financial incentives. Ministers sneered at the profit motive. ('I don't work for profit', George Brown once told me. 'Why should anyone else?'). They stopped sneering as time went on, and Mr Ray Gunter, then Minister of Labour, actually went as far as telling trade unions in August 1967 to 'stop equating profits with incest and lechery'. But the claim of bodies like the Institute of Directors and the CBI that Britain's very high top rates of taxation were harmful to the economy were always regarded with a very high degree of scepticism.

My own view is that, while such scepticism was understandable, it was carried much too far. Harold Wilson, George Brown, and Jim Callaghan allowed themselves to be ruled not by their heads, but by their emotions. This is pardonable to some extent, but in a mixed economy like ours it must not become the dominant factor. Wealth has to be created before it can be disposed of. And the creation of wealth depends, to a considerable extent, on what financial incentive there is to make the effort.

The CBI pointed out, in one of its surveys on the subject, that the ambitious man going to the top in Britain has to earn more than three times as much as in the United States to get £10,000 in take-home pay. And *The Economist* claimed, early in 1968, that 'this last generation of high marginal tax rates had added immeasurably to a stultification which was an infection of the

British social system even before the war'. By the 1930s, it said, the way of life of the successful British business man – with a house in Surrey and a son at Eton – was so nice that he was not inclined to take risks to get anything better.

Meanwhile his American counterpart would be pressing on past the earning of his first million to the earning of his tenth million, with the eventual aim of buying his son Jack the Presidency of the United States. 'A lot of Britain's relative economic decline in our lifetime', the paper declared, 'is explained by that'.

This may be an exaggeration, but one cannot deny that *The Economist* had a point. Making money may seem an immoral pastime to some people, but this is old-fashioned. It is both silly and pointless to look on 'profit', 'perks' and 'gains' as dirty words. The profit motive is a powerful driving force, both in the Boardroom and on the factory floor. And there is something to be said for the argument advanced by Mr Ronald Grierson, the former Managing Director of the Industrial Reorganization Corporation, that financial independence is a valuable asset for young executives. They must have the courage to assert their views even at the risk of being asked to resign, and they must be ready to take up daring new challenges on which their reputations might be made and could also be lost. Our tax system makes it difficult to secure such independence if one doesn't have inherited wealth; few men can accumulate substantial savings by the time they are 35, or build up capital through stock options. At the same time, though, I think it would be a mistake to blame *all* our economic ills on the alleged lack of incentive, as the Tories tend to do. Countries like Japan also have high personal taxation, but it has not pushed them into crisis after crisis, or prevented businessmen from being successful. The same is true in Britain: it would be absurd to suggest that men like Joe Hyman, Sir Frank Kearton and Arnold Weinstock are dragging their feet because of our surtax rates, and that they would double their efforts if the Chancellor did an about-turn. What is needed, surely, is a realistic assessment of the role which financial incentives can and should play in our kind of society. It is a mistake to start from the basis that the desire for reward represents 'selfish acquisitiveness' which must be stamped out. It is equally a mistake to see financial incentives as a universal panacea.

Mr Jenkins, fortunately, seems to be very much aware of this. He rejects the crude arguments about incentives (most of them are aired over long and costly lunches) but acknowledges that there is a strong case for selective action. In his first Budget speech, he indicated that his own reforming zeal will be directed chiefly at the field of personal taxation. His inclination, he said, was towards fewer loopholes and 'somewhat lower rates'. Britain's direct taxation on earned incomes, he acknowledged, was 'comparatively high'. His first Budget was not the occasion to 'contemplate reductions', but he hoped to do something about it in future years. It seems reasonable to assume, therefore, that if and when the time comes to relax, the new Chancellor will give high priority to earned incomes. An additional incentive for doing so, nearer to election date, will no doubt be the fact that it could steal some of Mr Heath's thunder. As General Booth said, Why should the devil have *all* the good tunes?

22 A Floating Pound?

SHOULD BRITAIN HAVE a floating exchange rate, as in the thirties? This was one of the questions discussed at the first Cabinet meeting Mr Wilson held, and was later raised every time there was a sterling crisis. It was again carefully considered before the November 1967 decision to devalue. Mr Reginald Maudling has publicly stated that he has 'always been attracted by the arguments for it', and Mr Enoch Powell has made it the subject of more than one of his sermons on the merits of free-for-all.

Basically, it amounts to nothing more than letting the pound find its own level. The Bank of England would stop using those precious gold and foreign currency reserves to defend a fixed parity, and we would all stop fretting about the prospect of a crisis every time the pound drops $\frac{1}{16}$ of a cent against the dollar. Sterling would stand or fall by our trade performance.

The obvious question is why, if this is such a simple solution, Mr Wilson's Government has rejected it for the past $3\frac{1}{2}$ years.

One answer is that it removes a major deterrent to domestic inflation. If the Government can no longer nag us about the plight of the pound, or 'prove' that British goods are on the point of being priced out of export markets, how can it sell us deflationary measures and an incomes policy? Another is that 'floating' is difficult for a reserve currency.

Our sterling area partners, and other people, hold their money here on the basis that we are prepared to defend a *fixed* exchange rate. Mr Wilson was persuaded by his advisers that, if we decided to float, we would almost certainly lose the sterling balances. This threat was, indeed, the most powerful point against it. Over the past few years, sterling's value under floating rates would simply *not* have been determined just by our trade performance. It would have been at the mercy of many factors including speculation.

The pound would have floated in the wrong direction. An additional point – thought to have clinched the argument – was that the confusion caused by a decision to float would do great damage to the international monetary system. Initially it would have had much the same effect as devaluation to a new fixed rate. Other countries might have followed suit, and the dollar would have come under strong pressure. Two alternative proposals were rejected for much the same reason. One was that we should seek a change in international rules that would permit currencies to fluctuate within a wider range. Another was that we should try to move towards a scheme of 'creeping devaluation', under which currencies would be adjusted by, say, 1% in any twelve month period. All these ideas had certain theoretical attractions, but were not really practical under existing circumstances.

It is possible to argue that the 1967 devaluation, and the important Basle arrangement made in the summer of 1968, have significantly changed the picture. Devaluation has given Britain a good chance of getting a healthy balance of payments surplus in 1969 and subsequent years. If and when that happens, confidence in sterling should be fully restored and it would probably float in the right direction – upwards. Its exposure to money movements should also be considerably reduced by that time. The days of sterling's world role are numbered. Its use in international trading has declined since devaluation, and this trend may well continue. The Basle scheme, which amounts to an 'insurance policy' for holders of the sterling balances, has virtually removed the threat of any sudden switch from sterling. Some of the key objections to 'setting the pound free' are, therefore, disappearing.

There would, of course, still be some confusion on the international monetary scene – floating exchange rates are disliked by central bankers, mainly for this reason – and it is possible that our trade might suffer. Some stability could, however, be maintained by continuing to use the exchange equalization account to iron out speculative fluctuations arising from the movement of capital.

Rigid exchange rates may be good for discipline, but they can also demand too much sacrifice. A floating pound may not have been feasible before, but the Government would do well to keep an open mind on the subject – if only because, on the evidence of the past three years, there is something to be said for leaving a wide margin for unexpected developments.

23 Will it Work?

'I HAVE NO INTENTION', Mr Roy Jenkins announced when he took over the Treasury, 'of presiding over an economic slither'. That is just as well. The devaluation gamble is Labour's last chance: if it fails, the Government is unlikely to survive.

Devaluation leads to a once-and-for all improvement in a country's competitive trading position. A 14·3% adjustment, such as we had in November 1967, is a very modest one. In 1949, Stafford Cripps devalued by no less than 33⅓% and many economists would have been happier if, having decided to take the plunge, Mr Wilson and his colleagues had gone for a bigger adjustment this time. They took the view, however, that a 14·3% change which was not followed by any of Britain's main competitors was better than a larger one which would, inevitably, have produced chain-reactions all over the world.

Industrialists were quick to point out that higher raw material costs, and removal of the export rebate and manufacturers' premium, had substantially reduced the advantage of the modest 14·3% devaluation. Many of them reckoned that, allowing for this, the extra advantage was nearer 7% or 8%. They said they would not cut their selling prices, but use the extra margin to absorb future cost increases and spend more on sales promotion and after sales service. Mr Tony Crosland, the new President of the Board of Trade, accused them of being unduly pessimistic, and *The Wall Street Journal* caused a commotion on both sides of the Atlantic by questioning whether – in all the circumstances – devaluation was likely to achieve its primary aim.

Other influential voices were more cheerful. M Pierre-Paul Schweitzer, the Managing Director of the International Monetary Fund, noted that devaluation was 'a powerful weapon' and that Britain had 'at last a real possibility of transforming its economic and external financial position'. The OECD, which had been so sharply critical of Mr Wilson's policies in earlier years, said that 'on any normal assumption about trade and price changes, the benefit of devaluation to the trade account should be substantial – and could, over time, even exceed the Government's target of an improvement of £500 million'. These are the kind of assessments which ministers cling to. They like to think that devaluation day represented the lowest point in their fortunes, and that everything will be changed by the time the next general election has to be held in 1970 or early 1971.

They are, however, very much aware that devaluation by itself cannot solve Britain's problems. It opened up a 'possibility', as M Schweitzer put it. The success or failure of the exercise, very much depends on the relative movement of costs, prices and the other factors such as delivery dates, design and salesmanship that determine competitive power in Britain and other countries. The cuts in Government spending announced in January 1968, and the tough Budget produced by Mr Jenkins two months later, were part of the textbook strategy for 'releasing resources for exports'. Home demand was deliberately cut back so that manufacturers would be forced to turn to export markets – which devaluation had made more profitable. The new Prices and Incomes Bill, too, plays a key role in ensuring that the benefits are not eroded. The aim is not simply to show a balance of payments surplus for a year or two, and then slip back into the same old mess. It is to retain the post-devaluation advantages for a very long time to come.

Britain's structural faults were not, of course, changed by devaluation. One would like to think that, as time goes on, the benefits of the work done by the DEA and Ministry of Technology will begin to show. Britain, for all her shortcomings, remains a powerful industrial nation, and the trend towards bigger units in the last few years has considerably strengthened her international competitive position. The quality of management, too, has greatly improved. But we are still bedevilled by restrictive practices and by out-dated attitudes to the world we live in. It may be that these could be more easily removed under a Conservative administration. While Labour remains in power, however, it has a duty to tackle these fundamental problems – regardless of electoral popularity. It is bound to be an uphill job.

The trade unions are restless. Businessmen have little confidence in the Government. The slogans which sounded so inspiring a few years ago have been discredited. But the effort has to be made, because a second devaluation would be disastrous not only for the Labour Government, but also for the country as a whole.

A firm line at home is all the more important because Britain continues to be vulnerable to events in the rest of the world. We devalued at a time when world trade was picking up strongly, after a period of slackness. The United States and Germany, two of our most important markets, were both recovering very nicely. But a forceful reminder that buoyant trading conditions cannot be taken for granted came early in 1968, with the gold crisis.

The crisis had been brewing up ever since General de Gaulle first started to swap dollars for gold. The General's well-publicized action drew attention to the yawning US balance of payments gap, and made millions of people wonder how long America's gold stocks would last if other countries followed his example. They concluded that, long before then, Washington would probably raise the price of gold, which had been fixed at 35 dollars an ounce way back in 1934. Anyone who bought while the going was still good would be sure of a nice profit if and when that happened. Hoarding increased considerably in 1966 and 1967, and US gold stocks dwindled to an alarming degree. But the enthusiasm for gold did not really develop into a fever until Britain devalued the pound.

Devaluation of one of the world's two reserve currencies was a resounding victory for the speculators, and a shock for the many people – including our sterling area partners – who had trusted the Government's word. The dollar promptly moved into the first line of defence. With the Vietnam war sapping America's financial strength, it was widely held to be only a matter of time before the dollar shared sterling's fate. Buying of gold in London and other centres rose to unprecedented levels. A reassuring statement from the world's central bankers failed to check the boom, and in the end Washington called a dramatic weekend meeting to decide what to do. They agreed that central banks should go on buying and selling gold to each other at 35 dollars an ounce, but that they would stop selling gold to everyone else. If speculators wanted to hoard gold, they would have to get their supplies on the free market. It was a make-shift arrangement that bought a little time, but it still left the future of the world's monetary system in doubt.

The crisis was, to a large extent, caused by an attempted speculative coup. But it also owed a great deal to that dangerous phenomenon: the credibility gap. Paper money, by itself, is worth nothing. Its value depends on what other people will give for it – and that, in turn, depends on the readiness of governments to follow sound economic policies. The remarkable post-war prosperity of the industrial countries was based on faith. People believed in the stability of the world-wide system of fixed exchange rates, and behaved accordingly. Dollars, in particular, were considered to be as good as gold. During the last few years, however, the willingness of politicians to adopt policies which would maintain the value of their paper currencies has been increasingly questioned. General de Gaulle's lectures on financial discipline struck a sensitive spot: many bankers and businessmen shared his concern.

The credibility gap is not a new invention, but it came to be strongly associated with President Johnson during 1965 and 1966. It arose because bankers, politicians and newspaper columnists felt no longer able to believe the figures they were being given about projected Government spendings, casualties in the Vietnam war, and other important issues. In Britain, Mr Wilson's critics quickly picked up the phrase. The Prime Minister's apparent inability to produce results to match his earlier promises seemed, to them, to make it just as difficult to believe what he was saying.

Mr Wilson's about-turn on devaluation, after three years of insistence that the 2·80 dollar parity would be defended to the last, was widely seen as confirmation that a politician's word could not be trusted. President Johnson's continued insistence that America would not raise the gold price was brushed aside: what guarantee did anyone have that Johnson would not 'do a Wilson'? The scramble to get out of paper currencies and into gold was an inevitable consequence. It was matched, particularly in Britain, by an equally big scramble to buy stocks and shares, antiques, jewellery and other 'tangibles' which it was felt would keep their value better than paper money.

Fear is a powerful force, and it feeds on itself. Few people stopped to think that, by acting the way they did, they were likely to bring about the very state of affairs which they were working so hard to protect themselves against.

Economists and bankers were, perhaps unwittingly, helping to spread the feeling of instability. Every pet theory about gold and monetary reform – no matter how ancient or improbable – was eagerly revived. Gloomy forecasts of an impending 'world catastrophe' were given wide publicity. *Fortune*, the US business magazine, said in March that it was 'painfully clear that the US dollar and the whole intricate monetary machinery that revolves around it are in deeper trouble than at any time since the early thirties'. British newspapers were, around the same time, predicting that 'the world was close to ruin'. All this did a good deal of damage to the dollar – and, because the two currencies remain closely linked, to the pound. The Bank of England revealed in 1968 that members of the gold pool countries, including Britain, sold more than $3,000 million worth of gold between the devaluation of sterling in November and the Washington conference. Heavy pressure on sterling, it said, led to a 'considerable loss of foreign exchange' and Britain made 'substantial drawings on central bank facilities'. In other words, we borrowed still more money to deal with a situation which had little to do with our basic economic problems. Britain was caught up in a world-wide phenomenon, and no-one could be sure what it would all lead to.

An ironic and unforeseen development in May 1968 was the sudden collapse of confidence in the franc, which forced General de Gaulle to re-introduce exchange controls and call a General Election. France – the country which had lectured the rest of the world on financial discipline and boasted of its strength – found itself almost overnight among the nations whose currency was 'suspect'. It happened because a group of noisy students had managed to inspire riots and mass strikes which threatened to undermine the French balance of payments. General de Gaulle's plight gave understandable satisfaction to many people in Britain and the United States, but it certainly did not please the money managers. The French crisis was another unwelcome reminder that in this supposedly enlightened world anything can happen, and increased the problem of shoring up a monetary system which had been tested and found wanting.

When the crisis blew up, I was in Japan, taking part in a world economic symposium. The Japanese have managed to perform the post-war miracle which has eluded us: their growth rate in the last couple of decades has been the envy of every other nation. Industrious, inventive, eager to learn and full of self-confidence, they made the most of the remarkable post-war growth in world trade. But they were very much aware, in this summer of uncertainty, that their progress could be abruptly checked if the international monetary system failed to hold together. This clearly applies to Britain, too. At its new parity, the pound is not an overvalued currency. Our exports are competitive, and the structural changes initiated in the past few years are beginning to produce results. But we also have sizeable debts, and at best devaluation is unlikely to produce a surplus of more than £350 million in 1969. If the world were pushed into a round of competitive currency devaluations, or into retrenchment such as we saw in the thirties, our chances of avoiding still further trouble would be very slim.

The Labour Government, said Mr Wilson after another round of by-election defeats in June, 'is determined to continue the policies which are known to be necessary until we reach a secure position where this country can expand production year-in year-out without relapsing into a balance of payments crisis. When we have that degree of economic security we will have great benefits, not only to the country's economic independence but to the standard of living and safeguarding of employment. The political consequences will then follow'.

After three years hard Labour, Mr Wilson was still chasing his elusive rainbow. He had no choice but to go on travelling along the road mapped out when the pound was devalued in November 1967, and he clung to the hope that somehow all would come out well by the time he had to call the next General Election.

The public has a short memory, and fortunes can change considerably over a period of years. His 1970 campaign speech was already mapped out in Wilson's mind. He gave a glimpse of it in the summer of 1968, when he lashed into his Tory critics at a rally of the faithful. Britain, he declared, has been experiencing 'the problems, the hardships, the tensions of an era of change'; 'a transformation is taking place in Britain's industrial society; we and every advanced nation are going through a technological revolution whose pace and capacity for social devastation far outstrips any era of industrial and technological revolution in our society'. This, we may be sure, will be his theme at the next General Election. Mr Wilson will cite the number of mergers, the rationalization of industries like shipbuilding, the growth in business schools, the increasing emphasis on research, and the elimination of a vast balance of payments deficit as evidence that we have indeed been through 'the second industrial revolution'. He will stress that, within the short period of six years, the Labour Government has made Britain 'blow away the cobwebs' and face up to its proper role in a changed world. He will acknowledge that there have been mistakes and disappointments, but add that he and his colleagues have been immensely handicapped by the Tory leadership and 'their allies in the Tory press' who brought on crisis after crisis by 'screaming their heads off in a campaign of distortion and misrepresentation'.

For good measure, Mr Wilson will go on to list his Government's social reforms, made in spite of all the financial and economic obstacles. He is hopeful that a vigorous campaign conducted on this platform, and aided by the skilful use of television, will convince the British public that the Government's mistakes should be forgotten, and that toughness will find its just reward. If all goes well, the Wilson formula may indeed carry the day.

But in the Prime Minister's nimble mind lurk several nagging questions. Will his colleagues decide that someone like Roy Jenkins should lead the Labour Party into the promised land? Will they accept that Harold Wilson is the real architect of the 'revolution' – the only man who saw the economy through both the bad years and the good? And even if they do, will all the strenuous economic effort of the past few years simply produce a solid financial base for another Tory Government? Back in the heady days of 1964, when the electorate had given him his first taste of power, he had told friends that he expected to be Prime Minister for at least sixteen years of consecutive rule. At the time, it seemed a reasonable expectation. But in the more sober atmosphere of 1968, it looked far from certain that his followers, and the electorate generally, would be prepared to forgive and forget.

Index